# THE
# BEDSIDE
# BOOK OF THE
# GARDEN

Published by Expert Books
a division of Transworld Publishers

The right of Dr. D. G. Hessayon to be identified
as author of this work has been asserted in accordance with sections
77 and 78 of the Copyright Designs and Patents Act 1988.

A catalogue record for this book is available from the British Library

TRANSWORLD PUBLISHERS
61–63 Uxbridge Road, London W5 5SA
A Random House Group Company
www.rbooks.co.uk

This title is an updated and revised version of
*The Armchair Book of the Garden* (1983)

Distributed in the United States by
∫∫ Sterling Publishing Co. Inc.,
387 Park Avenue South,
New York,
NY 10016-8810

ISBN 9780903505697 © D. G. HESSAYON 2008

Design: www.carrstudio.co.uk
Printed and bound by Clays Ltd, St Ives plc

THE

# BEDSIDE
# BOOK OF THE
# GARDEN

### Dr. D. G. Hessayon

Author of the best-selling *EXPERT* gardening series

**EXPERT BOOKS**

LONDON • NEW YORK • TORONTO • SYDNEY • AUCKLAND

## ALSO BY THE AUTHOR

THE BEDDING PLANT EXPERT

THE BULB EXPERT

THE CONTAINER EXPERT

THE EASY-CARE GARDENING EXPERT

THE EVERGREEN EXPERT

THE FLOWER EXPERT

THE FLOWER ARRANGING EXPERT

THE FLOWERING SHRUB EXPERT

THE FRUIT EXPERT

THE GARDEN DIY EXPERT

THE GARDEN REVIVAL EXPERT

THE GREENHOUSE EXPERT

THE HOUSE PLANT EXPERT

THE HOUSE PLANT EXPERT BOOK TWO

THE LAWN EXPERT

THE ORCHID EXPERT

THE PEST & WEED EXPERT

THE ROCK & WATER GARDEN EXPERT

THE ROSE EXPERT

THE TREE & SHRUB EXPERT

THE VEGETABLE & HERB EXPERT

# CONTENTS

# INTRODUCTION

THE trouble with most gardening books is that they always tell you to do something – go out and prune the shrubs, spray the apple trees, plant the cabbages and so on. Or they tell you to go out and buy things – the most up-to-date lawnmower, the newest weedkiller or the latest rose varieties which are so much better than the ones growing in your garden.

All of this expert wisdom is of course very useful, but there are times when we just want to read about our hobby and not be badgered with advice. We just want to lie back and read about plants we may never grow and look at gardens which we can never hope to match. We want to read about the way they did things in the past and about people long since dead who gave us the plants and great gardens of today.

To everyone who would like to know something more about the plants, people and places rather than just the practical side of gardening, *The Bedside Book of the Garden* is dedicated.

# PEOPLE

Gardening, like any other field of human endeavour, has its Hall of Fame. It is filled with a highly varied assortment of geniuses and charlatans, aristocrats and paupers, workers and dreamers. Their achievements have been equally varied – some have hunted for plants, others have created famous gardens and a handful of immortals achieved immortality by evolving a new

style which changed the face of gardening. Writers, patrons, plant breeders, nurserymen – neat pigeon-holes for the great names in horticulture, but people cannot always be classified so simply and some giants have achieved greatness in several different spheres of activity.

To the plant hunters of the past we owe our basic garden flowers. The first ones to appear in the Hall of Fame were the men fired by the adventurous spirit of the Renaissance – in the 16th century the Frenchman Belon combed Turkey, Egypt

and the Holy Land, and the Austrian de Busbecq (page 183) brought tulips and other plants back from Turkey. In the 17th century they went further afield – the Tradescants (page 47) collected in Russia and the New World, and Kaempfer was the first Western botanist to collect plants from Japan.

In the 18th century the trickle of plant collecting became a fast-flowing stream. John Bartram (page 12) was the first of the American-born plant hunters, de Tournefort collected in the Near East, Masson brought back pelargoniums from S. Africa and both Cuninghame and d'Incarville opened Western eyes to the wonders of the Chinese flora.

The 19th century saw the stream of plant discovery turn into a flood. Fortune (page 19) went into the interior of China, von Humbolt collected in S. America, Cunningham and Drummond collected in Australia. David Douglas was sent by the

Horticultural Society of London to N. America in 1825 and the flowers, shrubs and trees he collected are considered to have had more effect on our gardens than the discoveries of any other plant hunter.

The search goes on. 'Chinese' Wilson (page 50) and George Forrest brought back plants from the Far East at the beginning of the 20th century, and even today expeditions travel to the remoter parts of the world in search of new varieties.

Many of these plant hunters were not gardeners, and the early names in the realm of garden design were not plant lovers. Bramante (page 106) designed in Italy the first of Europe's Grand Gardens – for him

a garden was a place for stone, stairs, statues and water. After him there was the mighty Le Nôtre in France (page 34) who became the garden master of Europe in 1661. He created long canals, colourful beds and breathtaking views, but to him flowers and trees were merely blocks of colour. This indifference to flowers was replaced by definite antagonism when 'Capability' Brown (page 14) took over as Europe's garden master in the 18th century. Repton (page 37) softened this hard line and the early Victorian John Loudon (page 140) and the mid-Victorian Shirley Hibberd brought back flowers into the garden.

In 1870 the fiery Irishman William Robinson started the Modern School on which our present-day ideas are based (pictured and on page 40). Others, such as Gertrude Jekyll (page 22), modified his extreme view that gardens should be completely informal, and so the long line of garden designers beginning with Bramante has led us to the semi-formal garden outside your window.

Walking through that garden you may feel at one with Nature, but there is nothing natural about the craft of gardening – it has to be learnt. For this reason the writers and educators belong in the Hall of Fame – Theophrastus, who wrote the first gardening book (page 138), Thomas Tusser, who wrote the first horticultural 'best seller' in 1573, Parkinson, Miller, Loudon, Robinson and finally to the radio and T.V. personalities, beginning with Mr. Middleton and leading to today's teachers – Alan Titchmarsh, Expert books, Peter Seabrook and the rest.

These educators have only been able to draw on the knowledge of the day. From the time of Theophrastus before the birth of Christ there was little discovery or original thought prior to the 17th century. The great trio from the Low Countries – Clusius (page 17), L'Obel and Dodoens – discovered numerous new plants and described many others, but it was men like Linnaeus (page 29) and Mendel (page 32) who helped to create the modern science of horticulture.

So far the Hall of Fame has included people whose work has spanned the world in its influence, but some of the great names are best remembered for a single spot of earth which they turned into a garden. Vita Sackville-West at Sissinghurst (page 45) and Major Johnston at Hidcote (page 109) are good examples.

Gardening and gardens have been created by people using the earth and its resources – stone, water and plants to produce an oasis – a place of relaxation in a desert thousands of years ago, a French valley hundreds of years ago or 24 Acacia Drive today. To do this we have drawn on the work or genius of people in the Hall of Fame, but the gardens were actually made and cared for by millions of unknown people … and that includes us.

# JOHN BARTRAM

## THE FIRST OF THE AMERICAN PLANT HUNTERS

*M*ANY OF the people described in this section of the book are well-known. Josephine, Capability Brown, Linnaeus and so on are familiar names, but it is almost certain that you will never have heard of John Bartram.

He was the first American-born plant hunter and was described by Linnaeus as 'the greatest natural botanist in the world'. Others had collected plants around the areas of settlement, but Bartram roamed into native American territory from Canada to Florida to find new plants.

More than 150 new varieties were sent to England and some, like Witch hazel, have become household names. He created the first botanical garden in America and carried out the first experiments in hybridisation. He introduced the Linnaean System of plant classification to the Colonies and he was the first man to recommend the use of gypsum for improving the soil.

Yet he is largely forgotten both in Europe and America. The reason is that he never wrote a book nor an article, because he was always conscious of his lack of schooling.

YOUNG JOHN BARTRAM felt that there must be more to life than ploughing his farm near Philadelphia. Plants were his passion, but he had no formal education and so hired a schoolmaster to teach him Latin. Now he could read Linnaeus and the herbals; he had studied the trees and flowers throughout his native state of Pennsylvania and was ready to make plant hunting in the American Colonies his life's work.

The year was 1732 and he was 33 years old. He had started to correspond with Peter Collinson, a fellow Quaker and English woollen merchant, and for the next 34 years Bartram collected from virgin America seeds and plants which he sent back to his British patron. For five guineas a box he supplied a vast and varied collection to Collinson and Philip Miller. This money enabled Bartram to spend long periods away from his farm. In return the English collectors claimed the credit for the new introductions, despite the fact that they had never set foot in the natural haunts of the plants!

Bartram's collecting and letter-writing abilities must have been immense. He wrote to and collected plants for botanists and gardeners in Britain, Holland, Sweden, and the American Colonies. There were honours too – Collinson wrote to him in 1765 that 'this day I received certain intelligence from our gracious King (George III) that he hath appointed thee his botanist (in America) with a salary of £50 a year.' Dr. Dillenius at Oxford gave the name *Bartramia* to one of the mosses sent to him.

We can only guess at the full extent of the list of new varieties sent by Bartram to his English patrons. Plant historians love to argue over the merits of the various claims – the introduction of the Michaelmas daisy is often claimed for Bartram but there is little doubt that it was introduced into Britain before John started collecting. There is no doubt, however, that *Magnolia grandiflora, Kalmia latifolia* and *K. angustifolia, Hydrangea arborescens* and *Hamamelis virginiana* were first sent to Britain by Bartram, together with scores of less well-known trees and shrubs. For the flower garden there were varieties of lily, phlox, iris and bergamot which had not been seen in Europe before.

Not all of Bartram's efforts were devoted to shipping plants to his patrons. In 1731 he had planted the first trees and shrubs at his farm in the Schuylkill Valley, and this was to become the first botanical garden in America. In order to stock it he claimed to 'have collected seed of almost every tree and shrub from Nova Scotia to Carolina.' A gross exaggeration, of course, but he did criss-cross the vast tracks all over the land in search of new plants. He never liked nor trusted the native Americans, calling them 'the most barbarous creatures in the universe', but there is no record of him being injured by the natives, French militia, fever-ridden swamps, poisonous snakes or deprivations he had to face.

In 1777 the British troops were advancing on his beloved garden. It was all too much for the aged plant hunter and he died, saddened by the War of Independence and disappointed in his son William. And yet it was William who had helped him on the later journeys and was to preserve his memory by writing in 1791 an account of their travels. And the Redcoats never did destroy the house and garden – they still remain today.

# CAPABILITY BROWN

## GENIUS OR VANDAL?

*A*SK A group of people to name a famous landscape gardener and most of them will say Capability Brown. The more knowledgeable members of the group will tell you that he invented the Landscape style of gardening ... and they will be wrong.

He developed and popularised the style and became its arch-priest, but he did not start it. Nearly 200 gardens bear his stamp, and in many of them all the existing formal features such as avenues and rectangular canals were destroyed. In their place he put man-made countryside – grass, clumps of trees, streams, irregular lakes and low hills.

So was he a genius or a vandal? The argument has raged from his heyday until the present day. There is no simple answer – page 16 sets out the facts and expresses an opinion or two ...

LANCELOT BROWN surveyed the estate. Its owner wanted it transformed into the new and fashionable Landscape or 'Landskip' style, and Brown had an experienced eye. The parterres and flower beds would have to go and so would the straight paths. Some earth would have to be moved and the stream dammed to make a lake. He was a good gardener but an even better businessman. His reply was always the same – 'It has great capabilities'.

Thus he became 'Capability' Brown – Sheriff of Huntingdon, gardener to George III, friend of princes and ministers, and the virtual dictator of gardening fashion for 30 years. Nothing in his beginnings suggested that he would reach such heights. Born in 1716, the son of a Northumberland farmer, he went to work as a gardener at 16 to learn his craft.

Seven years later he was ready to seek his fortune, and the ambitious Lancelot moved south to Buckinghamshire. One year later, in 1740, he went to the new garden being created at Stowe and met there the man who was to influence the future course of his life – William Kent.

Kent had come back from Italy with grand ideas ... 'he leapt the fence and saw that all Nature was a garden'. At Stowe he was creating for the owner a new type of garden, a naturalistic garden. It was to be a Grecian landscape, with green hills, a lake, winding pathways, clumps of trees and lots of temples.

---

## His reply was always the same – 'It has great capabilities'

---

The Landscape School was being born before young Lancelot's eyes, and he was a quick learner. He became Head Gardener of Stowe and Lord Cobham allowed him to improve the garden and prepare plans for others, such as Warwick Castle. In 1751 he was ready to start on the career which was to bring him immortality – Capability Brown of Hammersmith, landscape gardener. He developed the Landscape ideas of Kent, Bridgeman, Gibbs and others with whom he had worked at Stowe. He didn't want a series of Grecian tableaux within the garden – he wanted a single piece of countryside. Everything associated with formality and straight lines had to go, even the terrace around the house. Fences were taboo – a sunken fence, the ha-ha, was used instead.

Some of Brown's alterations may seem lavish. Artificial hills were created and one of his most famous achievements was to dam the River Glyme and so create the lake at Blenheim. But Brown was always the

---

## THE CAPABILITY BROWN GARDENS

More than 170 gardens were created or strongly influenced by Brown. Not all remain, and some have been drastically changed. Listed below are some notable Brown gardens which still exist.

Audley End, Essex
Berrington Hall, Herefordshire
Blenheim, Oxfordshire
Bowood, Wiltshire
Broadlands, Hampshire
Charlecote Park, Warwickshire
Chatsworth, Derbyshire
Chilham Castle, Kent

Corsham Court, Wiltshire
Harewood House, W. Yorkshire
Heveningham Hall, Suffolk
Ickworth, Suffolk
Longleat, Wiltshire
Luton Hoo, Bedfordshire
Nuneham, Oxfordshire
Petworth House, W. Sussex

Ragley Hall, Warwickshire
Sheffield Park, E. Sussex
Syon Park, Greater London
Trentham Gardens, Staffordshire
Warwick Castle, Warwickshire
Wrest Park, Bedfordshire

hard-headed businessman and never the artist without thoughts about cost. He drove a hard bargain with his subcontractors, bought trees from the lowest bidder and personally supervised the work.

Fame and fortune came to Brown and he died at his official residence in Hampton Court in 1783. Genius or vandal? He has been criticised over the years and his most famous enemy was Sir William Chambers, a contemporary landscape architect remembered for his work at Kew.

Chambers wrote 'Peasants emerge from the melon grounds to the periwig and turn professor', and followed this slur on Brown's humble origin with an attack on his zeal – 'There will not be a forest tree left standing in the whole Kingdom'.

Chambers had a point, for Brown's zeal meant that native trees were swept away if they did not fit in with his plan. Flowers had to be walled away and the kitchen garden set about half a mile from the house … even the tradesman's entrance was an underground tunnel to the kitchen. When asked to remodel a garden in Ireland, he replied 'I haven't finished with England yet!'

On the credit side, it must be recognised that Brown produced many beautiful landscapes and popularised the first truly British style of gardening. We gained international prestige for the first time, and there is no doubt that some of the formal gardens which he swept away would have been too costly to maintain. Brown's sin, if he had one, was his desire to destroy the old style and not just create a new one.

# CLUSIUS

## Father of the Flower Garden

> ERY FEW garden books mention Clusius, and yet our debt to him is incalculable. He was the most important member of a trio of immortal plantsmen in the Low Countries – Clusius, L'Obel and Dodoens.
>
> These men wrote, taught, collected plants, distributed new species and were the Founding Fathers of the Ornamental Garden. Their work spanned much of the 17th century and their achievement was dramatically simple – before them the European garden was a place for herbs and vegetables ... after them it was a place for flowers.
>
> In the age of Clusius there was no British botanist of any merit and our gardens were poor compared to their Continental counterparts; England's reputation as a nation of gardeners was still centuries away. It is interesting that Clusius spoke Flemish, German, French, Italian, Greek, Latin, Spanish and Portuguese but not English. English, it seems, was not important for a scientist in those days ...

HIS NAME was not Clusius, it was Charles de l'Ecluse. The latinisation of his surname was a sign of respect for this distinguished naturalist, in the same way that Carl von Linné became Linnaeus to his own and later generations.

L'Ecluse was born in 1526 at Arras. His family were staunchly Protestant, which was to lead to religious persecution, and he suffered from a bone defect, which was to lead to broken limbs during his early life and crippling lameness when he was in his sixties. But as a boy he was blessed with a searching mind and outstanding intelligence, and his family were wealthy enough to send him to the great teaching centres in France and Germany.

It was a fine life for a young man – collecting plants in Spain, writing books, going on the Grand Tour of Europe – and then the axe of persecution fell. The L'Ecluse estate was confiscated, his father fled to Antwerp and Charles now knew poverty for the first time. It was time to work and no longer to enjoy the constraint-free life of the man of means, so at the age of 47 he accepted the position of Superintendent of the Royal Gardens in Vienna.

He became a man of eminence. He visited the Ottoman Empire to gather new plants, Britain to talk to Sir Francis Drake about the plants of the New World and other countries in his ceaseless quest to enrich the gardens of Europe. This was a good period for L'Ecluse, but in 1587 he left Vienna – perhaps religious persecution had once again reared its head. In Frankfurt he found a patron and at last, in 1593, the 67-year-old revered Clusius returned to the Low Countries

as Professor of Natural Science at Leyden University.

Now he could teach and write – his plant-hunting days were over. His monumental work *Rarorium Plantarium Historia* was published in 1601. This compilation of his earlier works provided information on about 600 plants which had not been described in detail before. Here we find cloves and nutmeg, rhubarb and camphor with the finesbotanical illustrations of the age.

It would be quite impossible to list the

achievements of Clusius – many have been lost to us and the ones we know would fill many pages. It is only possible to pick out a few of the more important contributions he made to gardening. He did collect a

few plants which he found growing in the wild and transformed them into garden plants – cyclamen from the Austrian Alps and auricula from the mountains of Germany are examples. His work in introducing or re-introducing plants to Europe which he found growing as garden plants in the Ottoman Empire is perhaps of greater significance – in this group we have the hyacinth, ranunculus and fritillary. Of course, he will always be remembered for growing the first tulips in Europe and thereby founding the Dutch bulb industry, but he was also responsible for the acceptance of the runner bean and perhaps the potato in Central Europe.

## He was blessed with a searching mind and outstanding intelligence

Despite all his achievements he never did solve the problem of Plant Classification – that had to wait for Linnaeus. But he did take the knowledge of plants a step further, and he did bring flowers to our gardens as a result of his influence and work at Vienna and Leyden.

# ROBERT FORTUNE

## The First Plant Hunter into China

CHINA WAS still a closed book to the plant hunter when Queen Victoria came to the throne. Europeans were not allowed to travel inland – the only exceptions were the French Jesuit missionaries who were permitted to travel into the mountains and plains of the forbidden country.

These missionaries managed to send some seeds and dried specimens to Europe, and over the years both sailors and travellers brought back a number of beautiful and unknown garden plants from the coastal towns. These discoveries whetted the appetite of the Horticultural Society of London. What wonderful garden plants there must be inside China. If only …

The chance came when the Opium War ended in 1842. By the Treaty of Nanking, England was granted right of entry to the interior. In 1843 the first of the European plant hunters set sail. His name was Robert Fortune.

ROBERT FORTUNE landed in Hong Kong in 1843. The island had recently been ceded to Britain and he was about to set out into the interior of China in quest of new garden plants.

The Horticultural Society had made an odd choice for their first collector to go to China. Fortune was born in 1812 in Scotland, and served his apprenticeship as a garden boy in the Edinburgh Botanical Gardens. Later, as Deputy Superintendent at the Horticultural Society's gardens at Chiswick, he had learnt a great deal about plants but he knew no foreign languages and had no experience of travel to out-of-the-way places. And yet here he was, the

first plant hunter in a mysterious land, surrounded by people to whom he had taken an instant dislike.

His instructions were extremely precise. He had been given a list of garden plants which were known to grow in China and he was to contact nurserymen in order to obtain supplies for shipment back to London. He was the first of the plant hunters to carry Wardian Cases (see page 154), which meant that he could send back living specimens.

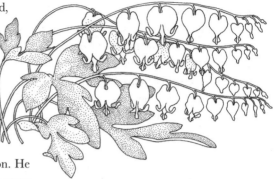

The 1843–1846 expedition was a success. He collected many plants which were unknown in Britain and learnt the secrets of chrysanthemum culture, the dwarfing of conifers and other techniques which were unfamiliar in his native land. On his return he was appointed Curator of the Chelsea Physic Garden, but this was not to last for long. Fortune was now an adventurer and he was not to settle in Britain until he was 50 years old.

## He was the first of the plant hunters to carry Wardian Cases

Leaving the Chelsea garden in 1848 he set sail for China once again on a simple but highly dangerous mission. He was to learn the secrets of tea growing, a secret closely guarded by the Chinese, and then smuggle plants to India so that cultivation could start there.

His adventures read like a story out of *Boy's Own Paper*. Disguised as a Chinese native he accomplished his mission, founding the tea industry in India and Sri Lanka.

There were further expeditions, including a journey to Japan, before he retired and became a farmer in Scotland. The year was 1862 and he was now reasonably wealthy from the sale of plants and curios. He had written several successful books, such as *A Residence Among the Chinese* (1857), and could now look back on his achievements.

He had learnt their language and their customs and had been given the Chinese name of Sing Wah. He had collected many new plants and some were destined to become very popular. But as the first serious hunter to travel into the heartland with the facility to collect living plants, his collection was surprisingly small. Many later plant hunters, like Wilson and Forrest, were far more successful in terms of new species gathered, so had he been a failure?

The truth is that he succeeded in his allotted task, but this had been distinctly limited. His job was to gather garden plants which had been bred in China over the centuries and he was not able to wander too far into remote regions. In achieving this end he sent back Winter jasmine, *Weigela*, Bleeding heart, Winter honeysuckle, Japanese anemone, Pompon chrysanthemum and others. Only *Rhododendron fortunei* was collected from the wild – it was left to the later plant hunters to journey to the remote areas and collect the wild trees, shrubs and flowers which flooded into Britain.

# GERTRUDE JEKYLL

## The First Lady of Gardening

IT IS AN unwritten rule for gardening writers that they can criticise anyone they like but they must not criticise Miss Jekyll. He can call Capability Brown a vandal for destroying so many formal gardens or he can call Le Nôtre a stonemason because of the Frenchman's disdain for flowers. He can suggest that the reason why the great designers London and Wise planted so many trees 300 years ago was because they owned a tree nursery ... but he must not criticise Miss Jekyll.

Obviously the 21st century garden owes much to this remarkable woman. It is partly due to her that the garden of today has a more informal and simpler air than its Victorian counterpart. Both colour and year-round effect have a new importance, and the perfection of the herbaceous border was perhaps her most memorable gift to us. But it is strange indeed that so very, very few of the 300 gardens she designed have been maintained in their original form.

It could be that her general ideas are as valid as ever, but her actual plans are far too labour-consuming for a world where armies of gardeners no longer exist.

MISS JEKYLL was 50 years old and she suddenly had to take stock of her life. She was comfortably rich, had a wide circle of friends and was an excellent painter as well as an expert embroideress. She was interested in but not passionate about gardening and she had just been told that she was going blind.

Born into a cultured and artistic family in 1843, she had grown up in the Surrey countryside where she learnt to identify the flowers, trees and birds. She wandered the lanes and grew to love the cottage gardens with their jumble of flowers. At 17 she entered the Kensington School of Art and her talents as a craftswoman and painter began to flourish. Nothing at this stage of her life suggested that she would become the First Lady of Gardening, but there were two occurrences which perhaps sowed the seed.

## Her first book, *Wood and Garden*, appeared in 1899

She met William Robinson, the fiery Irishman who was ranting against the formal style in his magazine *The Garden*. His views greatly influenced her and she

> In garden arrangement,
> one has not only to acquire
> a knowledge of what to do,
> but also to gain some
> wisdom in perceiving what
> is well to let alone.
>
> *Gertrude Jekyll*

became a popular contributor in 1875, which gave her the opportunity to meet and exchange ideas with many of the leading horticulturalists of the day. Secondly, her father's death in 1876 meant the return of the family from Berkshire to Surrey, and here she was involved in the design of the house and garden at Munstead.

Now she was 50 years old and her eyesight was failing. In order to avoid blindness it would be necessary to give up embroidery and painting. So she made the decision which helped to change the face of British gardening – she would in future paint her pictures by using flowers in a garden rather than paint on paper or canvas.

A few months earlier she had met Ned Lutyens, a 22 year old architect at the start of his career. This odd couple formed a professional partnership – he would design the house and garden, and she would design the planting arrangement. This partnership lasted for more than 30 years and its success was phenomenal. During that time she was involved in the design of about 300 gardens, ranging from large estates around mansions to modest plots around suburban villas. Young Ned became Sir Edwin Lutyens, one of the leading architects of the day.

The ground plans of the gardens created by Lutyens were strictly formal, leaving Miss Jekyll a range of geometrical features to be clothed with plants. She never had Robinson's slavish worship of the natural look, but she did aim for the homeliness and informality of the cottage gardens she had loved as a child. The plants she used were often old favourites but the planting design was not left to

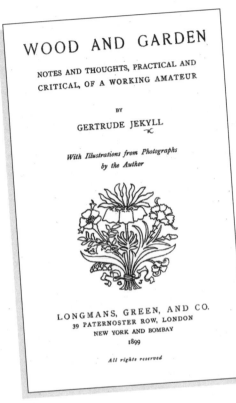

picture of pleasing colours and harmonious shapes which rose in tiers from the front of the border to the back.

Her first book, *Wood and Garden*, appeared in 1899 and it was a great success. She

## The careful blending of colours and shapes was her special magic

described it simply as 'Notes and thoughts, practical and critical, of a working amateur, with illustrations from photographs by the author' but the public wanted more. *Home and Garden* followed, filled with stories from her Munstead Wood home, and there was a stream of other publications. An important departure was *Flower Decoration in the Home* in 1907, which helped to encourage flower arranging as an art form.

Miss Jekyll's life was a full and long one and came to a close in 1932. Lutyens' memorial in the churchyard has the simplicity she would have wanted. No flowery verse, just

# GERTRUDE JEKYLL
## ARTIST
## GARDENER
## CRAFTSWOMAN

chance – the careful blending of colours and shapes was her special magic.

Many features were pioneered by her in these gardens. The single-coloured border, the use of grey-leaved plants, the year-round effect beginning with bulbs in the spring and ending with the Michaelmas daisies and golden-hued leaves of autumn. And, of course, there was the development of the herbaceous border. According to her rules this had to be a carefully blended

# JOSEPHINE

*A*S EVERY schoolboy knows, Josephine married Napoleon and became the Empress of France. But she was more than that – she was also the Queen of Roses.

She had a dream. The dream was as simple as it was breathtakingly bold. Her plan was to obtain specimens of every rose species and every rose variety growing anywhere in the world and to create with them the greatest rose garden ever made.

To contemplate such a task today with all the miracles of modern travel and communications would be a vast operation. To have undertaken such a scheme at the beginning of the 19th century was like reaching for the stars. No aeroplanes, no telephones, no fast ships … just war-torn France locked in a mighty struggle with the rest of Europe.

Yet she succeeded. On the outskirts of Paris the world's first great rose garden was created … it was called Malmaison.

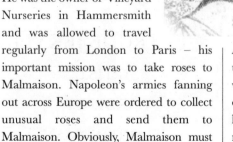

MR. KENNEDY felt quite safe as he sailed from England to France; the two countries were at war but he carried a Letter of Immunity. He was the owner of Vineyard Nurseries in Hammersmith and was allowed to travel regularly from London to Paris – his important mission was to take roses to Malmaison. Napoleon's armies fanning out across Europe were ordered to collect unusual roses and send them to Malmaison. Obviously, Malmaison must have been a very special place.

The story began in 1799, when the marriage of Napoleon and Josephine was on the point of collapse. Three years earlier the young and ambitious army officer had married the wilful and extravagant widow of Alexandre, vicomte de Beauharnais. The union began disastrously – while he was winning glory for France on the battlefields of Italy and Egypt his passionate love letters lay unopened and unanswered. His return in 1799 was a time of joy and sadness for him – home was the hero, poised to become First Consul of France, but he also came home to his wife's debts and the stories of her love affairs.

Napoleon forgave her. Instead of divorce there was to be a new interest and a new challenge for Josephine – the Château de Malmaison and its several hundred acres of parkland. Here, eight miles away from Paris, she could indulge her life-long passion for flowers.

She gathered around her some of the great botanists and horticulturalists of the day. There was Thomas Blaikie to landscape the grounds, André Dupont to

take charge of the search for roses and the artist Pierre-Joseph Redouté to record them for posterity. Josephine, now Empress of France, frequently visited her garden to advise, admire, argue and perhaps wish she could spend more time there. Her wish was soon to be granted.

---

## Malmaison contained about 250 different types of roses

---

Napoleon's desire to father a line of Emperors was even greater than his love for Josephine. She had failed to give him a son and in 1810 he had the marriage annulled. The ex-Empress now moved permanently to Malmaison and devoted herself to her plants.

If you could go back in time to 1810 and walk along the paths of Malmaison with the silken-clad ladies, you would probably have been disappointed. You would have seen none of the vibrant colours, the repeat flowering, the high-centred blooms nor the compact bushes of a modest suburban garden of today. Instead you would have found large,

---

## THE MAN WHO PAINTED HER ROSES

PIERRE-JOSEPH REDOUTÉ was born in 1759, the son of a travelling artist. His professional career began when he was 13 years old; it finished nearly 70 years later as he was showing a young student how to capture a flower's beauty in paint. Redouté was dead, leaving behind more than 5000 flower paintings, an international reputation and one of the greatest collections of botanical illustrations of all time – *Les Roses*.

His fame was due to his work at Malmaison. Josephine had commissioned him in 1805 to paint the plants which grew there; he was already a distinguished artist, having served as Drawing Master to Marie Antoinette. Surprisingly, it was to the lilies and not the roses he turned his attention, and between 1805 and 1817 the eight-volumed *Les Liliacées* was produced. In 1817 the first volume of *Les Roses* appeared, and about 170 of the Malmaison roses are illustrated in the three volumes. The descriptive text was by Claude Antoine Thory but it is the pictures we all know.

We see Redouté roses everywhere – framed prints, table mats, biscuit tins and so on – but there is an ironic twist: Josephine, creator of Malmaison, died three years before the first Redouté rose print appeared.

spreading bushes which bore a single flush of flowers each year.

Malmaison contained about 250 different types of roses and the dominant ones were the Gallicas. This was the classic Red Rose in all its forms, growing in beds alongside the Albas or White Roses. There were tough Rugosa Roses, graceful Burnet

## *Every* great Rose Garden in the world is a memorial to Josephine

Roses, Blood Roses from China and Virginia Roses from America. The finest fragrance would have come from the Damask Roses, and the Centifolias would have certainly impressed you with their large, globular blooms. But the overall absence of bright colours would have been a surprise – white, pink and red everywhere. If you had looked carefully you would have found a bed or two of dull yellow or dark orange roses from Persia – roses which were due to play an important part in the breeding of the modern colourful rose.

Josephine entertained lavishly and both royalty and aristocracy walked among her roses. Never before had there been such a collection and soon every château had to have its *roseraie*. The Rose Garden was born, and when the war was over the fashion spread to the grand gardens of Britain and then to North America.

Now the gardens of Malmaison are no more. Josephine died in 1814 and without her driving force they steadily declined until they were destroyed by the Prussians in the 1870–71 War. But not all is lost – the Malmaison collection has been recreated at La Roseraie de l'Hay-les-Roses in Paris. Not just this one, but *every* great Rose Garden in the world is a memorial to Josephine.

# LINNAEUS

## The Inventor of the Modern Naming System

CARL LINNÉ was born in South Sweden in 1707. He was a rather dull child but worked hard and at 34 became Professor of Medicine and then Botany at the University of Uppsala. Today he is remembered neither as Linné nor as a doctor. He has been immortalised by his Latin name – Carolus Linnaeus.

This is appropriate, because he evolved the modern system of Plant Classification, whereby each plant has basically two Latin names, the first one (the genus) is like a person's surname and the second one (the species) is similar to a Christian name. A simple idea, but before it there was great confusion and afterwards the door was opened for scientific plant breeding and the advance of botanical thought. 'God created the plants and animals, and Linnaeus put them in order.'

WHEN HE was 23 years old the son of the pastor at Råshult was offered the job he really wanted. His father had hoped that he would be ordained and his schoolmaster had thought that he would be more suited to mending shoes than going to University. But he did study at Uppsala and now he had been appointed a lecturer in botany.

Plants had always been the first love of Carl Linné. He had been given the nickname 'the little botanist' when he was a small child and whilst still at school he began to collect and press all sorts of plants. Their variations fascinated him – why couldn't there be a *simple* way of classifying and naming them?

The classification systems in use when Linné took up his post at Uppsala were many and varied. Some were over-simple (Albertus Magnus had just two groups – trees and shrubs) and others were hopelessly complex. None allowed an understanding of relationships nor a way of grouping them together. Young Linné hit on the solution – plants should be grouped according to the make-up of their flower parts. Closely-related plants had the same

# Eine Blumen-Uhr

number of petals, sepals, stamens etc., which meant that grouping had nothing to do with colour, size, use or any of the other ideas which had been proposed.

Linné talked about his ideas to the students at Uppsala and in 1735 the new system was published as the *Systema Naturae*. He travelled to England, France etc. to talk to prominent scientists and enough of them supported him to establish his reputation.

The naming of plants was as clumsy as their classification had been. The system in vogue was to give each plant a brief description in Latin and that was its scientific name. This was about as effective as calling people 'John the Shoemaker' or 'Arthur who farms by the brook' – family relationships were lost and confusion was inevitable. Linné once again had the answer. His new Binomial System gave a *genus* name to plants which were very closely related in terms of their flower parts – thus all roses were put in the genus *Rosa*. Next, the various sorts had to be separated and Linné gave these specific names – these were the *species*. The White rose became *Rosa alba*, the Dog rose became *Rosa canina* and so on. Brilliantly simple – a two-name system for all plants.

In 1737 Linné set out the basic principles in his *Genera Plantarum* and then turned his back on natural history. He went to Stockholm to practise as a doctor and in 1741 he was appointed Professor of Medicine at Uppsala University. But 'the little botanist' could not keep away from his plants, and in 1742 relinquished his chair in medicine so as to take up the more lowly post of Professor of Botany.

His days were spent teaching and classifying, and in 1753 the first edition of the *Species Plantarum* appeared. Within its pages were the Linnaean names of more than 6000 plants, and even today you can tell the ones he named by the letter 'L' printed after each one in textbooks.

The *Species Plantarum* is one of the most important books in the history of mankind (or *Homo sapiens* using the Linnaean System of naming animals). It is taken as the

CAROLI LINNÆI
EQUITIS DE STELLA POLARI,
ARCHIATRI REGII, MED. & BOTAN. PROFESS. UPSAL.;
ACAD. UPSAL. HOLMENS. PETROPOL. BEROL. IMPER.
LOND. MONSPEL. TOLOS. FLORENT. SOC.

# SYSTEMA NATURÆ
PER
REGNA TRIA NATURÆ,
SECUNDUM
CLASSES, ORDINES,
GENERA, SPECIES,
CUM
CHARACTERIBUS, DIFFERENTIIS,
SYNONYMIS, LOCIS.

TOMUS I.

EDITIO DECIMA, REFORMATA.

Cum Privilegio S:æ R:æ M:tis Sveciæ.

HOLMIÆ,
IMPENSIS DIRECT. LAURENTII SALVII,
1758.

starting point of the modern way of naming things and the modern science of horticulture would be unthinkable without it.

In 1761 he was raised to the nobility – it was now Carl von Linné, but it had long been Carolus Linnaeus in scientific circles. In 1778 he died, and his enormous collection of pressed flowers, shells, minerals, insects and books were bought a few years later by James Smith, a young English naturalist. The collection was housed in Chelsea and it is now preserved by the Linnaean Society of London.

# GREGOR MENDEL

## ABBOT OF BRÜNN AND THE FATHER OF GENETICS

*T*HE ABBOT of the Brünn monastery in Moravia (part of the Czech Republic) died in 1884. Fr. Gregor Mendel was mourned by his monks and the townspeople, but the world outside the area had never heard of him.

Success and fame have been the rewards of many of the great scientists and philosophers who have changed our view of the universe. Einstein, Aristotle, Darwin and others were recognised and appreciated in their own lifetime, but not Mendel. Strange, because the work and discoveries by this Austrian-born monk gave us our first knowledge of the way in which heredity works. His first laws of heredity (Mendelism) were the foundation stones of scientific plant and animal breeding and the start of the science of genetics. He sent his findings to the great libraries of the world, but for 33 years nobody listened ...

JOHANN MENDEL (he did not adopt the name Gregor until he was ordained as a priest) was born in 1822. He grew up on his father's farm and despite his love of plants and the soil he entered the monastery at Brünn in 1843.

The next part of his life serves as an inspiration to all who have failed in academic achievement – Mendel, destined to become one of the immortals of biology, did not achieve his teaching diploma ... because of low marks in biology! Despite this setback he did teach for a short time and in 1856 started his classical experiments on hybridisation in the monastery gardens.

Of course, the concept of hybridisation had been known for thousands of years before the birth of Mendel – the Chinese had been breeding camellias and roses for many hundreds of years and any observer could see the effect of crossing dissimilar strains by looking at a mongrel dog. In fact, the word 'hybrid' was coined to describe such dogs.

Before Mendel people had the wrong idea about what happened in a hybrid. It was assumed that the two dissimilar properties blended together and it was this blend which was passed on to the next generation. A white dog mated with a black one might give rise to a spotted puppy, and this 'spottiness' was transmitted to its offspring. They were wrong, and in the little garden at Brünn the reason why was to become plain.

Mendel's first trials were with garden peas. He chose varieties which differed in height, flower colour, seed shape, seed colour, etc. His first discovery was most interesting. When a tall variety was crossed with a short one, then the resulting progeny were all tall. A smooth-skinned pea variety produced smooth-skinned progeny after it had been crossed with a wrinkled variety. This, he reasoned correctly, must mean that some characteristics of living things were 'dominant' and others 'recessive'.

So the idea that characteristics were blended in a hybrid was obviously wrong. He felt that there must be genetic factors (we now call them genes) which pair up when fertilisation occurs. If the new seed gets two 'talls', or one 'tall' and one 'short', it would give rise to a tall plant – 'tall' being dominant. Only the seed receiving genetic factors which were both 'short' would produce short-growing plants.

It was an easy idea to test. If tall hybrids (one 'tall' and one 'short' genetic factor) were crossed, then by simple arithmetic you should get 75% tall and 25% short plants from the seeds. Mendel found that this was indeed the case. What now? He presented his results to the local natural history society in 1866. He was not modest about the findings – 'among all the numerous experiments made, not one has been carried out to such an extent ...' – and copies of the report were sent to many scientists. But nobody listened.

Mendel's scientific activity now steadily declined. In 1868 he was elected Abbot, and became a revered administrator. Unfortunately, about a year later he used hawkweed to try to confirm his laws of heredity, and the results failed to do so. Mendel's laws were basically correct but the mechanism of genetics is more complex than his simplified version. The simple laws did not apply to hawkweed.

So he spent less and less time on his experiments and perhaps in the end accepted his failure to be recognised. Fifteen years after his death the importance of his discoveries at last came to light. There is some argument over who should get the credit. Perhaps it belongs to the Royal Horticultural Society – it was at their meeting in July 1899 that the work of Mendel received its first public airing. Or perhaps it belongs to one or other of three scientists (Correns, van Seysenegg and de Vries) who in 1900 claimed to have obtained similar results to those in the research paper standing forgotten on the library shelf.

# LE NÔTRE

## GARDEN MASTER OF EUROPE

*T*HE SPIRIT of Le Nôtre infected Europe from the middle of the 17th century to the middle of the 18th century. In Britain, Germany, Italy, Russia and Austria as well as in his native France his monumental style was the height of fashion. The design of Washington D.C. was influenced by the layout of Versailles.

André Le Nôtre shone like the sun in the gardening sky, and yet for the first half of his long life he was unknown outside his native Paris. Even when fame came he remained as gentle and unassuming as ever. When Louis XIV suggested that he should have a coat of arms he refused, saying that he already had one – 'Three slugs surrounding a spade, crowned with cabbage leaves.' Noble families throughout Europe wanted his services, but there is little evidence that he ever left France apart from a trip to improve the Vatican Gardens. Simple and unassuming, maybe, but also immortal.

ANDRÉ LE NÔTRE was born in Paris in 1613 and from his baptism he was steeped in the gardening tradition. His father Jean was the Royal Gardener at the Tuileries and his godmother

ANDRÉ LE NOTRE

was the wife of Claude Mollet, one of France's great garden designers.

Young Le Nôtre was at first apprenticed to Vouet, the Royal Painter, and in this studio learnt the principles of perspective and architecture which were to stand him in such good stead. But the artist's life was not for him and he returned to his father's trade.

There is some disagreement about the ability and seniority of Le Nôtre during these early years as a gardener at the Tuileries. Some historians have him tending the shrubs and climbing plants, but it is on record that he was appointed Designer to the King's Gardens in 1640 and was involved in creating the vast avenue which is now the Champs Elysées.

Whatever the truth is about his early work in Paris, the world had certainly not heard of him when Finance Minister Fouquet asked him to design the garden at Vaux-le-Vicomte. The story of this ill-fated garden is told on page 123, but there was nothing ill-fated about it for the history of gardening.

Vaux-le-Vicomte gave Le Nôtre his chance to create *le jardin français*. Everything had to be on a scale which had not been contemplated before. The strict geometric shapes currently in vogue were maintained but the house was to be the centrepiece – cleared of trees and other obstructions so that it could be clearly seen in the midst of its grandeur.

The key feature was the wide central vista. This stretched from the courtyard at the front of the house to the distant horizon. Along or across this vista was the Long Canal which could extend for a mile

> He worked for private individuals and for the King with the same industry: his only thought was to aid Nature, and to reduce the truly beautiful to the lowest cost.
>
> *Le Nôtre's Epitaph*

or more, and the layout was decorated with complex parterres of dwarf box together with massive fountains and classical statues in ornate stone. Another important feature was the *patte d'oie* – a 'goose-foot' pattern of avenues radiating from a central point.

## LE NÔTRE'S GARDEN

Le Nôtre's garden at Versailles beggars description. Started in 1662, it took 36,000 workmen and 95 sculptors to create the ultimate French garden. They toiled for nearly 16 years under the watchful eye of André Le Nôtre and it cost an astronomical £50,000,000. The Versailles of today is not quite the same as Le Nôtre left it but you can see nearly all of the old glory and rather more flowering plants. There is the mile-long Grand Canal, The Royal Alley lined with marble vases, the Neptune Fountain and the vast parterres.

Trees were arranged in geometrical patterns well away from the house and conical evergreens were planted and clipped to serve as living green statues along the avenues. But plants did not have a basic role in the Le Nôtre garden – he preferred glass beads, coloured sand or porcelain flowers to living plants within his parterres. If flowers were used then their purpose was to provide a splash of colour of the correct size and hue – coloured carpeting, nothing more.

Vaux-le-Vicomte saw the first flowering of the new style. It cost the owner his liberty, but it provided Le Nôtre with his greatest challenge. Louis XIV ordered him to build a garden at Versailles, a swampy estate of about 15,000 acres. The rules of the game were simple – it had to be the greatest garden that the world had ever known, a vast outdoor palace which could accommodate thousands of people.

He was about 50 when he started the task and over 65 when it was completed. It was a masterpiece and the world marvelled. Louis' favourites were the fountains, although there was never enough water to make them all work satisfactorily. Le Nôtre died in 1700, in his beloved Paris. France had been his canvas and his masterpieces were many – St. Cloud, Fontainebleau, Rambouillet, Sceaux, St. Germain-en-Laye. His own favourite was neither Vaux-le-Vicomte nor Versailles – it was Chantilly.

There are, of course, many 'Le Nôtre' gardens in the world. St. James's Park in London, Het Loo in Holland, Herrenhausen in Germany, the Peterhof in Russia and Le Granja in Spain are all examples, but there is little doubt that they are the work of pupils and imitators and not the Master himself.

# HUMPHRY REPTON

## The Link Between the Landskip and the Bedding Plant

*T*HE 'LANDSKIP' was at its height when Capability Brown died. The previous style of rectangular lakes, long avenues and complex parterres had been the work of artists-turned-gardeners – the severely simple style of the Landscape School had been perfected by the practical gardener Lancelot (Capability) Brown.

Brown's successor as the leader of gardening fashion was basically an artist and not a gardener. He did not deviate greatly from the Brown pattern; maybe he had neither the inventiveness nor the courage, but he did soften it. He did not despise straight lines and flowers in the same way as his predecessor and his greatest achievement was to get the gardening world ready for the Gardenesque approach which was to appear shortly after his death. In this style plants became important and did not merely serve as garden furniture.

CAPABILITY BROWN died in 1783. For decades this man of boundless energy and fixed opinions had dictated the style of garden design. Nobody had challenged his emphatic belief that all formal features had to be swept away and replaced by idealised countryside, and his death left a void which at first nobody attempted to fill.

Obviously, the future of the Grand Garden hung in the balance. The new dictator might have even stronger views than those of Brown about the need for naturalness or he might order a return to the geometrical shapes and stiff formality of the 17th century. The mantle was to fall upon Humphry Repton, who believed in neither of the extreme views.

Unlike Brown, he had received no training in horticulture and had not worked as a gardener. Repton was born in 1752, and after schooling became an

apprentice and then a merchant in Norwich. His main interests, however, were the countryside and his water colours and so he moved to rural Norfolk.

It was an enjoyable time for Repton – sketching, walking, surveying his small estate, surrounded by his loving children. Unfortunately he did not have the resources to remain a gentleman of leisure and the Repton family moved to Hare Street in Essex where father could find some form of employment. In 1788 the calling cards were printed – H. Repton, landscape gardener. Brown had been dead for five years and Repton believed that 'the art could only be perfected by the united

## THE HUMPHRY REPTON GARDENS

Gardens of all shapes and sizes were designed by Repton and in some cases, such as Welbeck Abbey and Sheringham Hall, he was involved in the design of the house as well. Some have been destroyed, others partly altered but sufficient remain in their original form to provide a living demonstration of the Repton style.

| | | |
|---|---|---|
| Antony House, Cornwall | Rudding Park, | Tatton Park, Cheshire |
| Ashridge, Hertfordshire |   N. Yorkshire | Uppark, W. Sussex |
| Attingham Park, | Sheringham Hall, Norfolk | Welbeck, Nottinghamshire |
|   Shropshire | Stanage, Wales | Woburn Abbey, |
| Bulstrode, | Stoneleigh Park, |   Bedfordshire |
|   Buckinghamshire |   Warwickshire | |
| Cobham, Kent | | |
| Holkham Hall, Norfolk | | |
| Luscombe Castle, Devon | | |
| Rode, Cheshire | | |

powers of the landscape painter and the practical gardener'. He combined the two terms (if not the two skills) and as a self-styled landscape gardener wrote to his friends for commissions.

---

## He prepared detailed paintings of the garden at the 'before' stage and then paintings of the proposed 'after' stage

---

His local work was soon followed by designs prepared for William Thomas Coke at Holkham, the Duke of Portland at Welbeck Abbey and Lord Petre at Buckenden House. Repton was now established, and for the next 30 years he was Brown's successor as the trend-setter in gardening style.

His success was due more to his originality in presentation than the quality of the designs. He prepared detailed paintings of the garden at the 'before' stage and then paintings of the proposed 'after' stage. These proposals were often in the form of fold-over flaps, so the client could actually see his new garden develop by turning over the pages. These paintings and the text were handsomely bound in red leather and the Repton Red Book was often sufficient to persuade the rich and influential to put their estate in the landscape gardener's hands. About 400 Red Books were prepared but only 200 remain – a gardener's dream to own one but only the very rich can hope to buy one of these valuable collector's pieces.

The originality of presentation was not matched by any originality of ideas. Capability Brown's son had passed his father's notebooks to Repton, and in the beginning the principles of Brown were rather slavishly followed. In a short time a Repton style did evolve, which meant that the British garden stepped back from the brink of extremism.

The landscape concept remained, but on a much smaller scale. No longer did it have to encompass everything and no longer did all traces of formalism have to be destroyed. Commenting on a fine avenue of trees in a 17th century garden, Repton said 'a better reason than fashion must be advanced for cutting down large trees'. Brown would rather have died than say such a thing!

In Repton's style trees and shrubs were planted in greater numbers and exotic varieties were included. Terraces around the house were restored and flowers were no longer banished. In 1818 Repton died, and the Landscape School died with him. With his modifications of this severe style he had gently led the British garden towards the stage when trees, shrubs and flowers would become important in their own right.

# WILLIAM ROBINSON

## FATHER OF THE GARDEN OF TODAY

EVERY AGE has its own style of gardening and the mid-Victorian era was no exception. Architects like Barry and Nesfield had dictated that gardens must be strictly formal in design; plants should be bedded out in neat blocks and strictly disciplined like the children of the period.

The 21st century model is quite different. Everywhere there is an informal air — rockeries, naturalised bulbs, hardy perennials planted in a jumble of colours and shrubs planted in groups rather than straight lines. The founder and arch-priest of this style was William Robinson.

Like all revolutionaries he went too far. His belief that wild flowers should be a basic part of the garden scene was never really accepted and his call for the abandonment of Latin names met a similar fate. But his basic message was accepted — a garden should be a piece of the countryside with informal planting of shrubs and herbaceous perennials playing a dominant role. Others took up his message and a few improved on his ideas, but the title of Father of the Garden of Today belongs to Robinson.

WE KNOW practically nothing about the early life of William Robinson because he never talked about his humble beginnings and his boyhood in Ireland. He was born in 1838 but details of location, schooling and family background are not known.

We pick up the threads in 1859 when Robinson was in charge of the greenhouses in a Co. Kerry garden. Two years later he performed his first act of protest against the Old Order — he raked out the fires and opened all the windows in mid-winter and left for London. Robinson the Rebel had arrived.

He was employed by the Royal Botanic Gardens at Regent's Park — obviously references from previous employers could not have been important in those days! The turning point in his career came in 1867 when he was sent by *The Times* to cover the Paris Exhibition — from now on

Robinson was to be a pioneering writer, not a practical gardener.

His first book, *Gleanings from French Gardens*, appeared in 1868 and two years later *The Wild Garden* set out his belief that the flowers of the countryside belonged in the garden. These titles were interesting enough but Robinson was about to launch on the venture which enabled him to popularise his beliefs – he founded a magazine.

The first issue of *The Garden* appeared in 1871 and it attracted contributions from leading horticulturalists. The cry against strict formalism was now being heard, but there was still a need for a book to put it all together – a bible for the new movement. *The English Flower Garden* answered this need when it was published in 1883.

The peasant boy from Ireland was now a rich man. His writings, investments and inheritance (his father had made good in America) meant that in 1884 he could buy the large estate of Gravetye Manor in Sussex. He was 46 years old and the rest of his life was devoted to making his garden at Gravetye, updating *The English Flower Garden*, editing his magazines (*Gardening Illustrated* had started in 1879), writing more books and advising others in the application of his principles. This period was to last for more than 50 years, the last 30 of them being spent in a wheelchair. In 1935 William Robinson died – paralysed, 97 years old but a man of firm opinions and outspoken ideas to the end.

What are we to make of this man? It is hard to explain his friendship with Gertrude Jekyll – the arch-priestess of the movement towards informality in the garden. The aggressive, self-made Irishman who believed that paper plans were nonsense first met in 1875 the gentle, cultured 'Auntie Bumps' whose profession in later years was to draw up plans for other people's gardens. Yet the friendship never wavered and nearly fifty years later this man at 94 travelled in winter to say good-bye at her funeral.

As he got older this lover of the simple flower and the simple cottage garden produced ornate books and a pompously expensive magazine, *Flora and Sylva*, which soon failed. A life full of paradoxes – even Gravetye was not as natural as the ideal garden he promoted – but it was a life full of passionate zeal for a new way of gardening. Its memorial is outside your living-room window.

# THE ROTHSCHILDS

## A FAMILY OF WEALTH AND GREEN FINGERS

*I*F YOU think that the name Rothschild belongs in a book on banking but not gardening, take a trip to Exbury in Hampshire. The garden is open to the public between February and November, and in it you will find the largest and most varied collection of azaleas and rhododendrons in the country. It was the creation of Lionel Nathan de Rothschild, who began it after World War I and by the time of his death in 1942 had bred a number of outstanding rhododendrons and had created the world-famous Exbury strain of azaleas.

But Lionel was just one of the gardening Rothschilds. It is Edmund who controls the commercial nursery at Exbury these days, despatching azaleas, rhododendrons and camellias all over the world. Edmund is the latest chapter in the story of the gardening Rothschilds in Britain. The story began with Alfred.

THE ROTHSCHILD saga is a tale of power intertwined with public service on the grand scale. Baron Nathan Rothschild raised the money which enabled Wellington to defeat Napoleon, and Lionel lent Disraeli £4 million so that the British Government could pay for the Suez Canal.

It was only natural that the first British Rothschilds to be involved with gardening should do things on a grand scale – Alfred de Rothschild moved into the Halton mansion in Buckinghamshire and the formal gardens with their 50 greenhouses required a staff of 60 gardeners. Baron

Ferdinand de Rothschild built Waddesdon Manor during the 1880s in the style of a French château and the grounds around the house were designed by a French landscape gardener. Waddesdon was bequeathed to the National Trust in 1957, so you can visit this Victorian grand garden with its spectacular aviary amid the flower beds, terraces, statuary and fountains of the period.

The only interest shown by these early Rothschilds in gardening was as a means to provide a fine setting for their stately houses. Look inside Waddesdon Manor and you will see the true interests of Ferdinand – the paintings, tapestries, porcelain and furniture which adorn the mansion.

Towards the end of the 19th century a true interest in gardening crept into the Rothschilds and this seed was destined to flourish and eventually flower at Exbury. The first member of the family to show this awakening interest in horticulture was Leopold de Rothschild (1845–1917). At Gunnersbury House in London he created a famous fruit collection and at Ascott in Buckinghamshire he laid out a 30 acre garden with advice from Sir Harry Veitch. Ascott is one of the finest examples of the late Victorian garden in existence – it is now administered by the National Trust and you can visit it between April and September. There you will see the grass terraces, topiary sundial, unusual trees, pools and rockeries which Leopold de Rothschild created.

## Lionel Nathan de Rothschild employed more than 200 labourers and gardeners

In 1868 the 2nd Baron, Lionel Walter Rothschild, was born and the great naturalist tradition of the modern Rothschilds was established. Lionel Walter collected his first butterflies when he was seven and went on to become a distinguished zoologist. He created the superb gardens around his home in Tring Park, but he is remembered as the man who gathered the largest natural history collection ever amassed by one person and his museum at Tring is now part of the British Museum.

Lionel Nathan de Rothschild was born in 1882 and planted his first garden at the age of five. Once again the early start bore fruit – Lionel became a world authority on rhododendrons and orchids. In 1919 he began work on a 200 acre garden at his home at Exbury and in the 1920s began to breed rhododendrons. From this work came many fine varieties such as 'Hawk', 'Lady Chamberlain' and 'Lady

the millionaire tradition. This even spilled over into horticulture – during its heyday there were over a million plants in the Exbury garden.

> Our England is a garden,
> and such gardens are not made
> By singing – 'Oh, how beautiful!'
> and sitting in the shade,
> When better men than we go out
> and start their working lives
> At grubbing weeds from gravel
>   paths
> with broken dinner-knives.
> Then seek your job with
>   thankfulness
> and work till further orders,
> If it's only netting strawberries
> or killing slugs on borders;
> And when your back stops aching
> and your hands begin to harden
> You will find yourself a partner
> in the Glory of the Garden.
> Oh, Adam was a gardener,
> and God who made him sees
> That half a proper gardener's work
> is done upon his knees;
> So when your work is finished,
> you can wash your hands and pray
> For the Glory of the Garden,
> that it may not pass away.
>
> *Rudyard Kipling*

Bessborough'. Even more important was the introduction of the Exbury strain of deciduous azaleas which combined floral beauty with fragrance.

## There were over a million plants in the Exbury garden

Lionel Rothschild employed more than 200 labourers and gardeners when he was creating Exbury and so carried on the family tradition of doing things on the grand scale. But it had not always been so – Meyer Amschel was born in the ghetto at Frankfurt in 1744. He took the house sign of a red (*rote*) shield (*schild*) as his adopted name and rose from poor fatherless apprentice to rich banker. He sent one of his sons, Nathan Meyer, to London to start the Rothschild Bank there, and so began

# VITA SACKVILLE-WEST

## CREATOR OF SISSINGHURST

> *T*HE Hon. Victoria Sackville-West was appointed the Gardening Correspondent of the *Observer* in 1947. Each Sunday she wrote about the happenings in the garden she had created – Sissinghurst Castle.
>
> She had been the driving force and the gardener, her husband the designer of the six acre garden which was destined to be one of the most beautiful and influential gardens in Britain. Others like Gertrude Jekyll had pioneered the concept of informal planting within a strictly geometrical design; Major Johnston had created a series of linked garden rooms at Hidcote – Vita Sackville-West put it all together at Sissinghurst.
>
> Her biography reveals an extremely complex personality, a partner in a most unusual marriage but above all a gardener extraordinary.

IN 1930 Sir Harold Nicolson and his wife, Vita Sackville-West, bought Sissinghurst Castle in Kent. They were a distinguished couple – Sir Harold was a diplomat and writer, his wife was a novelist and poet (*not* poetess, a term she detested). Both were the children of titled parents, but like millions of married couples before and since, they set out to turn a neglected wilderness into a garden.

Looking around their new home in 1930, they found an old castle-like mansion which had been built in Tudor times but was now derelict, and a weed-infested wilderness surrounding it. Others would have seen a depressingly hard task, but all Vita could see was wonderfully rich soil and the chance to create a fairyland.

It took about two years to clear the site, and then the work of garden construction began. The plan was to have long walks running to each point of the compass, with small gardens opening into these corridors 'like rooms of an enormous house'. Writing in the R.H.S. *Journal* in 1953, Vita Sackville-West recorded the style they chose – 'the strictest formality of design with the maximum informality in planting'. Harold was the landscape architect, Vita the landscape gardener – his work was soon finished but her task continued for the rest of her life.

By 1934 the garden had been built and planted. Its success is one of the legends of

gardening. Sissinghurst Castle, now the property of the National Trust, is regarded as one of the most important of our gardens. Sir Harold acknowledged only one as superior – Hidcote Manor. If you join the 100,000 people who visit Sissinghurst each year you will see the world-famous White Garden, filled with silvery and grey plants, and the Nuttery, a hazel orchard carpeted with primroses. There is a Cottage Garden and an excellent Herb Garden. Vita's Tower stands like a sentinel over the flowers and trees, looking down on so many interesting features. There is a thyme lawn, herb-covered garden seats, the yew-fringed circular areas of lawn known as roundels and many other unusual items. A garden, like its creator, which is filled with surprises.

The Hon. Victoria, the only child of Lord Sackville, was born in 1892 at Knole in Kent. She was a tomboy forced into the strict mould of Edwardian ideas about the role of a woman of quality, and after an unhappy childhood she married a young diplomat, Harold Nicolson, in 1913.

> The size of the garden has nothing to do with it; twenty acres or one acre or half an acre, it is all the same.
>
> *Vita Sackville-West*

There were two sons, Ben and Nigel, and we are indebted to Nigel Nicolson for the biography of his mother. It revealed the complexity of her character, providing an insight into her extraordinary marriage. Before the purchase of Sissinghurst there were prolonged absences – Harold served at the Embassies in Teheran and Berlin, but Vita did not accompany him. The ultra-feminine role of a diplomat's wife abroad would have been quite impossible for her.

This was a time of writing and tempestuous love affairs with other women, but despite this side of her nature and the fact that they spent most of their lives apart, their relationship was extremely close. From the date of their meeting to her death in 1962 they corresponded at almost daily intervals, pouring out their worries, joys … and love.

# THE TRADESCANTS

## The Father and Son who Changed the British Garden

*J*OHN TRADESCANT the Elder began his horticultural career with the Cecil family at the beginning of the 17th century. Eventually he became a gardener to the wife of Charles I, and he was succeeded in this post by his son.

They did not write about horticulture, nor did they create a new gardening style. Yet by the time that John Tradescant the Younger died in 1662, their achievements had transformed the British Garden.

The Tradescants have been described as the fathers of English Gardening, which is perhaps too fanciful. They were, in fact, collectors *par excellence* – the first of the British plant hunters who combed the world looking for new varieties.

The list of plants they brought to our shores for the first time is a long one, but recent research indicates that it may well have been overstated in the past. Many of the plants which have been credited to them were already in Britain. Their greatest success may well have been the way they popularised their own as well as other people's discoveries. In this way scores of botanical rarities were turned into garden plants.

JOHN TRADESCANT the Elder was born about 1570 somewhere in Suffolk. His father was a farmer, but practically nothing else is known about him before he appears in the records as a gardener to the Cecil family. In 1609 the plans for the gardens of Hatfield House were prepared by Mountain Jenings, and Tradescant was sent overseas to collect plants.

The nurseries and gardens of France and Holland were his suppliers and the detailed accounts exist to this day.

Tulips at ten shillings the hundred, 'flowers called anemones', 'sypris trees at one shilling the peece', mulberries, vines and many, many more. His employer, who was now the Earl of Salisbury, must have thought highly of his efforts – a figure which is thought to be John Tradescant is carved on a newel post on the staircase at Hatfield House.

The job at Hatfield was short-lived – the Earl died in 1612 and Tradescant moved to the gardens of Sir Edward Wotton at Canterbury. In 1618 he got the chance he had always wanted – a plant-hunting trip to a far-off land. He was appointed naturalist to a mission to Russia and was

---

A figure which is thought to be John Tradescant is carved on a newel post on the staircase at Hatfield House

---

responsible for preparing the first-ever list of Russian flora. Obviously he brought some plants back to these shores, but the old story that he introduced the larch is now doubted.

Other exciting trips followed, such as hunting pirates along the Algerian coast in 1621. The booty he brought back was not recaptured jewels; it was the apricot and other shrubs and trees. After a spell as gardener to the Duke of Buckingham he was appointed Keeper of His Majesty's Garden at Oatlands.

In 1629 he leased a house and large garden in Lambeth and his appointment as gardener to Charles I in the following year meant that he now had the money, time and prestige to establish a large collection of objects and oddities from all over the world. This was Tradescant's Ark – a 'closett of rarities' which included Henry VIII's stirrups, hawks' hoods and hawking glove donated by Charles I.

John Tradescant's full and rewarding life came to an end in 1638. We shall never know the full list of plants he brought for the first time to our gardens – the flowers, vines, fruit trees, shrubs and so on, but his contemporaries did know. The 17th century author John Parkinson wrote that

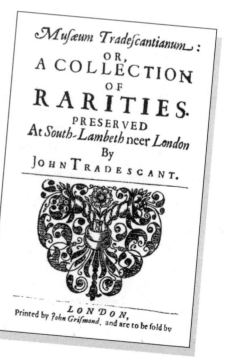

Musæum Tradescantianum:
OR,
A COLLECTION
OF
RARITIES.
PRESERVED
At South-Lambeth neer London
By
JOHN TRADESCANT.

LONDON,
Printed by John Grismond, and are to be sold by

Tradescant 'wonderfully laboured to obtain all the rarest fruit he can hear of in any place in Christendom, Turkey, yea or the whole world.'

The post of Keeper of the Royal Garden passed to his son, John Tradescant the Younger. He was 30 years old when he succeeded his father in 1638, and had inherited the passion for plant-hunting from the man he had served as an assistant for 15 years.

The passion was the same but the location was completely different – John the Younger had turned to the New World. He was on a plant-hunting expedition in Virginia when his father died, and was to make further trips to North America in 1642 and 1654.

The list of plants he brought back to Britain for the first time is lengthy and varied, and includes such familiar names as the Tulip tree, Plane tree and Red maple. For a much longer list of American plants Tradescant was not the discoverer but was responsible for their acceptance as garden plants – examples are the lupin, bergamot, rudbeckia, Virginia creeper, False acacia and walnut.

It is right that the Tradescants should have been immortalised by Linnaeus who coined the name *Tradescantia* for the spiderwort. It is strange, however, that they should be remembered in the name of an American plant with which their connection was slight rather than for their collection so painstakingly gathered at the Ark.

The Tradescant Trust was formed in 1977 to preserve the memory of our earliest plant collectors. Its home is at the church of St. Mary-at-Lambeth, next to Lambeth Palace in London, and in the graveyard is the family box tomb of the Tradescants. On its top you will find their epitaph and round the side symbolic carvings to represent their travels.

A Museum of Garden History has been created together with a Memorial Garden which contains examples of the plants growing in the Tradescant garden in 1656. The Garden is maintained by volunteers and is open throughout the year from Tuesday to Sunday (open 10.30–17.00; closed Mondays and over the Christmas period).

Elias Ashmole, a friend of John the Younger, had long envied the collection and managed to persuade Tradescant to sign a deed of gift. So the collection passed to Ashmole on John's death in 1662 and in turn was bequeathed to Oxford by Ashmole where it formed the nucleus of Britain's first museum. They called it the Ashmolean Museum after its donor ... not the Tradescantian after its collectors. The name is wrong, but it is still a testimony to the father and son team who changed the British Garden.

# E. H. WILSON

## THE FACE THAT LAUNCHED A THOUSAND PLANTS

*A*T 21 Ernest Henry Wilson was a bright young botanist ready to start his career as a lecturer at the Royal College of Science. He had seen Gloucestershire, Warwickshire, London ... and little else.

Before his fortieth birthday he was the legendary 'Chinese' Wilson, famed for his travels in the East. Quite simply, he was to become the most prolific plant hunter of all time. Before his tragic death in 1930 he had discovered 3000 new species – about 1000 of which were brought back for cultivation in the gardens of Europe and the United States. About 600 of them are still grown today, and both nurserymen's catalogues and our shrub borders would be thinner if he had taken up the post as lecturer at the Royal College of Science instead of accepting Mr Veitch's offer.

IN 1898 the Managing Director of the famous Veitch Nurseries asked the Director of Kew Gardens to recommend a young man who would be willing and able to travel to China and find the Handkerchief tree. Pressed specimens of the leaves and curious white flowers had been sent to them – now they wanted seeds in order to raise and then introduce the tree to British gardens.

> If you have two loaves,
> sell one and buy a lily.
> *Chinese Proverb*

The Director recommended Ernest Wilson. The choice was either a fortunate guess or a piece of inspired selection. There had been nothing in the boy's career to suggest that he had the outstanding toughness required or the ability to obtain the cooperation of people in a strange and hostile land.

His application letter to Mr. Veitch set out his unadventurous life story. Born at Chipping Campden in 1876, he had worked at Birmingham Botanical Gardens and studied at the Technical School. He had obtained a position in 1897 at the Royal Botanic Gardens at Kew, there was a lectureship in the offing – but he was willing to go to China to hunt for plants.

His first expedition lasted from 1899 to 1902 and was extremely successful. In the mountainous region of N.W. China he found the Handkerchief tree (*Davidia involucrata*) and much more besides – the Primrose jasmine, *Magnolia delavayi*, the Chinese Hill cherry, the Paperbark maple … a collection of nearly 400 plants.

## His most famous discovery during these later expeditions was a lily

In 1903 Mr Veitch sent him off again, this time to find the Yellow poppy (*Meconopsis integrifolia*). Once again he found and brought back to Britain many plants which had never been seen before. New rhododendrons and roses, new primulas and poppies – the reputation of Ernest Wilson was now established.

He was 30 years old when his connection with Britain and the Veitch Nurseries came to an end; his new home was to be the United States. His new patron, Professor John Sprague Sargent, was the famous Director of the Arnold Arboretum in Boston. America's greatest tree collection needed new specimens, and Wilson was the man to find them. So 'Chinese' Wilson went off on his travels again, to Japan, Korea, Australia, New Zealand, India, Africa and, of course, China.

The search was for trees for the Arboretum, but his most famous discovery during these later expeditions was a lily, *Lilium regale*. He found it growing in a remote valley on the borders of Tibet and in 1910 sent back 7000 bulbs. At last there was a lily which was easy to grow in any garden – white trumpets crowded on top of 1.5 m stems. It was quickly established as a favourite garden flower and has remained so ever since.

It was inevitable that when Professor Sargent died his successor would be Ernest Wilson. This occurred in 1927 and the great plant hunter's travelling days were over. Now he could look forward to a long and distinguished career in charge of the Arnold Arboretum.

After all, he was a born survivor. His first expedition to China was at the time of the anti-European Boxer Rebellion and the country was infested with bandits. He came to no harm as he had a remarkable ability to allay suspicions and create friendships with the people he loved, the Chinese peasants. Instead of cutting his throat, they showed him where the secret flowers grew.

Sometimes the location of these plants was almost inaccessible. *Lilium regale* could only be reached by crossing a narrow gorge. A falling rock smashed his leg and as he lay motionless each one of his 50 mules gingerly stepped over the shattered limb without touching it. An English surgeon would have amputated the crushed leg, but the missionary doctor saved it.

A born survivor in one of the most dangerous corners of the world, but not on the streets of Massachusetts. In 1930 his car skidded on a wet highway and both he and his wife were killed.

Who, that has reason, and his smell,

Would not 'mong roses and jasmin dwell,

Rather than all his spirits choke,

With exhalations of dirt and smoke,

And all th' uncleanness which does drown

In pestilential clouds a pop'lous town?

*Abraham Cowley*

The works of a person that builds begin immediately to decay; while those of him who plants begin directly to improve. In this, planting promises a more lasting pleasure than building.

*William Shenstone*

# PLANTS

THE RANGE of decorative flowers and shrubs grown in Elizabethan times was remarkably small – in Shakespeare's plays the references are generally to wild flowers and herbs and not to the plants you can find at your local garden centre.

The reason for this is quite simple – very few of our garden favourites existed in those far-off times. It is not the purpose of this chapter to describe the virtues and uses of the thousands of popular plants with which we are now blessed – study a nurseryman's catalogue or visit the garden centre mentioned earlier in order to appreciate fully the enormous range of sizes, shapes and colours now available.

The range may seem limitless and yet our choice is often surprisingly narrow. Just look at a group of gardens and you will so often find that the same varieties are present and they are being used in the same way. The function of this section is to try to widen this horizon a little by introducing you to the less familiar side of the garden plant world.

There are several surprises in store. For instance, there is the basic fact that plants require to be kept in moist soil or compost in order to stay alive – a basic fact, but not universally true. There are plants you can grow (page 55) which never need watering and others (the Bromeliads) which can be kept watered by topping up the cup at the base of the leaves. Another basic fact – plants obtain their food by the action of sunlight on the foliage together with salts absorbed through the roots … yet some plants can obtain nourishment by ensnaring and then digesting insects (page 66).

Obviously we can widen our view on the way plants feed and drink, and we can also extend the varieties which we grow in the garden. Each year the same top ten vegetable seeds are usually chosen and each year the chance of trying a new taste is rejected. But there are many unusual vegetables (page 93) which are worth a trial and squashes, so well known in America, should certainly be more widely grown (page 89). Perhaps new flavours don't interest you but you would like to impress your friends – then growing Beefsteak tomatoes weighing 500g or more (page 59) would be a worthwhile idea.

Being adventurous need not be restricted to the vegetable plot. Orchids may sound too difficult for the living room, but the details on page 78 will show you that they need not be as difficult as their reputation would have you believe. The same is true for palms on the doorstep (page 81).

In the garden itself we should not always buy green-leaved shrubs which bloom in spring, summer or autumn. Think of leaf colour as well as the flowers – a splash of silver or golden foliage throughout the growing season or even throughout the whole year can add enormously to the beauty of your garden. This virtue of silvery-leaved plants (page 86) and golden ones (page 71) is quite well known, but the virtue of choosing a variety with beautiful bark (page 57) is less widely appreciated.

Words of encouragement, then, for you to try some of the less usual plants which are available and a word of caution on bonsai (page 63) which is not quite as easy as it seems. But a bedside book should not really tell you to go out and change anything. Perhaps you would rather read about some of the exotic beauties of the plant world which you will never grow. If so, turn to the King protea (page 74), Passion flower (page 83), Bird of paradise (page 62) and the Sacred lotus (page 84).

Plants from the four corners of the earth, and each year new varieties appear in the catalogues and on the benches of the garden centre. There is, of course, a thrill in growing a new plant which you have never seen before, but don't forget the old favourites. There are Sweet violets (page 91) and old Shrub roses, now pushed into obscurity by showier cousins … but their fragrance remains to remind us of days gone by.

It is curious, pathetic almost, how deeply seated in the human heart is the liking for gardens and gardening.

*Alexander Smith*

# AIR PLANTS

PERHAPS YOU have never heard of the Bromeliads, but you will certainly know one of them – the pineapple. Columbus was offered this delicious fruit as a symbol of hospitality. He thought it looked like a pine cone and it was given the Spanish name *pina-las-India*, corrupted in English to 'pineapple'. These fruits became a symbol of affluence in 17th century England, and carvings of them appeared on the furniture and gateposts of the wealthy.

The pineapple is one of the Bromeliads which grows on the ground, but most of the members of this vast family of tropical plants attach themselves to other things. Such plants are called epiphytes, and these epiphytic Bromeliads are spread from the southern states of the U.S. down to Argentina.

The range of homes they choose is bewildering. Their favourite habitat is the jungle where they attach themselves to large trees, but some can be found on barren rocks or even on telephone wires in town. They can grow at sea level or higher than 4 km, at near freezing or at 40°C. The general pattern is a flat rosette of leaves with a central 'vase'. This receptacle collects water, insects and even small lizards – food and drink for a plant which

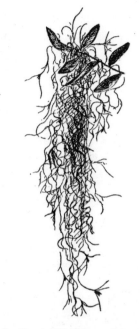

has no feeding roots. Some of these rosette Bromeliads have brightly coloured leaves and showy flower heads, and not surprisingly they have become popular house plants. *Aechmea*, *Billbergia* and *Vriesia* belong here.

There is one group of Bromeliads which has taken the ability to be self-sufficient one step further. These plants have no central collecting cup – instead their leaves are covered with absorbent furry scales which can take up water from the humid air, and nutrient salts from its dust content. They are called Air Plants – plants which literally live on air.

The most important group of Air Plants are species of *Tillandsia*, and to find most of them in the wild you would have to search the rain forests of tropical America. One of them, however, is a common sight from Georgia to Rio de Janeiro and has many picturesque names, such as Spanish moss, Old Man's beard and Vegetable horsehair. All these common names of *Tillandsia usneoides* are highly descriptive of the masses of grey, stringlike festoons which hang from trees in the cities and countryside. Another Air Plant you will see on a trip to the southern states of the U.S. is the Ball moss (*Tillandsia recurvata*) which forms spherical mossy clumps on telephone wires.

All of this sounds as if you must be a jet-setter if you are ever going to see these strange plants, but Air Plants are available in Britain and can be grown as house plants which never need watering. You may be able to find one or two varieties in your garden centre – if not, write to Vesutor Ltd, The Bromeliad Nursery, Marringdean Rd, Billingshurst, W. Sussex for their catalogue.

The one you are most likely to find is *T. caput-medusae*, the Medusa's Head Air Plant – thick and twisted leaves arise from a bulbous base. For a flowering variety choose *T. aeranthos* – pink and blue flowers appear above the carnation-like leaves. Many other types are available from specialist nurseries or garden centres, and all will require attachment to a stout support – driftwood, coral, shell, stone and pottery are all used. Push the base of the plant into a crevice or stick it onto the support with a small dab of glue.

Maintenance is very simple. Mist the plants with water every couple of days and stand the display in a bright spot away from direct sunlight. At monthly intervals add an orchid liquid fertilizer to the water used for misting. These plants are remarkably tolerant of wide temperature fluctuations, but if the room is warm you should mist daily; reduce this to twice weekly if it is unheated in winter.

The Air Plants will not win any prizes in a House Plant Beauty Contest, but they are interesting novelties which cannot fail to fascinate the children and impress the neighbours.

> I had not the smallest taste for growing (plants), or taking care of them. My whole time passed in staring at them, or into them. In no morbid curiosity, but in admiring wonder, I pulled every flower to pieces till I knew all that could be seen of it with a child's eyes.
>
> *John Ruskin*

# BEAUTIFUL BARK

FLOWERS AND foliage provide the colour in the shrub garden, borne aloft by trunks, branches or twigs. But bark can be an interesting or colourful feature, too, if you choose the right varieties.

Beautiful bark on tree trunks comes in several forms. A few trees have brightly coloured trunks but it is more usual to find trees where the bark peels away to reveal a different colour underneath – birch and plane trees are common examples. There are several varieties with 'snake-skin' bark, looking somewhat like the skin of a python. Finally there are the 'whitewashed' trees with chalky white trunks and branches.

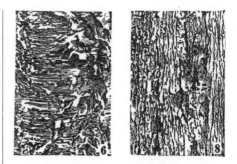

Beautiful bark is not restricted to trees. A number of shrubs, notably dogwood, bramble and willow, have numerous upright branches which are brightly coloured. Tree or shrub, you can find a wide variety of beautiful barks.

Woody plants display their bark in winter when the leaves have fallen and when there is a shortage of colour in the garden. Always site the plants close to the house or near a main path – otherwise only the robins will enjoy them!

> Except during the nine months before he draws his first breath, no man manages his affairs as well as a tree does.
>
> *George Bernard Shaw*

# THE BEAUTIFUL BARK DICTIONARY

*Acer davidii* (Snake-bark maple)
Small tree with shiny, dark green leaves.
BARK IS GREEN WITH WHITE LINES.

*Acer griseum* (Paperbark maple)
Small tree; leaves turn red in autumn.
BARK FLAKES TO REVEAL DARK ORANGE BELOW.

*Acer grosseri* (Snake-bark maple)
Small tree; leaves turn red in autumn.
BARK IS OLIVE-GREEN WITH WHITE LINES.

*Acer palmatum* 'Senkaki' (Coral Bark maple)
Rounded bush; leaves deeply lobed.
SHOOTS ARE BRIGHT CORAL-RED.

*Acer pensylvanicum* (Moosewood)
Small tree; leaves turn yellow in autumn.
BARK IS GREEN OR REDDISH BROWN WITH WHITE LINES.

*Arbutus andrachnoides*
Slow-growing tree; white flowers in autumn.
BARK IS CINNAMON-RED.

*Betula papyrifera* (Paper birch)
Large tree; leaves turn yellow in autumn.
BARK SMOOTH, PEELS IN PAPER-LIKE SHEETS.

*Betula pendula* (Silver birch)
Popular tree; diamond-shaped leaves.
BARK IS WHITE AND ROUGH.

*Cornus alba* (Red-barked dogwood)
Tall shrub with many upright stems.
SHOOTS ARE RICH RED.

*Cornus alba* 'Sibirica'
Tall shrub with many upright stems.
SHOOTS ARE CRIMSON – BRIGHTER THAN *C. ALBA.*

*Cornus stolonifera* 'Flaviramea'
Tall shrub with many upright stems.
SHOOTS ARE YELLOW WHEN YOUNG.

*Eucalyptus niphophila* (Snow gum)
Small tree with large, grey-green leaves.
BARK IS GREEN WITH WHITE PATCHES.

*Platanus hispanica* (London plane)
Large tree with maple-like leaves.
GREY BARK FLAKES TO REVEAL CREAM BELOW.

*Populus alba* (White Poplar)
Large tree; leaves white below.
BARK IS PALE GREY WITH HORIZONTAL ROWS OF BLACK MARKINGS.

*Prunus serrula*
Small tree with willow-like leaves.
NEW BARK LOOKS LIKE POLISHED MAHOGANY.

*Rubus cockburnianus* (Whitewashed bramble)
Bush with long, arching stems.
SHOOTS ARE COVERED WITH A WHITE BLOOM.

*Salix alba* 'Chermesina' (Scarlet willow)
Tall shrub, sometimes called 'Britzensis'.
SHOOTS ARE BRIGHT SCARLET.

*Salix alba* 'Vitellina' (Golden willow)
Tall shrub; prune regularly.
SHOOTS ARE GOLDEN YELLOW.

# BEEFSTEAK TOMATOES

—⟶⊳●⊲⟵—

WE ALL know what a tomato is. In Britain it is a small or medium-sized fruit we use as a vegetable. It has large cavities within it and these are filled with juice and numerous seeds.

Say 'tomato' in the United States and you conjure up quite a different picture. To the American a tomato is a large fruit which is often flattened and ridged. Within it the cavities are small and numerous and they bear few seeds – the flesh is thick and meaty. For the minority who might want something different there is the 'bite-sized' tomato – small, round and juicy. This is our old friend, the 'English' tomato.

The Giant tomato is available in Britain, but it has never become popular. Seed catalogues offer one or two varieties and you should find a box of large Dutch tomatoes at your supermarket.

The question of taste is always a difficult one. For juiciness and sweetness the traditional tomato scores, but for a meaty filling for sandwiches the Giant varieties come out on top. For cooking and frying nobody can tell you which is best – it is a matter of personal taste.

There are three types of Giant tomato. The largest of all belong to the Beefsteak group, and new varieties with 'beef' or 'steak' in their names have appeared in recent years. Pages 59-60 tell you about the Giant tomato varieties and provide a tip or two on how to grow them successfully.

---

THE BEEFSTEAK varieties are the largest of all tomatoes. The average weight is about 400 g, but single fruits weighing 1 kg or more can be grown. For a sandwich, merely cut a slice and place between two large slices of bread! But even these figures pale when compared with record breakers – such as the 3 kg fruit of the Beefsteak variety 'Delicious'.

There is nothing new about this group in their American homeland. Ponderosa has been around for generations and is available in red, pink, yellow and white forms. Over the years a steady stream of new Beefsteak varieties have appeared – Delicious, Oxheart, Pennheart, Beefmaster and so on, but very few have reached British shores. Seeds of the American Beefsteaks *are* available in Britain, but you will have to search the catalogues to find one of the varieties named above.

Cultivation is quite straightforward, but they are late-maturing and that means that you will have to grow them under glass. Treat the plants as any other greenhouse variety – water, feed, deleaf etc. in the usual way. Remember that your aim is to grow a limited number of giant tomatoes, so stop the plants when the fourth truss has set.

One of the drawbacks of the American Beefsteaks is that they are poor pollinators and the fruit set can be distinctly disappointing. For this reason it is a good idea to tap the flowers on a bright day to aid pollination.

Just two or three fruit weighing 500 g each can be a serious strain on the flower stalk, so the truss should be supported by staking. Use a piece of cloth and not string to tie the truss to the cane or wire.

A new generation of Beefsteaks has been bred by the Dutch, and varieties such as Dombito are available from some seed suppliers. These Dutch Beefsteak varieties have the advantage of setting fruit rather more easily than their American counterparts.

In the U.S. the popular group of Giant tomatoes are not the Beefsteaks – they are the Large $F_1$ Hybrids. Big Boy is the favourite and it has the same vital statistics as the Beefsteaks – fruits which average 400 g and the chance to grow 1 kg fruits.

However, the $F_1$ Hybrids never produce the record-breaking mammoths. Big Boy has red fruit and like the others in this group must be grown under glass. Seeds of Big Boy are available from some specialist suppliers in Britain, but in the U.S. you can buy the whole family – Better Boy, Ultra Boy and Wonder Boy.

In the U.S. you will also find the Girls. Big Girl is similar to the original Big Boy – round, smooth and meaty but with the added advantage of high disease resistance. The other Large $F_1$ Hybrids are less attractive and somewhat smaller. Spring Giant and Supersonic produce ridged fruits which weigh about 150 g.

The third group of Giant tomatoes are the large fruits you find when you go to Spain or Italy on holiday. These are the Marmandes, and you can find Marmande seed without much trouble in Britain. Marmande will never win any prizes in a beauty contest – the fruits are large and misshapen, but they do weigh up to 500 g each and their flavour is excellent. An added advantage is that it is an outdoor tomato and an unusual feature is that it is a determinate variety – a technical term which means that it stops growing after about five trusses.

Beefsteaks, Large $F_1$ Hybrids and Marmandes – each group offers you a chance to grow a new type of tomato which should certainly dwarf the puny fruits you have grown in the past ... but there is always a catch – do not expect the same numbers you have been used to picking in the past.

## The Story of the Tomato

In 1544 the first strange fruits arrived in Italy. They had been sent from Central America by the Spanish missionaries, and we know that these tomatoes must have been a yellow-skinned variety. They were given the name *pomodoro* (golden apple) and this word remains the Italian for tomato.

Our word is derived from the native *tomatl*, a description given by the native Americans to the fruits they used for food and as an aphrodisiac. The Italians were trusting and ate them, but other Europeans were not. The first tomatoes arrived in Britain in about 1580 and were regarded with grave suspicion. They looked like Deadly nightshade and grazing animals would not touch them. The tomato quickly earned the name Love apple, perhaps because of its use in love philtres but much more likely because of its early Latin name *Poma amoris*.

For 250 years we could not make up our minds whether to trust it or not. It was grown as a tender ornamental climber which bore colourful fruits. Even in the 1820s a distinguished gardening authority described the various pretty shapes and colours, and noted that only the large red ones could be used in the kitchen. The 1870 seed catalogues in the U.S. placed tomatoes in the Ornamental Flowers section.

Breeders began to improve the insipid or bitter taste of the wild fruits and the doubts about safety at last disappeared. The result is that the tomato is the most popular of all the raw vegetables consumed in the U.S. and Europe.

# THE BIRD OF PARADISE

IN 1773 a spectacular plant was sent from South Africa to Kew Gardens in London. It was easy to find a suitable common name – the orange and blue flowers rose up from the horizontal bract and the 15 cm long flower-head looked like some exotic bird in flight, so 'Bird of Paradise' was obvious.

The Latin name also posed no problem. Such a strikingly beautiful flower would have to bear the Queen's name. Queen Charlotte was keenly interested in botany and she actively assisted the development of the Botanic Gardens at Kew. The cultivation of apples was her main interest – the popular dessert 'Apple Charlotte' is thought to have been named in her honour.

The 'Bird of Paradise' was worthy of such a Queen, and so it was called *Strelitzia reginae* to commemorate her family name – before her marriage to George III she had been the Duchess of Mecklenberg-Strelitz.

## A PLANT FIT FOR A QUEEN

In many tropical and sub-tropical countries you will see this colourful member of the Banana family in parks and private gardens. It is the emblem of Los Angeles, which indicates its popularity in the warm areas of the United States, but it is too tender to be grown outdoors in Britain.

To see the Bird of Paradise in all its glory you should visit one of the larger Botanical Gardens. There are fine specimens in the Temperate House at Kew, and you may also see them offered for sale by large garden centres and specialist nurseries.

They are surprisingly easy to grow as house plants, provided that you remember their needs. Space is essential – a mature plant will grow about 120 cm high and will need a 25 cm pot. You will also need patience – a newly-rooted *Strelitzia* will not flower for about 3 years. But in the meantime it will be no trouble. All it needs is average warmth and a rather cool place (13°–16°C) in winter, watering thoroughly when the top of the compost is dry and an occasional misting of the leaves. Do not repot mature plants – root restriction is vital for annual blooming.

Your reward will be vivid flowers, about 15 cm across, which last for several weeks on top of tall stalks surrounded by large paddle-shaped leaves.

# BONSAI

M ANY WRITERS wax eloquent on the subject of bonsai, and the beautiful specimens on display at major flower shows justify their enthusiasm. A Red-leaved maple with stout trunk and glowing leaves, a Crab apple bearing tiny crimson fruits or a wizened old Chinese juniper looking like a living Japanese painting. We would buy one straight away … if it were not for the price.

> ## If you are willing to devote care and time to a collection then it can be a rewarding and enriching hobby

By far the easiest way to acquire a bonsai is to buy a mature specimen from a reputable supplier. It will have taken a number of years to grow and train, which means that it will be costly, but that is not the only drawback you must consider. First of all, it cannot be used as a house plant – it belongs in the garden or on a balcony and may only be brought indoors for a few days at a time. Secondly, it will mean a lot of work – from spring to autumn it will need frequent watering and in warm, dry spells you will have to take the watering can out at least once a day.

Bonsai is obviously not for the casual admirer. But if you are willing to devote care and time to a collection then it can be a rewarding and enriching hobby – well-grown specimens increase in value every year.

If you feel that bonsai may be for you, let us begin at the beginning with a definition. The Bonsai Kai of the Japan Society of London state that 'a bonsai is essentially a tree encouraged to conform in all aspects with ordinary trees, except for its miniature size. The technique of growing bonsai is, in essence, a simple one, and consists of keeping the tree confined to its pot by pinching out the top growth and pruning the roots to strike a balance between the foliage above and the roots below, and at the same time to develop a satisfying shape.'

And that, in a nutshell, is bonsai. The art began over 1000 years ago in China and spread to Japan. At the end of the 19th century specimens began to trickle into the West, but this method of cultivating trees did not become popular in America and Europe until after World War II. The word *bonsai* means 'planting in a shallow container' and this underlines the importance of the pot. As a rule of thumb the volume of the container should be

# THE BONSAI DICTIONARY

## Evergreen foliage

*Abies* (Fir)

*Cedrus* (Cedar)

*Chamaecyparis* (False cypress)

*Cryptomeria* (Japanese cedar)

*Juniperus* (Juniper)

*Picea* (Spruce)

*Pinus* (Pine)

*Sequoia* (Californian redwood)

*Taxus* (Yew)

*Thuja* (Arbor-vitae)

## Deciduous foliage

*Acer* (Maple)

*Betula* (Birch)

*Fagus* (Beech)

*Ginkgo* (Maidenhair tree)

*Larix* (Larch)

*Nothofagus* (Antarctic beech)

*Quercus* (Oak)

*Salix* (Willow)

*Tilia* (Lime)

*Zelkova* (Grey bark elm)

## Flowers or Fruit

*Azalea* (Azalea)

*Berberis* (Barberry)

*Camellia* (Camellia)

*Chaenomeles* (Japonica)

*Cornus mas* (Cornelian cherry)

*Cotoneaster* (Cotoneaster)

*Crataegus* (Hawthorn)

*Malus* (Crab apple)

*Pyracantha* (Firethorn)

*Sorbus* (Mountain ash)

*Styrax* (Snowdrop tree)

*Wisteria* (Wistaria)

about one third of the total volume of the trunk and top growth. Its width should be greater than its height and it must be sound – there should be no cracks and you should check with the supplier that it is frost-resistant. The colour should be subdued and the inside must be unglazed. At the bottom there must be at least one drainage hole. The pot will need soil – first put plastic mesh over the hole and anchor it down with a layer of gravel, then add a soil-based compost such as John Innes

Seed and Cutting Compost. Cover the surface around the plant with moss or small stones.

Now for the plants themselves. A vast number of hardy trees and shrubs can be grown, but types with large leaves are rarely suitable. Well-known bonsai trees and shrubs are listed in the dictionary on the left but you can try others. The most expensive method is to buy a ready-grown bonsai, the cheapest is to dig up a seedling from the garden. Don't go out into the countryside to do this – it's illegal. You can raise plants from seed but a good method is to go to the garden centre and hunt for a small plant with an interesting shape.

> I like trees because they seem more resigned to the way they have to live than other things do.
>
> *Willa Cather*

Pot, soil, plant – now you have to look after it. Its home must be outdoors and if you have a collection they should be sited so that you can see them from the window. A low slatted table is best, with some protection from high winds and heavy rain. In Japan they say it takes three years to learn how to water a bonsai, so don't regard it as a job to do whenever you remember. Daily watering is necessary in summer but in winter once or twice a month is sufficient. Use rainwater, not tapwater, and include a little liquid feed in spring and summer.

Root and stem pruning are arts you must learn. In March take the plant out of its pot and see if its roots have started to encircle the soil ball. If so, cut them back by about a third and remove some of the old soil – for conifers this root pruning should be less drastic. Put the plant back in its pot with some fresh compost and protect from strong winds until it is re-established. Now carefully prune the shoots – removing the tip will stimulate branching and removing lower side shoots will create the trunk. Copper wire can be used to shape the trunk but you must remove this wire when it starts to cut into the stem. Branches can be made to weep by hanging weights on them.

Bonsai can have a spell indoors for up to four days. Place the pot in a well-lit area and mist the leaves with water every day. The art of bonsai is rather like keeping a dog. It will have to be cared for every day and you will have to keep watch on its progress, but because you have to expend so much effort the attachment can become very close.

# CARNIVOROUS PLANTS

PLANTS OBTAIN their requirements for nitrogen and other nutrients from the soil. We learnt this simple fact in our first botany lesson, but it is not always true. Some plants grow in situations where the roots cannot obtain sufficient plant nutrients.

In tropical rain forests you will find colourful plants with strap-like leaves growing on trees. The roots are for attachment and not for feeding, so our first botany lesson is of little use to the plant. It has to find another way, and in the centre of each rosette of leaves you will find a natural vase. This is filled with rainwater and the drip from the leaves, and in the water are dead insects which decompose to provide the vital nutrients.

Plants growing in acid bogs and swamps have a more difficult life. Their roots cannot obtain enough nitrogen from the wet peaty ground but these plants cannot just wait for passing insects to drop in – insects are not as abundant as they are in the jungle. So many of these bog plants have had to evolve mechanisms which will ensnare insects – these are the carnivorous or flesh-eating plants. The organic matter in the insect's body breaks down and the simple salts produced are absorbed into the plant's tissues.

There are several methods of insect capture. The most dramatic method is used by the **Fly Traps**. These plants bear spine-edged leaves which are hinged in the middle. When an insect crawls on to the sensitive hairs in the centre of the leaf, the trap snaps shut. The prey is tightly held and its efforts to escape stimulate secretion so that the insect is drowned. Digestive juices then attack the body and after one or

## After one or two weeks the trap reopens so that rain can wash away the empty shell

two weeks the trap reopens so that rain can wash away the empty shell. If the prospect of owning such a gruesome pet appeals to you, buy a Venus' fly trap (*Dionaea muscipula*) and keep it on the windowsill. A winter temperature of 10°–13°C is required and good light is necessary. There are a few general rules for growing any carnivorous plant indoors – use rainwater and not tapwater, stand the pot in a saucer of water, repot into an acid peat/sphagnum moss mixture and do not use a fertilizer, feed instead with tiny bits of meat.

Less sophisticated but equally effective is the mechanism adopted by the **Sticky-leaved Plants**. The Sundews (*Drosera* spp.) are the most common type – the leaves bear glandular hairs which secrete a glistening, sticky fluid. This attracts insects, and once the fly is caught the hairs turn inwards and digestive fluids are secreted. You can grow a Sundew on the windowsill if you follow the rules given on page 66 for the Venus' fly trap. Less common than the Sundews are the Butterworts (*Pinguicula* spp.) which have a delicate appetite. Their leaves bear very fine hairs which produce an oily substance and gnats, attracted by the fetid smell, are ensnared. At the other end of the scale is the Australian sticky-leaved plant *Byblis gigantea*. It has the heartiest appetite of all – the small insects caught on its long, sticky leaves merely serve as bait for its diet of small lizards.

The most spectacular of the flesh-eating types are the **Pitcher Plants**, even though their insect-killing activity cannot be observed. The leaves of these plants are shaped like tall funnels and are either lidded or bent over at the top in order to keep out excessive rainwater. Insects are attracted by the bright colours or the smell of the nectar-like secretion, and once inside the entrance they are doomed. Losing their footing on the smooth interior they fall into the fluid at the base and are drowned. In some cases

ordinary decomposition takes place – in others digestive enzymes are secreted. The easiest Pitcher to grow outdoors is the Huntsman's cap (*Sarracenia purpurea*). In the Cobra plant (*Darlingtonia californica*) the pitchers have a snake's head appearance – it can be grown outdoors in sheltered districts. Unfortunately neither of these plants is easy to grow indoors and the most eye-catching of all (*Nepenthes* spp.) are distinctly difficult. They require a winter temperature of 16°–21°C and very high humidity.

Some people consider the collecting of carnivorous plants quite fascinating. In this strange world there are pitchers over 1 m long and some with tiny bladders which are less than 2.5 mm in length. Other people find the idea rather gruesome – plants are not supposed to eat insects. Anyway, the insects have the last laugh. Many carnivorous plants are particularly susceptible to attack by greenfly and caterpillars!

# CONSIDER THE LILIES

> *'Consider the lilies of the field, how they grow;*
> *they toil not, neither do they spin:*
> *And yet I say unto you,*
> *That even Solomon in all his glory*
> *was not arrayed like one of these.'*
>
> Matthew 6, 28 and 29

THE BIBLICAL writer obviously appreciated the beauty of the lily, but it was admired and held to be sacred long before the start of the Christian era. Lilies were painted on the walls of Cretan palaces about 1500 years before His birth, and the Assyrians adopted it as their symbol of royalty.

To the Greeks it was the symbol of purity, arising from the milk which fed the infant Hercules, and this association with purity passed into Christianity when the lily became the flower of the Virgin Mary.

This revered lily was the Madonna lily, pure white and deliciously fragrant, which has been cultivated for over 3000 years. Until the 16th century it was our only garden lily, but since then there has been a series of introductions and nowadays lilies can be found in a wide variety of sizes, shapes and colours.

FOR MANY gardeners the lily is a flower they see in other people's gardens, not their own. Perhaps the reason for this lack of widespread popularity is its reputation for being difficult to grow. There is some truth in this view as some of the older species are rather fussy about growing conditions and are prone to disease. For example, the Golden-rayed lily will fail if the soil is not deep and lime-free, and the Madonna lily suffers badly from botrytis.

These days, however, the 'hard-to-grow' reputation for all lilies is quite unfounded. During the past century a number of hardy and tolerant species have been discovered and in the past 70 years the Hybrid lilies have set new standards in flower size, vigour and disease resistance. The most famous Hybrid lilies have been bred in Oregon by Jan de Graaf, and one of the best of these

Oregon hybrids is 'Enchantment' – 15 cm wide orange flowers on long spikes.

You can now find flowers in nearly every colour, from purest white to deepest red. There are trumpet-shaped types, such as the Regal lily and Madonna lily, and there are Turk's cap flowers with swept-back petals, like the Martagon lily.

## Most lilies prefer free-draining soil which is rich in humus

Most lilies prefer free-draining soil which is rich in humus, and they like to stand their heads in the sun and their roots in the shade. But this is only a generalisation and you can now find varieties which will thrive under all sorts of conditions. The golden rule is to check on the likes and dislikes before you buy.

Lilies may be bought as bulbs. Choose the variety carefully, because it may grow to 30 cm–3 m depending on your choice. There are both lime-tolerant and lime-hating types – if you don't know the lime content of your soil, choose one of the many lime-tolerant varieties.

The bulb is not quite like a daffodil or tulip; it has no outer protective cover and must not be allowed to dry out. So plant it; don't store it. This will be in late summer or autumn for most soils, but it is better to wait until the spring if your soil is rather heavy.

Lilies and really heavy ground don't mix. Poor drainage is perhaps the greatest

The flower sweetens the air with its perfume; yet its last service is to offer itself to thee.

*Rabindranath Tagore*

enemy of these plants – if your garden is composed of sticky clay then grow them in pots or tubs.

Before planting, dig the site thoroughly and work in plenty of well-rotted compost. Then plant the bulbs on a bed of coarse sand. There is no general rule for planting depth – stem-rooting varieties need 15 cm of soil on top of the bulb; base-rooting types need only 5 cm of soil over them and the Giant and Madonna lilies should have their bulb tips just below the surface.

# What were 'The lilies of the field'?

For many years the 'lilies of the field' mentioned in the New Testament were thought to be anemones. Twentieth century research, however, indicates that they may have indeed been Madonna lilies (*Lilium candidum*), although other scholars are convinced that they were a variety of iris.

The true nature of the national flower of France is also a matter of controversy. It is now the lily, of course, but the origin of the *Fleur-de-lis* was an iris. The banner of Louis VII was this wild flower, and his badge was called *Fleur-de-Louis* which was later corrupted to *Fleur-de-lis*.

For a time the lily was outlawed in France. It was the sign of the Royal family, and to wear or carry one during the Revolution meant certain death. When Napoleon came to power he ordered the removal of all carved lilies from monuments and their replacement by eagles.

Be guided by your supplier or his catalogue.

Lilies call for little attention when growing. Don't hoe round the plants – use a mulch of compost or bark instead. Keep down the important pests – slugs, lily beetle and greenfly. If staking becomes necessary, take care not to damage the bulb. And then, when flowering is over, make sure that the dead blooms are removed before the large seed pods are formed.

Leave them alone and they will bloom year after year. Divide up the bulb clusters in autumn every five years and you will be able to increase your stock of this Queen of Flowers.

# GOLDEN FOLIAGE

TREES AND shrubs with golden leaves are a vital part of any planting scheme. Yellow flowers may produce a bold splash of colour on a bush, but yellow foliage lights up the whole plant. That is not all – yellow flowers fade and die when their season is over but the yellow leaves of an evergreen tree or shrub keep it colourful all year round.

Nothing else can brighten up the winter garden in quite the same way, and nothing else can provide such a startling contrast for plants with dark green foliage. The

For maximum effect plant all-yellow varieties next to or in front of plants with dark green foliage

Dictionary on the next page lists a few of the more popular yellow- and golden-leaved varieties. There are excellent trees such as the yellow *Robinia pseudoacacia* 'Frisia' and the golden *Gleditsia triacanthos* 'Sunburst'. The shrub list is larger, varying in size from the tall Golden elder to the small Golden heather. There is an extensive range of golden conifers and

there is even a golden ivy called Buttercup.

Not all the trees and shrubs in the Dictionary on pages 72–73 have all-yellow or all-golden leaves. Some have green leaves marked with yellow or gold – these are the variegated varieties. The yellow may be in the form of an edging, a series of blotches or an inset – all of these types are represented in the list on pages 72–73.

Many of the variegated shrubs are grown primarily for their attractive foliage – good examples are *Elaeagnus pungens* 'Maculata', *Euonymus japonicus* 'Ovatus Aureus' and Golden privet. Some popular flowering shrubs, however, have varieties which bear variegated leaves and these are often a good choice, providing colour before and after the flowering season. An example here is *Vinca minor* 'Variegata.'

The golden trees and shrubs span a wide range of plants and so precise rules

# THE GOLDEN FOLIAGE DICTIONARY

*Acer pseudoplatanus* 'Worleei'
Medium-sized tree – the Golden sycamore.
LEAVES YELLOW, TURNING GOLD AND FINALLY GREEN
WITH AGE.

*Aucuba japonica* 'Variegata'
The popular Spotted laurel used for
hedging.
LEAVES GLOSSY AND OVAL – SUCCEEDS ANYWHERE.

*Chamaecyparis lawsoniana* 'Minima Aurea'
One of the best of all dwarf conifers.
BRIGHT YELLOW FOLIAGE FORMS A SLOW-GROWING,
ROUNDED PYRAMID.

*Elaeagnus pungens* 'Maculata'
Popular evergreen shrub grown for its
leaves.
AN EXCELLENT CHOICE FOR BRIGHTENING UP THE
WINTER GARDEN.

*Erica carnea* 'Aurea'
A variety of heather bearing pink flowers
in March.
FOLIAGE BRIGHT GOLD IN SPRING AND EARLY
SUMMER.

*Euonymus japonicus* 'Ovatus Aureus'
Easy-to-grow, dense bush with shiny leaves.
USEFUL EVERGREEN – SUNSHINE NECESSARY FOR
BRIGHTEST COLOURS.

*Gleditsia triacanthos* 'Sunburst'
Medium-sized tree – the Golden Honey
locust.
FERNY LEAVES ARE GOLDEN WHEN YOUNG.

*Hedera helix* 'Buttercup'
The best golden form of Common ivy.
LEAVES YELLOW, LATER PALE GREEN. USE AS A
CLIMBER OR GROUND COVER.

*Ilex aquifolium* 'Golden Queen'
One of the popular Golden hollies – the
other is 'Golden King'.
A MALE VARIETY DESPITE ITS NAME – DOES NOT
BEAR BERRIES.

*Juniperus communis* 'Depressa Aurea'
Wide-spreading, prickly conifer – the
Golden Canadian juniper.
USEFUL DWARF VARIETY – GOLDEN IN SUMMER,
BRONZE IN WINTER.

*Philadelphus coronarius* 'Aureus'
A yellow-leaved form of Mock orange.
EXCELLENT MEDIUM-SIZED SHRUB; WHITE FLOWERS
IN JUNE AND JULY.

*Robinia pseudoacacia* 'Frisia'

One of the best of all yellow-leaved plants.

MEDIUM-SIZED TREE – RICH GOLDEN-YELLOW FROM SPRING TO AUTUMN.

*Sambucus racemosa* 'Plumosa Aurea'

The Golden elder with deeply cut, serrated leaves.

MEDIUM-SIZED SHRUB – BEARS RED BERRIES IN AUTUMN.

*Taxus baccata* 'Elegantissima'

The popular Golden yew – very slow-growing.

WITH AGE, THE ALL-YELLOW FOLIAGE CHANGES TO GREEN WITH YELLOW EDGES.

*Thuja occidentalis* 'Rheingold'

A popular conical conifer for the rockery or heather bed.

FOLIAGE IS OLD GOLD IN COLOUR, TURNING COPPERY IN WINTER.

*Vinca minor* 'Variegata'

A variegated form of the popular periwinkle.

USEFUL GROUND COVER; BRIGHT BLUE FLOWERS IN SPRING.

> Nothing else can brighten up the winter garden in quite the same way, and nothing else can provide such a startling contrast for plants with dark green foliage

are impossible. Yellow leaves are attractive to look at but they do reduce the plant's ability to manufacture carbohydrates – chlorophyll is the key to this process and yellow leaves have less chlorophyll. This means that the yellow-leaved variety usually needs more light than its all-green relative. If all-green branches appear on your golden shrub or climber then cut them off when they are first seen.

For maximum effect plant all-yellow varieties next to or in front of plants with dark green foliage. But don't let anyone try to give you precise rules about planting arrangements – remember that it is *your* garden!

> What a man needs in gardening is a cast-iron back with a hinge on it.
> *C. D. Warner*

# THE KING PROTEA

SOME PEOPLE love roses whereas others only admire them. It is different with King proteas – you will either love them or hate them. The flower heads are enormous, up to 30 cm across, and extremely long-lasting. The encircling bracts are red, varying from pale pink to deep crimson depending on the conditions. These bracts are covered with silky down and the centre of the bloom is a soft dome of white florets.

To some it is one of the most spectacular of all flowers – it was highly prized in Britain for about 50 years after its introduction in 1774. To others it is gross and vulgar – a cross between an artichoke and a daisy.

THE KING PROTEA is the national flower of its homeland, South Africa. Here it grows to perfection in dry, acid soils which are baked by the summer sun and moistened by winter rain. You will also find them growing in Australia, California, Madeira and many other subtropical areas. Nearer home they grow in the Tresco Gardens in the Isles of Scilly. If you are adventurous and live in a particularly favoured spot in the southern counties, you can try to cultivate one outdoors. Perfect drainage is essential (add compost and plenty of coarse sand to the soil) and so is abundant sunshine – if the summer is a poor one there will be no blooms. High temperatures are not essential and an established plant can withstand several degrees of frost.

For the British gardener, apart from the lucky few who can grow subtropical plants outdoors, the King protea is a plant for the cool greenhouse or conservatory. Grow it in a 30 cm pot, filling the bottom third with crocks and the rest with potting compost which has been enriched with coarse sand and peat. Give the plant direct sun and make sure that there is good ventilation. Water moderately in summer and sparingly at other times and stand the pot outdoors between June and August. Your reward should be a succession of large blooms in early summer on a 1.2 m evergreen shrub.

You will have to search to find a King protea – write to a nursery which specialises in exotic plants. You will find it easier to buy seed – sow in spring in a cool greenhouse. Cuttings can be taken in July, using young shoots about 10 cm long. The flowers of King protea are sought after for flower arrangements.

# LIVING COLUMNS

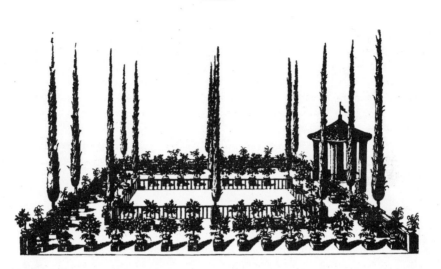

UPRIGHT TREES have a special role to play in the garden. Most plants have a rounded or spreading growth habit, and a well-placed upright tree or conifer set in their midst adds a point of interest – it adds a strongly vertical touch to a horizontal scene. There are other uses – a solitary upright tree makes an excellent focal point, and such specimens are often planted at the entrance to a driveway or close to the front door. The use of column-like trees is frequently for the purely practical reason of saving space rather than a great regard for upright plants – in many small gardens a tall upright tree is feasible whereas a tall spreading tree would cause serious shade problems.

Various terms are used to describe these living columns – upright, fastigiate, columnar and so on. The words are usually used indiscriminately in catalogues, but for the purist they do mean different things. Upright trees are of two types. In *columnar* varieties the branches arising from the main stem are short and horizontal like a bottle brush, or long and downswept, like the spokes of an umbrella which is stood on its handle. Some conifers, such as Incense cedar, are columnar.

The other type of upright tree is *fastigiate*, where the branches grow strongly upwards against the main stem, like the spokes of a closed umbrella stood on its point. Upright deciduous and evergreen

# THE LIVING COLUMN DICTIONARY

*Betula pendula* 'Fastigiata'
An erect form of the Silver birch.
MEDIUM HEIGHT — GOOD FOR SMALL GARDENS.

*Carpinus betulus* 'Columnaris'
An erect form of the Common hornbeam.
SMALL TREE — USEFUL WHERE SPACE IS LIMITED.

*Chamaecyparis lawsoniana* 'Columnaris'
One of the best of all column-like conifers.
MEDIUM HEIGHT — BLUE-GREY FOLIAGE.

*Crataegus monogyna* 'Stricta'
An erect form of the Common hawthorn.
SMALL, VERY HARDY TREE — BROADENS WITH AGE.

*Fagus sylvatica* 'Dawyck'
An erect form of the Common beech.
AN EXCELLENT TALL TREE — BROADENS WITH AGE.

*Ginkgo biloba* 'Fastigiata'
An erect form of the Maidenhair tree.
MEDIUM HEIGHT — FAN-SHAPED LEAVES TURN
YELLOW.

*Ilex aquifolium* 'Green Pillar'
An erect form of the Common holly.
AN EXCELLENT SPECIMEN TREE — DARK GREEN, SPINY
LEAVES.

*Juniperus communis* 'Compressa'
An excellent choice for the rockery.
DWARF — GREYISH-GREEN BRANCHES ARE CLOSELY
PACKED.

*Juniperus virginiana* 'Skyrocket'
One of the narrowest of all conifers.
MEDIUM HEIGHT — BLUE-GREY FOLIAGE.

*Libocedrus decurrens*
The Incense cedar — bottom branches
are retained.
TALL TREE — ONE OF THE MOST IMPRESSIVE OF ALL
LIVING COLUMNS.

*Malus tschonoskii*
An erect form of the Ornamental crab.
AN EXCELLENT SPECIMEN TREE — MORE CONICAL
THAN PENCIL-LIKE.

*Populus nigra* 'Italica'
Narrowly fastigiate — the familiar
Lombardy poplar.
TALL AND PENCIL-LIKE — DO NOT PLANT THIS TREE
CLOSE TO HOUSE FOUNDATIONS.

*Prunus* 'Amanogawa'
An erect form of the Ornamental cherry.
AN EXCELLENT SPECIMEN TREE — PINK FLOWERS IN
MAY.

*Quercus robur* 'Fastigiata'
An erect form of the English oak.
AN EXCELLENT TALL TREE — BROADENS WITH AGE.

*Sorbus aucuparia* 'Fastigiata'
An erect form of the Mountain ash.
A SLOW-GROWING TREE — LARGE, DARK GREEN
LEAVES.

*Taxus baccata* 'Fastigiata'
The Irish yew — broadens with age.
MEDIUM HEIGHT — BLACKISH-GREEN FOLIAGE.

smaller ones for the suburban garden and these should be chosen where space is limited. In the catalogues and at garden centres you will find a number of excellent upright dwarf conifers which can be used to break up the flat appearance which bedevils so many rockeries.

> I have not read of any virtue the birch tree hath in physic, howbeit, it serveth for many good uses, and for none better than for beating of stubborn boys that either lie or will not learn.
>
> *New Herbal (William Turner)*

trees are usually fastigiate.

An upright growth habit can be distinctly effective, but unfortunately it may not last throughout the lifetime of the tree. Sometimes it comes later – the Incense cedar is quite bushy at first and only with age does it adopt the column-like habit which is such a spectacular sight at Westonbirt and other tree gardens. All you need is patience here, but that won't help with other upright trees which are a delight when young but then acquire a middle-aged spread. In this case careful clipping is the only answer.

The description of a tree as column-like conjures up a picture of a tall, stately specimen towering above the lowly trees and bushes clustered around its base. Such fine trees exist, of course, but there are

# ORCHIDS ON
# THE WINDOWSILL

*P*EOPLE GENERALLY regard orchids as the most exotic and difficult of plants. We
   know that they are all jungle plants, require greenhouse conditions to be
really happy and require green fingers to make them bloom again.

These are just three of the myths which have grown up around this mysterious
plant family. We regard them as flowers with a limited range of species, but they
make up the largest family of all flowering plants. There are about 30,000 species
and 100,000 hybrids, which range from the arctic to the equator, with flowers as
small as a pinhead or as large as a dinner plate.

It is true that there are jungle orchids which are difficult and require the
steamy conditions of a warm greenhouse, but there are others which cannot stand
jungle-like conditions and detest warm nights. These are the house plant orchids.

F*ROM THE* beginning of the 21st century
there has been a dramatic increase in
the popularity of orchids. Several types are
sold in florists, garden centres and DIY
superstores everywhere – these are the
High St. varieties and are listed on page 79.
Just one of them is responsible for the
orchid revolution. The Moth Orchid
(*Phalaenopsis*) easily outsells all the other
High St. ones – very often it is the only type
on offer. The reason for this popularity is its
ability to thrive in a centrally-heated room
where it can be expected to stay in flower
for months. For an unheated room you
should choose a cool-house type such as
*Cymbidium* or *Miltoniopsis*.

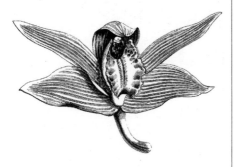

The High St. varieties are not delicate. For a plant to grow and bloom satisfactorily it should have a drop in temperature of at least 5°C at night – pamper it like an invalid and it will deteriorate quite rapidly.

Carefully examine the orchid you have bought. You may find that the stem bases are swollen – these pseudobulbs are capable of storing water. The Moth and Slipper Orchids are exceptions. The orchid is quite used to spending short periods without receiving any water, and overwatering is the main reason for the death of these plants. The surface of the special compost used for orchids dries out very rapidly so do not use it as a guide – in most cases the top half of the compost should dry out between waterings. Once a week in summer and less often in winter is a general guide but it is certainly not a hard-and-fast rule. Orchids are fussy about what they drink – the water should be soft (use rainwater if you live in a hard-water area) and it must be at room temperature. Always water before noon.

Feeding will not be a problem (apply dilute liquid fertilizer with summer waterings) but air humidity will be. Orchids need a relative humidity of about 50%, which means that summer air will be moist enough, but winter air in a centrally-heated room will be too dry. A pebble tray is the answer – place a 3 cm layer of gravel at the bottom of a tray on the windowsill and keep the bottom of the stones wet at all times. Stand the pots on the surface of the gravel.

Light is, of course, all-important. Ample daylight is essential, but you must shade the plants from strong, direct sunlight. Turn the pots occasionally.

If you are a beginner, buy a well-grown plant which is already in flower and has several buds. There will probably be several roots growing out of the pot – don't worry about this as it is a natural feature of this strange group of plants. Most orchids are epiphytes, growing on trees but not living off them. The purpose of the roots is to attach the plant and suck up moisture from the air, so when pushed into a pot the roots quite quickly try to get back to their natural element.

This strange mode of life gives a clue to the proper compost for orchids. The tree-living ones will not survive in wet compost – the role of the growing medium is to anchor the roots and provide a moist atmosphere. Ordinary peat composts won't do – buy a special orchid compost.

Don't be in a hurry to buy this compost – your plant must not be repotted for 2 or 3 years. Divide up the plant when repotting is essential – see *The Orchid Expert* for details.

Collecting orchids was once a craze in Britain – in Victorian times some varieties fetched a hundred times their present price. Now the madness has gone but the charm of the orchid remains. There are varieties which *will* grow on your windowsill and can be induced to flower again and again.

## THE SEVEN DEADLY SINS

### TOO MUCH FERTILIZER
Two rules – do not feed when plants are not actively growing and do not exceed the recommended dose.

### DIRECT RADIANT HEAT
Orchids should never be placed in front of a radiator. Too much heat leads to leaf collapse.

### WET LEAVES
Leaves which are left wet overnight are a common cause of fatal disease. Water and mist early in the day.

### OVERWATERING
The main cause of death. Follow the watering rules – do not assume lack of water is the cause of all ills.

### COLD DRAUGHTS
Draughts are not the same as ventilation. Draughts involve the rapid movement of air between one opening and another.

### DRY & STUFFY AIR
Some method of increasing air moisture is needed for most orchids and so is air movement around the plant.

### STRONG SUMMER SUN
Too much sunlight leads to scorching heat. Some direct sun may be recommended, but shade from midday summer sun is always required.

# PALMS ON THE
# DOORSTEP

No OTHER group of plants can quite match the palms as providers of an exotic touch to the terrace, garden or doorstep. There are over 2000 species, but for the British gardener the choice of palms that will survive outdoors all year round is strictly limited.

If you want to grow a tall palm tree in the garden and you are not blessed with a particularly favoured situation, you have an easy choice to make – only one species is suitable. The plant is the Chusan or Chinese Windmill palm (*Trachycarpus fortunei*), which came to us from China in 1830 and was reintroduced by Robert Fortune in 1849. You may find it in the catalogues as *Chamaerops excelsa* and the description may tell you that it is only suitable for mild locations, but this is not so. It is suitable for most parts of Britain except in the extreme north. You will find it on sale at garden centres and will see it in large gardens in many different parts of the country.

The brown, shaggy trunk of the Chusan palm will grow to about 10 m high and the large fan-shaped leaves are 60–120 cm across. Low temperatures are not a problem as it can stand many degrees of frost – the first plants sent to England were killed by stifling them in the Palm House at Kew. The secret of longevity is to protect them from biting winds and to make sure that the drainage is good.

If instead of a garden specimen tree you are looking for a palm to grow in a tub by the front door or on the terrace, then once again the choice is a simple one. The Australian palm (*Cordyline australis*) is the one to choose. It is not a true palm, but the straight trunk and crown of sword-like leaves make it a palm in the popular meaning of the word. Good drainage is vital, so make sure that the tub is raised from the ground to allow water to escape freely through the drainage hole. It will succeed in sun or partial shade, and if there is a particularly

tub plant. Other palms which succeed in pots and tubs are the Canary Date palm (*Phoenix canariensis*) and the Pygmy Date palm (*Phoenix roebelinii*). The Canary Date palms on the Isles of Scilly tower up to 15 m, but for nearly all the rest of us Date palms should be brought indoors for winter, as they can withstand only a few degrees of frost.

## Palms look their best when grown against a white wall

To complete the list of palms which will grow in the favoured South West or as winter-protected tub plants, there are the Chilean Wine palm (*Jubaea chilensis*), *Rhapis humilis*, Kentia palm (*Howea forsteriana*) and Jelly palm (*Butia capitata*). Not for you, perhaps, but nearly everyone can grow one or other of the two hardy ones in a sheltered spot. Palms look their best when grown against a white wall, but they are striking enough to look good almost anywhere.

cold snap in winter place a large transparent bag over the crown of leaves until slightly warmer weather returns. Remember to water when the weather is dry and feed occasionally – your reward will be a striking plant which grows about 50 cm each season and when mature will branch into two or three heads. After about a dozen years small, white and fragrant flowers may appear, showing that this 'palm' is really a member of the Agave family.

So for most of us the choice of palms is very narrow – the Chusan palm as a garden tree and the Australian palm as a tub plant. If, however, you live in the Western maritime fringe warmed by the Gulf Stream or are willing to move the tub into a cool greenhouse over winter, then the choice is a larger one. There is the Dwarf Fan palm (*Chamaerops humilis*), which is the only palm native to Europe. It grows to a height of only 1 m, so it makes a useful

> Where grow! Where grows it not! If vain our toil,
>
> We ought to blame the culture, not the soil.
>
> *Alexander Pope*

# THE PASSION FLOWER

*HERE IS* a legend that the early Spanish missionaries in South America looked around for the presence of Christ in the strange and exotic landscape. They found it inside a curious flower which grew on one of the climbing vines which clambered up the trees. There clearly laid out were the signs of Christ's Passion.

Leaving legend and turning to history, it is recorded that the Roman Catholic priests certainly used the Passion Flower to illustrate the story of the Crucifixion to the native American tribes they converted to Christianity.

THE PASSION FLOWER (*Passiflora caerulea*) need not be just a picture in a book – you can grow it as a house plant. Place the pot in a sunny spot and remember to keep the compost moist at all times. Move the plant outdoors occasionally in summer – in this way you will not only increase its vigour, but you will also be able to enjoy the flowers which appear between July and September.

In the winter the secret is to keep the Passion Flower in a cool room – it does not like a temperature above 10°C and detests central heating.

If you live in a mild district you can grow it as a climber against the house. Choose a south or west wall and provide wires or a trellis to support the twining tendrils.

# THE SACRED LOTUS

HE LOTUS plays no part in the life of people steeped in Western culture. The
yoga enthusiast adopts the lotus position in her exercises and the film addict
is used to the doe-eyed Eastern temptress being called Lotus Blossom. But for all
of us the Lotus flower is something we have heard of but can't quite picture ....

The situation is entirely different in the East. The Hindu Lotus is sacred for
both the Hindu and Buddhist, and this flower forms part of their everyday and
religious lives. The Lotus of the Nile was revered by the Ancient Egyptians.

These sacred lotuses are water lilies which bear their flowers well above the
water. This ability to rise above the mud must have been considered a divine
property, coupled with the fact that the roots and other parts of the plant could
provide food for the hungry.

## HINDU LOTUS

In the Hindu religion, the Lotus is the
centre of the Universe. In the beginning
this flower arose from the navel of the
Great God, and at the centre sat Brahma.

His role was to recreate the world after
the Great Flood, and to do this he used the
parts of the Lotus. The hills and the valleys

---

## In the Hindu religion, the Lotus is the centre of the Universe

---

and the rivers were formed, and within
each of the people who have inherited
this earth there has been the spirit of the
Lotus. Through yoga a higher level of
consciousness is reached and the highest of
all is the Thousand-petalled lotus. This
flower is not only sacred to the Hindus –
the Buddha appeared on earth on the leaf
of a Lotus.

It is not surprising that this flower
should have been universally used as a
decorative symbol throughout the East. In
every village in India its presence in rivers
and pools is preserved and its flowers
revered.

The plant is *Nelumbo nucifera*, which is widely distributed in Asia and N.E. Australia. It will grow outdoors in Southern Europe but requires winter protection in Britain. It spreads rapidly by means of rhizomes and the large, fragrant blooms are up to 30 cm in diameter.

## LOTUS OF THE NILE

The Lotus was the hieroglyphic symbol used to represent the land of Egypt. For the Ancient Egyptians this mystical flower which arose from the Nile after the rains was a sign of divinity; in their prayers they asked to become a lotus after death in the garden of the Sun God. Within the tombs of the Pharaohs well-preserved specimens of both species of the Lotus of the Nile have been found.

## The Lotus was the hieroglyphic symbol used to represent the land of Egypt

Contact was maintained with this plant at every opportunity. Its blossoms were painted on pottery, furniture and walls. Its stems were twined around the arms of people offering flowers and fruit to the gods and its open flowers were carried by guests as a sign of friendship.

Two types of Lotus were regarded as sacred by these ancient people. The Blue lotus of the Nile (*Nymphaea caerulea*) has narrow, pale blue petals which open during the day and the White lotus of the Nile (*Nymphaea lotus*) which has broad, white petals which open only at night. The blue species appears to have been the more important. The *Nymphaea* is the true water lily and many types will grow happily in Britain. Unfortunately, both the sacred ones of Egypt are too tender for our shores.

# SILVERY FOLIAGE

SILVERY AND grey-leaved shrubs and trees have a special fascination. When the summer garden is ablaze with bright colours they provide a sedate contrast, but in the winter months the evergreen silvery varieties have the opposite role to play. When surrounding plants are dull or bare, these pale-leaved ones provide a splash of interest.

The true silvery-leaved plants are covered by a coating of dense silky hairs or a granular powder. They are well-adapted to hot and dry conditions – they will thrive in sandy soil and full sun but a shady spot in heavy soil is bound to lead to disappointment.

Some gardeners like to grow these plants in a bed of their own, a fashion started by Gertrude Jekyll, but the effect can be positively dull. Plant them instead as points of interest within the green-leaved herbaceous or shrub border. Many of the silvery-foliaged varieties are herbaceous perennials, such as *Stachys lanata*, *Artemisia* 'Silver Queen' and *Salvia argentea*, but the list on pages 87-88 is restricted to woody plants.

There is no clear-cut dividing line between the silvery-leaved plants and the blue-grey ones. The Gum tree (*Eucalyptus gunnii*) and lavender illustrate this lack of a simple definition – some writers regard them as silvery-leaved plants whereas others regard them as greyish-blue ones.

## There is no clear-cut dividing line between the silvery-leaved plants and the blue-grey ones

Apart from the trees and shrubs which bear all-silvery or all-grey foliage there are many varieties which bear double-sided foliage. The upper surface of each leaf is green and the lower surface is white or grey. When the wind blows a shimmering effect is often produced – look at White poplar or Weeping Silver lime on a windy day to see how effective this can be.

# THE SILVERY FOLIAGE DICTIONARY

*Chamaecyparis pisifera* 'Boulevard'
One of the most popular of all dwarf conifers.
SILVERY-BLUE FOLIAGE FORMS A SLOW-GROWING, NEAT CONE.

*Cornus alba* 'Elegantissima'
Variegated variety of the Red-barked dogwood.
TALL SHRUB WITH MANY UPRIGHT STEMS.

*Euonymus radicans* 'Silver Queen'
Low-growing evergreen; leaves grey-green, edged white.
EXCELLENT AS A GROUND COVER OR WALL PLANT.

*Hebe pinguifolia* 'Pagei'
Low-growing evergreen; leaves silvery-grey.
WHITE FLOWERS IN MAY – USEFUL IN THE ROCK GARDEN.

*Hippophae rhamnoides*
The Sea buckthorn – a good windbreak for seaside gardens.
TALL, SPINY SHRUB; LEAVES WILLOW-LIKE AND SILVERY.

*Ilex aquifolium* 'Argentea Marginata'
The most popular Silver holly; leaves broad, edged white.
BUSHY GROWTH FORMS A DENSE PYRAMID. GOOD BERRY PRODUCTION.

*Ligustrum ovalifolium* 'Argenteum'
The Silver privet; leaves oval, edged creamy-white.
AN ALTERNATIVE TO THE MORE POPULAR ALL-GREEN AND GOLDEN VARIETIES.

*Picea pungens* 'Koster'
A Blue spruce which reaches about 2 m in 10 years.
FOLIAGE IS OUTSTANDING – INTENSE SILVERY-BLUE.

*Populus alba*
The White poplar – a large tree bearing lobed leaves.
UNDERSIDE OF FOLIAGE COVERED WITH WHITE WOOL.

*Populus candicans* 'Aurora'
Medium-sized tree – young leaves blotched white above, all-white below.
TO MAINTAIN COLOURFUL FOLIAGE PRUNE HARD EACH WINTER.

*Salix lanata*
The Woolly willow; leaves oval, covered with grey down.
ERECT CATKINS IN SPRING. LOW-GROWING, SUITABLE FOR THE ROCK GARDEN.

*Santolina chamaecyparissus*
Bush about 60 cm high – silvery foliage aromatic and finely divided.
YELLOW, BUTTON-LIKE FLOWERS IN SUMMER.

*Senecio* 'Sunshine'
Bush about 90 cm high – young foliage covered with silvery down.
YELLOW, DAISY-LIKE FLOWERS IN SUMMER.

*Sorbus aria*
Medium-sized tree – underside of foliage covered with white wool.
SEVERAL VARIETIES OF WHITEBEAM AVAILABLE; YOUNG LEAVES COATED WHITE.

Another combination of green and white is found in the variegated varieties. In nearly every case this is seen as a white or pale cream edge surrounding a green or near-green leaf, but in a few cases there are large white blotches scattered over the green surface. Some of these variegated plants are grown solely for their foliage but others, such as *Weigela florida* 'Variegata', are flowering plants with colourful foliage as an extra bonus.

The chlorophyll in variegated leaves and all-silvery ones is in short supply or hidden by a surface coating. This means that in general more sunshine is required for good health by these plants than their all-green relatives.

> The smallest garden may be a picture, and not only may we have much more variety in any one garden, but, if we give up imitating each other, may enjoy charming contrasts between gardens.
>
> *William Robinson*

> And the soul of the rose went into my blood,
> As the music clash'd in the hall:
> And long by the garden lake I stood,
> For I heard your rivulet fall
> From the lake to the meadow and on to the wood,
> Our wood, that is dearer than all.
>
> *Alfred Lord Tennyson*

# SQUASHES

IT IS NOT as if the British rejected all of the plants which the native Americans introduced to the world. Potatoes, French beans, chocolate, maize and tomatoes are all firm favourites over here, but one group has been left in the New World for the American housewife to cook and enjoy. The Amerinds called them 'plants eaten raw' – their word *askutasquash* was shortened to *squash*.

Various types of squash can be found in supermarkets throughout the United States. Hard and green, soft and yellow, they are part of the American diet. In Britain you can buy zucchini (courgettes) in the shops, but for the rest you may have to search for a supermarket which sells the more unusual types of squashes.

The squashes include all the edible gourds with the exception of pumpkins. There is no neat dividing line between squashes and marrows – the Patty Pan squash and the Custard marrow are exactly the same thing!

The one clear-cut feature is the distinction between summer squashes and winter squashes. Summer squashes are harvested in the summer before they are mature. Fried or boiled, they are eaten skin and all. The flavour is bland, and although they come in all shapes there is little difference in taste between them. The courgette has introduced us to this type of squash, but winter squashes are practically unknown on this side of the Atlantic. Hubbard or Acorn, Buttercup or Butternut, they are harvested at the end of the growing season and stored for winter use.

The problem with the winter squash is that our growing season is a little too short and a little too cool to ensure perfection, but it's well worth a trial if you are looking for a new taste. The squash is cut in half by slicing through the hard, inedible rind. The seeds are removed, the flesh brushed over with melted butter and then baked for about 45 minutes.

# Vegetable Spaghetti

You really can grow your own spaghetti! In a good summer these squashes will be ready about 70 days after sowing. Pick them when they are about 20 cm long and the skin has started to turn yellow. Boil for about 25 minutes and then cut in half. Remove the seeds and use a fork to scoop out the spaghetti-like strands from the inside. Season with salt and pepper – serve with butter, tomato or cheese sauce.

Study the seed catalogues and make your choice. The descriptions will tell you quite clearly whether it is a summer or winter squash and whether it grows as a bush or vining plant. Remember that the latter type will require either a support on which it can climb or space over which it can trail. Having made your choice, you can now prepare the squash 'hills' in the garden. Dig a hole about 50 cm deep and place compost or well-rotted manure in the bottom. Fill the hole with a mixture of soil and compost and leave the top as a mound about 10 cm above the surrounding soil. You have made your first hill – space the others about 1-1½ m apart.

In mid May push three seeds into the top of the hill, 2 cm deep and pointed end downward. Put a cloche or inverted jam-jar over each group of seeds and leave it in position until the danger of frost is past.

You must water freely when the weather is dry and put a 1 cm deep layer of compost or peat over each hill. When the main shoots of vining varieties are about 60 cm long, pinch out the tips to encourage the production of flowering side-shoots.

Squashes are the fastest growing of all garden vegetables and in a couple of months you will have the satisfaction of seeing the large, yellow flowers and the developing fruits. Proper timing of harvesting is essential. Summer squashes must be cut while the skin is still soft and you should never leave them to grow longer than about 20 cm – if you do then the plant will stop flowering.

The rules are quite different for winter squashes. Leave them on the plant until the stems turn yellow, which is usually when the first frosts have occurred. Cut off each squash with about 8 cm of stem remaining. Let them stay outdoors for a few days if the weather is dry and then store them in a dry, frost-free place.

# SWEET VIOLETS

EDWARDIAN POSTCARDS illustrate one of the popular tokens of friendship before the 1914–1918 War – a bunch of violets. Sweet Violets were part of the Victorian way of life in Britain – street hawkers offered them, ladies carried or wore them and Oil of Violets was the top-selling perfume. But interest suddenly declined with the outbreak of World War I and it has never returned. Nowadays you will find bunches of anemones and freesias

at the florist but the once-loved violet is now neglected – 'We don't get any call for them.'

It was once so very different. In Ancient Greece there were violet nurseries flourishing before the birth of Christ and this humble flower was the symbol of mighty Athens. In mediaeval times in Europe the Sweet Violet was more than a pretty flower and a source of perfume. It was a widely-used foodstuff – the blooms were one of the very few sweeteners available before the introduction of sugar and they were either cooked with game and beef or served as a sweetmeat. Violets were also used as a deodorant – large quantities of blooms were used to cover floors so as to mask the unpleasant smells of the age.

As a medicinal plant it was put to all sorts of uses. There were violet recipes to cure drunkenness, melancholia and sleeplessness, to improve the skin and even arouse desire. These assorted herbal uses declined steadily until they disappeared in our modern times, but the flower has remained a symbol of innocence and modesty from the time of the Ancient Greeks up to the present day.

The heyday of the Sweet Violet was in France after the rise of Napoleon. The intertwining of the life of the Emperor with this tiny flower is one of the most touching stories in the whole of history. It began when he first met Josephine – she threw a bunch of violets at the feet of the young officer as she left, and he kept the posy. During their marriage he sent violets to her on every wedding anniversary despite the pressures of battle and affairs of state. In defeat and after his divorce the violet remained. When exiled to Elba he promised 'I shall return in the spring with the violets.' He did, and as a messenger to his divorced wife at Malmaison he sent his small son carrying a bunch of the sweet-smelling flowers which had by then begun to appear in the woods of France. The saddest part of the story concerns his final days – captured and due to be exiled to St. Helena, he asked to visit the grave of Josephine. There he picked some of the violets and after his death the withered blooms were found in a locket around his neck. The Sweet Violet became a symbol

of the Bonapartists after his death and its popularity in France was remarkable. At the end of the 19th century more than 200 tons of flowers were harvested each year in a single region of the Riviera.

Now the age of the Sweet Violet has passed, but there is no reason why you should not grow this delightful plant in your garden – there is a whole generation which has never experienced the strong perfume which our grandmothers knew so well. Try to provide the same sort of conditions that it enjoys in the wild. Sweet Violet (*Viola odorata*) grows in light woodland and under hedges in humus-rich soil. It is a perennial which spreads by means of runners, growing about 10 cm high and producing purple or white blooms in early spring and occasionally in autumn.

# UNUSUAL VEGETABLES

T HE BEST-SELLER LISTS of vegetable seeds vary slightly each year, but you will always find the old favourites – Runner beans, tomatoes, lettuce, peas, cabbages, carrots, beetroots, Brussels sprouts, cauliflowers and Broad beans. No surprises, and certainly no unusual vegetables.

We have only ourselves to blame. An increasing number of out-of-the-way varieties ('queer gear' in the language of the wholesale produce markets) have come into the shops. The larger supermarkets and greengrocers now offer Chinese cabbage, Florence fennel, Kohl rabi, Winter radish and several others, so we can at least try some of the new ones. The seed houses are also playing their part in tempting us to be more adventurous – each year new root vegetables, unusual saladings and strange leafy varieties are offered … but we generally stick firmly to the old favourites when we decide on what to sow in the vegetable plot or on the allotment.

Why? Basically it is a fear of the unknown – will it succeed in my soil … will the family like the taste … will I look stupid if nothing comes up? Far too many gardening writers have scoffed at these fears, but some of the 'queer

> Garden Radishes are in wantonness by the gentry eaten as a salad, but they breed scurvy humours and corrupt the blood.
>
> *Nicholas Culpeper*

gear' were disappointing for a few years until experience showed which varieties were best. Furthermore, some have had a flavour which did not appeal to Mr. and Ms. Average. The rule is – try a small patch of any unusual vegetable and if possible buy some from your local shop and sample it before devoting land, time and effort to its cultivation.

Many of the unfamiliar vegetables are easy to grow and their flavours, although different, often provide a welcome relief from the monotony of carrots, caulis, beetroot, etc. First of all, the root and root-like vegetables. There is **Celeriac**, a bulbous 'root' with celery-like leaves. Plant out seedlings in May and harvest in winter. **Kohl rabi** is even easier to grow – just sow the seeds outdoors

between April and July, and harvest the swollen stem bases when they are the size of tennis balls about 11 weeks later. Like Celeriac, eat them grated in a salad or slice and boil them as a vegetable. The flavour is rather bland – for a distinct aniseed taste grow **Florence fennel**. Sow the seeds between April and July, and harvest the swollen leaf bases. Slice them as a salad or cook whole to replace cabbage or cauliflower. In the true root group there are **Salsify**, which is grown like parsnips but has a much nicer flavour, and **Scorzonera**, which is rather more difficult to grow and less appetising in appearance. If you want an unusual root crop which is really easy to grow, choose the **Jerusalem artichoke**. All you have

to do is plant the tubers about 10 cm deep and 30 cm apart in February and then dig up the knobbly artichokes in the winter.

Turning to leafy vegetables, there are several lettuce substitutes you can try. **Endive** (which needs blanching), **Sorrel** and **New Zealand spinach** (which are not to everybody's taste) and **Chicory** (which needs forcing) are the sorts of unusual vegetables which have disappointed people in terms of yield and flavour and so driven them back to the top ten. But there are salad novelties which are well worth trying. Begin by sowing a different type of lettuce – there is **Salad Bowl**, which is a cut-and-come-again variety, or the red-leaved type **Delicato**. **Chinese cabbage** looks like a large Cos lettuce with frilly-edged leaves and it can be eaten raw or cooked. Even radishes have their odd relations – as a change from old favourites like French Breakfast and Cherry Belle, try **Winter radish**. Sow in July, harvest in November and the roots will be the size of turnips or large carrots.

If you are going to try just one out-of-the-ordinary vegetable this year, make it the **Asparagus pea**. Grow it like any other dwarf pea variety, but pick the pretty winged pods when they are only 4 cm long and cook them whole. Delicious!

The list of unusual types and varieties could go on and on – yellow beetroots, striped tomatoes, red lettuce … try a few this year, if only to be different.

# GARDENS

❧

T HE GARDENS illustrated in this chapter span about 500 years, from the 14th century water gardens in Spain, where tinkling streams and tiles dominate the flowers (page 105), to the 20th century delight of Sissinghurst (page 45) where the flowers are everything.

In the beginning the garden was *within* the house, castle or monastery. For a reconstructed example of a garden in Roman Britain go to Fishbourne Palace (W. Sussex) – to see a monastery garden go to Newstead Abbey (Nottinghamshire). In 15th century Florence the garden moved outside – green squares with fountains and pathways, marble seats and hidden arbours. These early Renaissance gardens were places for quiet meditation like their predecessors, the Mediaeval gardens within castle and monastery walls. In 16th century Rome the style changed – spectacular fountains, ornate terraces and elaborate staircases provided places for entertaining on a lavish scale. The grand Renaissance garden had arrived, and you can see the prototype which changed the whole of the

European scene at the Vatican Gardens. There are other examples – Villa Lante and Villa d'Este (page 106) – Italy now led the gardening world.

## Early Renaissance gardens were places for quiet meditation

Our Renaissance gardens were pale in comparison but the Tudor garden (1530–1560) did at least found the outdoor garden in Britain with its terraces, mounts, statuary, fountains and box-lined knots. No complete Tudor garden remains, but you can see traces at Hampton Court (page 107). The Elizabethan garden (1560–1610) followed – similar to but grander than its Tudor parent. Once again none of the great gardens like Theobalds or Holdenbury remain but you can see either reconstructions or authentic fragments at Montacute (Somerset), Edzell Castle (Tayside) and New Place, Stratford-upon-Avon (Warwickshire).

The beginning of the 17th century saw

James I on the throne and the start of the Jacobean age of gardening. The Queen's Garden at Kew (page 113) will give you an excellent idea of the style of the time, but the reign of the Renaissance garden was about to end.

In 1661 the Frenchman le Nôtre created Vaux-le-Vicomte (page 123) and for 100 years his rules guided Europe's garden makers. The long vista, the avenues, the rectangular canal and the elaborately-patterned beds close to the house were now all-important. The formal *jardin français* had arrived. Versailles (page 34) remains its crowning glory, but you will find other excellent examples in France.

Charles II brought the style back to England when he was restored to the throne, and the nurseries of London and Wise were its main driving force. Throughout the land they sold trees and designs for large and not-so-large gardens, but though the French style took root it never really flowered. Charles transformed the Royal Gardens (page 107) but they were mere shadows of Versailles. Our parterres were described as the meanest in Europe, and long canals were never really popular. Melbourne (Derbyshire) gives the best impression of *le jardin français* in England.

Britain was still a second-rate copier of foreign patterns, but there was a wind of change. William Kent came back from Italy 'leaped the fence and saw that all nature was a garden'. He created his idealised countryside at Chiswick and Rousham (1741) and the Landscape garden had arrived. Stourhead (page 121), designed by Hoare, is our finest example, but Capability Brown was the arch-priest of the new style. The Great French gardens at Blenheim (page 97), Chatsworth (page 101) and elsewhere were swept away. No walls, no hedges, no flowers – the landscape became part of the garden and the garden became a classical picture.

This couldn't go on for ever, but it did last for nearly a hundred years. The Victorians, despite their faults, remembered that flowers make a garden, but their florid Neo-Italianate style and fussy bedding schemes gave way to the informal planting schemes of the early 20th century and at last Design and Plant had learnt to live together.

See these 20th century gardens at Sheffield Park (page 119), Nymans (page 117), Bodnant (page 99), Inverewe (page 111), Hidcote (page 109) and Sissinghurst (page 45). For a living garden history book go to Hampton Court (page 107) or Blenheim (page 97). If you want to learn about plants go to Wisley (page 125) or Kew (page 113), but if you want to see a series of garden tableaux visit homely Compton Acres in England (page 103) or the vast Longwood Gardens in the U.S. (page 115).

These few pages can do no more than give you a glimpse of some of the Grand Gardens of the Western World, but they do show the golden threads in the vast tapestry which was started thousands of years ago.

# BLENHEIM

MANY OF THE gardens open to the public represent a single page from the history book of garden design. There are the Elizabethan Garden at New Place in Stratford, the Landscape Garden at Stourhead and the modern Woodland Garden at Savill Gardens in Windsor Great Park.

Blenheim is different. As styles came and went, the layout of the garden was changed. Many great landscape architects worked there over a period of 200 years – Vanbrugh, Wise, Capability Brown, Duchêne – and each one has left his mark somewhere on this vast expanse of grass, trees, water, stone and flowers.

The story began in 1705 when a grateful Queen Anne presented her manor at Woodstock in Oxfordshire to John Churchill, 1st Duke of Marlborough and victor at the Battle of Blenheim. Here a spectacular palace was to be built on behalf of the nation, and the architect chosen was Sir John Vanbrugh.

Such a palace needed a garden which would match its grandeur and Henry Wise, gardener to Queen Anne, started work on its construction while the house was being built. We shall never know how much of the plan was due to Wise rather than Vanbrugh, but together they created a vast parterre, with a width and length of 800 m. This was a garden befitting a soldier – two avenues of stately elms, large stone enclosures, heroic statues and fountains, and a complex design of dwarf box hedges.

Now Sarah, Duchess of Marlborough, entered the picture. At her request a flower garden as well as the great parterre was created, for she wanted to walk amongst irises and carnations and not just through a grandiose tapestry of stone and topiary.

The famous argument between Duchess Sarah and her architect was not about flowers – it was about the bridge. Vanbrugh wanted to build an elaborate triumphal bridge on the approach road to the palace. It would be large enough to carry a series of rooms and would straddle

across – nothing! Below it there would be the tiny River Glyme and the surrounding swampy land. Sarah thought the scheme ridiculous, but Vanbrugh won the day and the imposing bridge was built.

Contemporary writers considered the French-style garden to be one of the great sights of Britain, but it was doomed in 1764 when the 4th Duke called in Capability Brown.

The formal gardens of Henry Wise were swept away and replaced by grassland, but the walled kitchen garden and the elm-flanked avenues were allowed to remain. Many garden historians have criticised Brown for his destruction of the parterres in his quest for naturalism, but all have praised his treatment of Vanbrugh's bridge.

Brown set out to give it 'something worth crossing'. He dammed the small river and created a large irregular-shaped lake – one of the most imposing man-made sheets of water in Europe. Brown was pleased – he said that the River Thames would never forgive him!

Times change, and in the 20th century the 9th Duke decided to restore the formal gardens which had once stood next to the house. He appointed the French landscape architect Achille Duchêne, and in 1925 a beautiful water parterre with black and gold fountains was created. It is the highlight of the garden – within it you will see complex scrolls of neatly-clipped box hedges and beyond it the terraces leading to the lake. Look for an oddity on one of the terraces – a stone sphinx bearing the head of the American heiress Consuelo Vanderbilt, who married the 9th Duke of Marlborough.

Blenheim continues to reflect the changing styles of garden design, and a modern addition has been the Spring Garden – an informal woodland garden of winding paths and attractive shrubs and trees … a purely 20th century garden, snuggling happily close to Wise's kitchen garden, Vanbrugh's bridge, Brown's lake and Duchêne's terraces.

> God Almighty first planted a garden. And indeed it is the purest of human pleasures. It is the greatest refreshment to the spirits of man.
>
> *Sir Francis Bacon*

# BODNANT

Some people consider that Bodnant is the finest garden in Britain, and there are sound reasons for this claim. There are sights and views to delight the eye of the visitor who knows nothing at all about gardens and gardening but who just wants a day out in the country. You need no knowledge of plants in order to enjoy the beauty of a long tunnel dripping with laburnum tassels or of a pool studded with rare water lilies. The view from the house is quite breathtaking – six great terraces stepping downwards to the wooded dell in the valley below, with the mountains of Snowdonia as a backcloth.

It is also one of our best gardens for people who are more interested in unusual plants than in wonderful views. In the cool Welsh air you will find an outstanding collection of azaleas, rhododendrons, camellias and magnolias, and everywhere there are rare shrubs and trees – a tiny rockery gentian at one end of the scale and a mighty 40 m Giant fir at the other. The rose garden, the rock garden, the carefully-labelled plants and a well-stocked garden shop all cater for the visitor who wants more than just a day out in the country.

Many of our grand gardens were started hundreds of years ago, with successive generations chopping and changing the styles and plantings. Not so with Bodnant – the first beginnings were in 1875 when Henry Pochin planted the conifers and it was his daughter, the first Lady Aberconway, who extended the garden to include herbaceous borders and shrubs as well as trees. Bodnant is really the work of the Aberconway family – it was the 2nd Lord who gave the gardens to the National Trust in 1949. The late 3rd Lord Aberconway, who was the President of the Royal Horticultural Society, lived at Bodnant.

Begin your tour at the garden entrance to the house. From this upper terrace, guarded by two wild-eyed sphinxes, you will have the most spectacular view that Bodnant has to offer – the wooded valley

with the mountains beyond. Walk down to the croquet terrace below – here you will find a wistaria-clothed fountain and several beautiful shrubs, such as the Small-leaved lilac and *Eucryphia nymansensis*. Continue downwards to the bow-fronted third terrace with its lily pond and stately cedar trees, and then down to the fourth terrace with its rare shrubs and nearby rose garden.

Another flight of steps and you reach the most famous terrace of all. Along the length of this grassy terrace, flanked with herbaceous plants, hedges and trees, is a long rectangular canal. At one end is the Pin Mill, an attractive gazebo built in about 1730 and used for part of its life as a factory making pins. The Aberconways bought this building shortly before World War II and transported it from Gloucestershire to Bodnant, where it was re-erected to grace the canal. At the other end of this stretch of water is the 'green theatre' – a raised lawn serving as the stage and a closely clipped yew hedge as the wings and backcloth.

Below the canal is the final terrace. Here you will find the magnolias in all their glory – *M. sieboldii*, *M. kobus*, *M. sinensis*, *M. wilsonii* and the rest. Now look back up towards the house and once again admire the formal Italian-style terraced garden through which you have walked. Turn around and the scene is completely different, for the path now descends into a woodland garden – apparently wild but actually carefully planted. Here you will find rhododendrons, camellias, azaleas, hydrangeas and so on clothing the valley and the hillside flanking the terraces. A stream flows into this dell, and along its banks grow moisture-loving plants.

Nearly 35 hectares of a gardener's paradise set in Gwynedd, close to Conway and Colwyn Bay. It is a place where you can enter free of charge if you are a member of the National Trust or the Royal Horticultural Society, and you can forget about time as you wander through the many gardens within a garden. But you will have to remember to leave your dog at home, because it is not allowed.

> Large or small, (a garden) should look both orderly and rich. It should be well fenced from the outside world. It should by no means imitate either the wilfulness or the wildness of Nature, but should look like a thing never to be seen except near a house.
>
> *William Morris*

# CHATSWORTH

THERE ARE scores of gardens you can enjoy if you have an afternoon to spare – a stroll around the flower beds, a sniff at the roses and a pause by the lake. Chatsworth is different – the house is such a treasure-store and the gardens so full of interest that you will need a whole day … and then perhaps a return visit.

The site is picturesque – the wooded valley of the River Derwent in the Derbyshire Peak District. The words of a standard tour guide sound rather dull – start at the Orangery and go past the flower borders to the large fountains. Then pass through Azalea Dell, so impressive in springtime, past the Ravine and enter the conifer and tree collections. The next stage is the impressive Great Cascade and the Cascade House, and finally back to the house through the woods. There are other sights along the way, some of which involve a detour. See the site of the Great Conservatory, now a maze, and visit the great ornamental rocks and the Display House.

Hidden behind these rather terse instructions lies the history of British gardening together with as many fascinating and unique sidelights as any garden has to offer. The first garden was made by unknown hands and virtually nothing remains – it was the Elizabethan garden, and all you will find is Queen Mary's Bower where part of the building is original.

Named landscape gardeners now enter the picture and these names were the greatest of the age. The 1st Duke of Devonshire called in the foremost nurserymen and designers, George London and Henry Wise, to create the formal gardens about his new house. The result was the French-style garden which was in fashion at the end of the 17th century – rectangular blocks of trees, straight avenues, complex parterres, long stretches of water and fountains.

The avenues and parterres were swept away by Capability Brown in 1760 when

into the air, Paxton's narrow greenhouse ('conservative wall') still grows camellias, the massive blocks of stone which were transported here remain as impressive as ever. The extensive tree collections which the two friends gathered from far-off lands have matured and become more impressive with time, but the star of the Paxton garden has gone.

## The Great Conservatory, completed in 1840, was the largest greenhouse in the world

he was called in by the 4th Duke to change the garden into a parkland landscape. Only some stonework was allowed to remain, but Brown was more cautious with the elegant waterworks. He removed most of the fountains but preserved the dominant feature of the garden which happily remains the dominant feature today. A Great Cascade had been built in the London and Wise garden – a sheet of water which slid down the hillside over a series of stone steps. Before Brown there had been nine fountains designed by the water architect Grillet, but today only the Sea Horse Fountain remains.

The glory of Chatsworth really began when young Joseph Paxton arrived in 1826 as the Head Gardener to the 6th Duke of Devonshire. The legendary friendship between these two men is told on page 146, and their achievements make a memorable list. The Emperor Fountain still hurls its jet of water nearly 100 m

The Great Conservatory, completed in 1840, was the largest greenhouse in the world. In 1919 it was blown up by the 9th Duke – one man's genius destroyed by another man's recklessness. The story since then has happily been one of continued development. Flower borders have been set out and a maze has been created on the site of the Great Conservatory. A Display House has been built so that orange trees and other exotic plants have returned to Chatsworth where once they flourished in the palace of glass. There is an adventure playground and a working farm to entertain the children. The Rose Garden with the sort of display you will find in many gardens is another feature. Then there is the floor plan of Chiswick House traced out in dwarf box on a lawn – the sort of display you will find nowhere else. Chatsworth is like that – a mixture of the usual and the unique.

# COMPTON ACRES

GARDEN PURISTS would not choose Compton Acres as their favourite garden. For them the great delight is to be able to wander freely from one area to another, leisurely or even aimlessly moving about and then chancing upon some unusual plant or interesting feature. A visit where you feel it is *your* garden.

Compton Acres is not like that. There are well-ordered and well-kept displays of gardens created in different styles. You move from one to another along a clearly marked route.

The fact that Compton Acres is set out as a series of living exhibits through which we are routed should not really arouse criticism. After all, that is just the way we see most of the stately homes in this country, moving from room to room along a roped-off passageway. One of the advantages of the Compton Acres approach is that people are sure to see all the points of interest – there is a beginning and an end to the tour, just as in the stately home.

In each of the distinct sections which make up the garden there is something to interest everyone. For the novice there is a clear demonstration of different styles – the water and stone of the Italian Garden, the lawns and borders of our own style and the essential features of the gardens of

Ancient Rome. For the knowledgeable who know these styles there are plant rarities to see – many tender varieties grow here.

## It would be worth going to Compton Acres to see just one of the five major gardens – the Japanese Garden

Compton Acres is a 4 hectare garden situated in the suburbs of Bournemouth. It was started after World War I by Thomas Simpson, but he never lived there and it was neglected during World War II. After the war it was restored and opened to the public in 1952. It soon became a popular attraction for both residents and holiday-makers, attracting 150,000 visitors each year.

It would be worth going to Compton Acres to see just one of the five major gardens – the Japanese Garden, which occurs close to the end of the tour. It was built by a Japanese architect using ornaments and plants imported from Japan. The style is authentic and the effect is quite delightful. For many visitors it is their first sight of this type of garden with all its symbolism and hidden meanings – the tinkling stream, the curious bridges, twisted willows, azaleas, pagodas, stone lanterns and squat figures. An excellent garden … even for the purist!

But that is only one of the garden rooms. Walk over to the Italian Garden with its spectacular lake and gardens. Here you will find statuary, urns and colourful bedding displays. It is also known as the Wedding Garden with the Italian Villa being used as a wedding venue.

Next there is the Wooded Valley with shady glades filled with bluebells, foxgloves and other woodland plants. Spring is the favourite time for visitors, when the bulbs, camellias and rhododendrons are in bloom. Nearby is the Rock and Water Garden, built in the 1920s and filled with a wide variety of alpines and bulbs, and in the corner is the Heather Garden with its newly-planted slopes and stunning views over Poole Harbour.

Five main gardens, but there are many more attractions. There are the Palm Court with its palms, jacarandas and mimosas, the Garden of Memory, the Roman Garden, Wooded Valley etc. Children have not been forgotten – there is a Kids' Play Area tucked away among the trees.

There are over 3000 different species of trees, shrubs and flowers at Compton Acres, and it is open 363 days a year. The question remains – is it an exhibition or a grand garden? The answer doesn't really matter – it provides an enjoyable day out for scores of thousands of people.

# GARDENS OF WATER

I T IS ONLY during the past 200 years that water has ceased to be an essential ingredient in the grand garden. At the start of Western gardening it was the *only* essential ingredient. The Persians regarded the garden as an oasis. Here they sat during the dry, intense heat of summer, listening to the fountains and looking at the cool water in the long, tiled canals. There were trees and flowers and hedges of myrtle, but water provided the paradise, and 'paradise' comes to us from the ancient Persian word for a garden.

The Persian concept of garden design spread eastwards to India and westwards to Spain. By A.D. 718 the Moors had overrun most of the Spanish peninsula and they created their gardens at Seville, Cordoba and elsewhere in Andalusia.

Most of these Moorish gardens fell into decay following the reconquest of Spain, but you can still see two outstanding examples at Granada. The Alhambra was completed in about 1390 and the most famous of its gardens is the Patio de los Arrayanes – a long pool lined by clipped myrtle hedges. Below it is the Patio de los Leones with its statues of lions and massive fountain. Even more fascinating are the picture-postcard gardens of the nearby Generalife, the white-walled summer palace of the kings of Granada. Here you will find the Patio de la Riadh which is nearly 45 m long with two lines of curving jets of water falling into the flower-edged central canal.

The mastery of gardening with water passed to the Italians in the 16th century. Pope Julius II, patron of Raphael and Michelangelo and founder of St. Peter's, was also the man who 'changed the whole conception of gardening in Europe'. His architect, Bramante, built the Cortile de Belvedere at the

Vatican. Like Le Nôtre's Vaux-le-Vicomte in France many years later, this creation transformed the garden scene and became the prototype for everything that followed.

Villa Lante at Bagnaia has long been considered to be the perfect Italian Renaissance garden. Built between 1566 and 1570, all the basic features are still to be seen – ornate terraces, grand staircases, complex parterres and an abundance of urns and statues. However, it is water and not plants which provides the major display. No flower garden, this, but there is a flowering of water – bursting forth from elaborate fountains, tumbling down water staircases, descending like sheets from cascades and lapping gently against the stone boats in the water parterre.

It was at the Villa d'Este that the water garden reached its pinnacle, and this estate at Tivoli remains the supreme example. Much of its glory and mechanical wizardry has disappeared over the years,

but enough remains to delight the eye … and the ear. The centrepiece is the Avenue of the Hundred Fountains – hundreds of small fountains and jets playing against and spouting upwards from a long, moss-covered wall. There is the Oval Fountain, the Neptune Fountain, the Rometta, the Baroque Organ Fountain and many more. The time to see the Villa d'Este is at night, when the fountains are floodlit and the water rises and falls to the sound of music.

In 1661 the French Style of gardening, *le jardin français*, burst into flower. The Long Canal, up to 1.5 km long, was a vital feature and fountains served as focal points in the grand design. About 100 years later it was the Landscape Garden which dominated the scene, and water became a feature to be treated in a natural manner – large lakes were created and streams were diverted but these water features always had the appearance of being untouched by human hand.

The Victorian and Modern gardens arrived and the heyday of water was over. Lakes, fountains, pools, waterfalls and the like were now optional extras … the garden henceforth was a place for trees and flowers and not for tinkling water as it had been in ancient Persia.

# HAMPTON COURT

IN 1838 Queen Victoria opened the gardens of Hampton Court to the public for the first time. Within a few months over 100,000 people had walked along the royal pathways, and ever since a visit to Hampton Court has been a favourite day out for Londoners and tourists.

There are the magnificent Palace, the Grand Maze, the Great Vine, vast lawns for the children to play on and beautiful flowers to admire. For the garden lover, however, there is much more ... the Hampton Court gardens are a unique living record of our gardening history.

And a long history it has been. In 1514 Cardinal Wolsey rented the Manor of Hampton and began to create a Palace and the first Grand Garden in Britain:

'The knots so enknotted it cannot be
　expressed,
With arbours and alleys so pleasant
　and so *dulce*,
The pestilent airs with flavours to
　repulse ...'

Wolsey's opposition to Henry VIII's marriage cost him both his position and his beautiful gardens. The King had no liking for the Cardinal's arbours and alleys – he built instead the garden of a man of action. Between 1530 and 1534 he created bowling alleys, archery butts, tennis courts and a tiltyard where jousting was practised. The crowning glory was the mount from which the whole garden could be surveyed. His 'awne darling' Anne Boleyn was not

forgotten – there was a rose garden to supply her with flowers.

Almost nothing remains of Wolsey's or Henry's Tudor garden. Close to the Broad Walk you will find a long building which is one of the 'tennis plays', used for Real or Royal Tennis. Stone 'Kinges Beastes' of the type used to decorate Henry's garden can be seen at the entrance to the Palace, and a Tudor Knot Garden was reconstructed in 1924. Spend a little time at this Knot Garden. It is one of the few good examples of this basic feature of the early English garden – complicated patterns of clipped box or yew infilled with coloured gravel or flowers.

Unlike the Tudor garden, the next phase of development does remain. Charles II restored the monarchy in 1660 after his exile in France, and he brought back with him the memory of great gardens like Vaux-le-Vicomte. Of course he did not have the money to attempt to remodel Hampton Court on such lavish lines, but he did set out to create Britain's first Grand Garden in the French style. A canal (the Long Water) was built, stretching eastwards for nearly 2 km. Lime trees from Holland lined the avenues. It was not Versailles, but it was an impressive new style in the British gardening scene.

But it was William and Mary and not Charles who made the most spectacular changes. Wren extended Wolsey's building, and between 1696 and 1700 the Great Fountain Garden was built at the east side of the Palace. The yew-lined avenues radiating from the portico remain as impressive as ever, but the complex flower beds have gone.

These parterres were swept away by the 'Landscape' look of the 18th century. Kent and Capability Brown both laid their hands on Hampton Court but they fortunately left the basic structure of the gardens unchanged. They did not bring in the lakes, hills and temples with which they destroyed so many formal gardens.

The last great feature which Britain introduced to the world of gardening was the herbaceous border, and one of the best examples is to be found by the Broad Walk. Three hundred metres long, it should not be missed by any keen gardener.

A garden then, and not just a palace. There is the large Priory Garden, filled with flowers, statues, lawns, trees, paths and a fountain. Stand there and look at the Thames through the magnificent wrought-iron grille of Jean Tijou. Nearby is the Sunken Garden and of course you won't forget to see the famous Hamburg Vine planted in 1769. It still bears more than 500 bunches of black grapes each year.

# HIDCOTE MANOR

HIDCOTE MANOR is quite different from the other grand gardens of Britain. First of all, it consists of only 4 hectares – you will find none of the breathtaking vistas and vast expanses of Blenheim, Stourhead or Chatsworth. It was created on a windswept, clayey field near Chipping Campden in Gloucestershire – there was no fertile or picturesque earlier garden on which to build. The most out-of-the-ordinary feature is that it reverses the normal nationality pattern. Each year crowds of American tourists pass through our gardens, such as Harewood House or Castle Howard, to admire the work of British landscape gardeners – at Hidcote Manor we have British visitors enjoying and being inspired by the work of an American.

> **The basic feature of Hidcote Manor is a central pathway which passes through a series of clearly-defined compartments or 'outdoor rooms'**

Major Lawrence Johnston left his native home and began his garden at the start of the 20th century. During the next 40 years he created there several new concepts in garden design. The features he incorporated have greatly influenced both landscape architects and ordinary gardeners in the way they group plants together, yet he remains virtually unknown. Perhaps the reason is that he spent his time making a garden rather than writing textbooks for others.

The basic feature of Hidcote Manor is a central pathway which passes through a series of clearly-defined compartments or 'outdoor rooms'. Within these hedge-lined compartments Lawrence Johnston broke with tradition. In 1907 the rule books clearly spelt out that there should be herbaceous borders of perennials, shrubberies of bushes and trees alongside rose gardens and flower beds … all with distinct boundaries.

At Hidcote the rules were ignored. For instance, in the Red Garden you will find trees such as the Purple-leaved plum and the Purple-leaved hazel, shrubs like *Berberis thunbergii atropurpurea* and red flowers such as *Lobelia cardinalis* and scarlet dahlias. Trees, shrubs and flowers jumbled up with red roses and purple-leaved alpines to give the desired effect – a living painting in bronze, red and purple. Such a mixed border seems commonplace today, but in the early 1900s it was heresy.

Of course, the Red Border is not the only outdoor room at Hidcote Manor – there are more than 20 others. There are a White Garden and also Mrs Winthrop's Garden, which contains the yellow flowers which Major Johnston's mother loved. There are a Holly Walk and a Pool Garden with its water lilies and goldfish. Some of the rooms are devoted to a single group of plants – you will find a Fuchsia Garden and a Rose Garden in which there is a superb collection of old-fashioned roses.

The largest room is the Theatre Lawn and one of the most interesting is the Stilt Garden – immaculately-clipped horn-beams with straight, bare trunks. Room after room – the Pillar Garden, the Kitchen Garden, the Stream Garden, the Lime Avenue and so on. Hidcote Manor is a place for the plant lover, for in its many rooms you will find a wide array of rare and interesting plants.

Do look at the hedges, because it was at Hidcote that the 'tapestry' hedge was

The kiss of the sun for pardon,

The song of the birds for mirth,

One is nearer God's heart in a garden

Than anywhere else on earth.

*Dorothy Frances Gurney*

created. Combinations of yew, hornbeam, holly, box and beech are planted together to give a mottled green effect in summer and a patchwork of green and brown in winter.

In catalogues you will find *Lavandula angustifolia* 'Hidcote' – one of the best varieties of lavender you can grow. There is *Hypericum* 'Hidcote' which bears the largest flowers of any garden hypericum. Major Johnston, who planned and planted the garden, has gained no such immortality. Plant breeders did not rush to pay homage to this horticultural innovator by naming new varieties after him. There is a 'Lawrence Johnston' rose – a vigorous, yellow-flowered climber which is still grown – but it was regarded as useless by the Frenchman who raised it, and he sold the only plant to the creator of Hidcote.

# INVEREWE

LET US SUPPOSE that you want to see a large and varied collection of sub-tropical plants growing outdoors without having to leave the shores of Britain. You want to see Tree ferns from New Zealand, the Pitcher plant from America, palms and palm-like plants from Australia and China, exotic bamboos from Asia and many, many more. Where would you expect to find such gardens – in a sheltered area in the south east of England or on the gale-swept strip along the west coast of Scotland?

The answer is the west of Scotland, and the secret is the Gulf Stream. This ensures frost-free winters – frost and ice, not cool summers, are the enemies of sub-tropical plants. You will find the plants you seek in the small botanical garden at Logan in the Mull of Galloway and also at Inverewe, a National Trust for Scotland property in West Highland.

The trip from Inverness or up the coast road is not an easy or quick one, and yet more people go to Inverewe each year than to the Cup Final at Wembley. It is a paradise for plant lovers wishing to see something different, but it was not always so.

In 1862 the Inverewe headland was bare rock and peat with patches of heather and crowberries. On the site where the garden now stands there was a single bush – a stunted willow. In that year Osgood Mackenzie, the Laird of Gairloch, decided to build his garden and the task was a daunting one.

The two prime needs were for wind-breaks and soil. Large trees such as Corsican pine and Douglas fir together with many shrubs like *Griselinia* and *Rhododendron ponticum* were planted to block out the Atlantic gales. Topsoil was brought in to cover the bare rocks.

Now there was wind protection and soil, so Mackenzie tirelessly collected plants from many parts of the world until his death in 1922. His daughter carried on with his work until 1953, when Inverewe was handed over to the National Trust for Scotland.

The Visitor Centre is modern, the guide book is well-written and informative, and in the area close to the entrance you will find well-ordered herbaceous borders. Beyond this is the real Inverewe, once aptly described as 'a wilderness of flowers'. A wooded wild garden, criss-crossed by paths, with strange plants on every side. The labelling is good, and you will see trees and shrubs which are probably new to you. *Hoheria* and *Gevuina* are trees and shrubs you won't find at your local garden centre!

## The two prime needs were for windbreaks and soil

At every turn there is so much to see. There are the views – the Atlantic Ocean, Lake Ewe, the hills, the villages of Brae and Inverasdale. There are the climbers clambering up the trees – unusual types such as *Berberidopsis* and *Eccremocarpus*. One moment you are looking upwards to see the stately Wellingtonias or the birds in the pines and the next moment you are bending down to see the blue flowers of the Himalayan poppy. Favourite areas are

> The Story of Mankind began in a garden and ended in Revelations.
>
> *Oscar Wilde*

the Giant Rhododendron Walk and the Bambooselum with its exotic trees and shrubs, but everywhere you will find unusual plants. Pride of place goes to the magnificent *Magnolia campbellii* which is 12 m high and is covered in pink flowers as big as soup plates – an unforgettable sight in March and April.

Inverewe is deservedly popular, even though it is tucked away in the north of Scotland. The semi-tropical garden at Logan in south Scotland is much less popular and it is smaller, but it has much to offer. The display of Chinese Fan palms and Australian Cabbage palms is spectacular, and an occasional pinch is necessary to remind you that you are nearly 500 km north of London!

# KEW

ALFRED NOYES wrote 'Go down to Kew in lilac time, it isn't far from London' and about one million people each year follow his advice. Not all of them go in late May or early June when the lilacs are in full bloom – the time of the year depends upon their interests.

For many people a trip to the Royal Botanic Gardens is an outing with the family during the summer holidays, the children enjoying the acres of lawn and playing hide-and-seek around the trees whilst parents admire the flowers. For others it is a spring pilgrimage, going early or late to enjoy the bulbs covering the Mound, the Flowering cherries in bloom or the matchless collection of alpines gathered from every corner of the earth and which now grow in the famous Rock Garden.

For many botanists there is no special time of the year for visiting Kew – their magnet is the largest collection of pressed flower specimens in the world and the world's most important collection of horticultural books in its library.

Once it was a private Royal Garden, created by Augusta, wife of Frederick, the Prince of Wales. It became a Botanic Garden in 1759, but it was only when George III inherited it (1772) and Sir Joseph Banks became its first Director that the Royal Pleasure Grounds at Kew earned an international reputation.

In 1840 Queen Victoria handed the renamed Royal Botanic Gardens over to the nation and Sir William Hooker (pictured) was appointed Director in 1841. This man of boundless energy increased the size from 9 to 200 acres and built the Herbarium, Library and Museums.

The 120 hectares which now make up the Royal Botanic Gardens border the River Thames and clustered in the northern part of the grounds are the more formal areas and the original gardens. Most of Kew is grassland and woodland, but planted in the open and under glass there are over 25,000 different species – one of the most comprehensive collections in the world.

You will find these plants in different situations. Some of the outdoor plants are grown as isolated specimens or in clumps – a tall Corsican pine, a clump of Darwin tulips and so on. Many more have their own special garden, and these areas are certainly worth visiting. A word of warning here – don't try to see all of Kew's features in one day – it would be easier to compete in the London Marathon. A partial list of these gardens includes those devoted to Heather, Bamboo, Chalk, Scree, Aquatics, Iris, Azaleas and Conifers.

A special word for one of these gardens – the Queen's Garden, opened in 1969. This superb reconstruction of a 17th century garden contains pleached alleys, a fountain, gazebo and a collection of herbs and other plants which grew in our gardens 300 years ago. All are labelled with their old names and stories – a place not to be missed even if your visit to Kew is a short one.

Apart from the individual gardens which are things of beauty there is the Herbaceous Ground which is a thing for study. Here the plants are grouped in parallel rows according to their family. Obviously design takes second place, but it is an important area for the scientifically-minded.

There is a great deal to see outdoors but perhaps Kew's greatest glory is its glass. The first greenhouse was the Orangery built in 1761, but the symbol of Kew is the giant Palm House built by Decimus Burton in 1844–1848. There are others – Fern Houses, the Water-Lily House, Orchid House, Australia House, Cactus House, etc.

The reconstructed Temperate House was opened in 1982 – the Victorian building has been improved and many new varieties have been planted amongst the old favourites – the palms, the orange and lemon trees, the Bird of Paradise flowers. In contrast there is the new Alpine House which was opened in 2006. This strikingly innovative building is a narrow glass-covered arch which houses an outstanding display of rockery plants from all over the world. The Princess of Wales Conservatory was opened in 1987.

So do go down to Kew in lilac time, it isn't far from London. There you will see the old favourites, like the Chinese Pagoda and the Palm House, and lots of new things, such as the Tree Walk and the Gallery of Botanical Art.

# LONGWOOD

THERE ARE many gardens open to the public which will provide an enjoyable day's outing. If you live close by or are visiting the area they will provide pathways to follow, sights to admire and plants to envy. But they are not unforgettable – only a handful of gardens are spectacular enough to be worthy of a pilgrimage – Longwood in the United States is one such garden.

Situated about 5 km north of Philadelphia, it gives an immediate impression of vastness. Over 400 hectares stretch around the Information Centre at the entrance, but this is no Landscape garden of lakes, woodland and pathways – about 120 hectares are carefully tended garden filled with plants.

The 2 hectares under glass are one of the great horticultural sights. Along the corridors and in some of the smaller conservatories you will find fascinating collections – the Orchid Case with its brilliantly-coloured rarities, the Tropical Terrace with its assorted ferns, bromeliads and insect-eating plants. The Fern Passage, the Palm House, the Desert House and so on, but you can have seen such things before. Maybe you have never looked at so many interesting plants under one roof, but they are still only collections of plants on display and not beautiful rooms decorated with plants and trees.

It is when you walk into the Main Conservatory that you see the breathtaking and unique beauty of Longwood indoors. Picture a large ballroom made of glass. The 6 m tall pillars are clothed in *Ficus pumila* and all around you is a vast room decorated solely with plants. At Christmas time there is a green turf carpet edged with white and red poinsettias. Tree ferns and orange trees stand like statues between the garlanded pillars, and the scene changes drastically in spring when the Calla lilies, foxgloves, apple trees and others take over. Autumn is a spectacular time when the dominant furnishing material is the chrysanthemum – carpets of small ones,

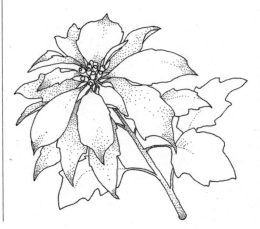

pots and tubs of large ones and tiny ones making up glowing chandeliers.

The Main Conservatory illustrates one of the basic attractions of Longwood from which other gardens could perhaps learn. The floral display changes with each season, and so do several other features in the garden. There are exhibitions of new varieties, home landscaping, garden history and so on and these displays are changed regularly. There is a large Open Air Theatre which seats 2100 people, and a series of plays are shown during the summer months.

All this means that you don't just visit Longwood once and then cross it off your list. It is treated rather like an attractive theatre with its own permanent charm but which is visited again and again to see the latest 'show'.

The permanent features are not all spectacular. There are lecture theatres, training courses, scientific research grounds, rose gardens, quiet walks among the flowering cherries and dogwoods, and so on. On the other hand there are many items of outstanding interest. The Water Gardens cover about 2 hectares and the illuminated fountain display at night is a memorable sight. An apparently static 'Eye of Water' high on the hillside feeds the waterfall and fountain displays, and a Waterlily Garden houses varieties which you will not have seen before.

The Longwood Story began in 1798 when two brothers, Joshua and Samuel Pierce, established a tree garden (arboretum). Their descendants extended the Pierce Garden and opened it to the public, and in 1906 Pierre S. du Pont bought the estate. At this stage the development of Longwood as we know it today really began. Fortunately some of the old trees planted by the Pierce family are still there – the original Ginkgo, Cucumber magnolias, Tulip trees and hemlocks have been retained.

There are many strange things to greet British eyes at Longwood. No ice-cream kiosks nor snack bars, the provision of guided tours, a plentiful supply of gardeners, the use of a water curtain on the stage of the Open Air Theatre … Longwood has been described as 'one of the most extraordinary horticultural showplaces in the world', but only you can judge whether the description is correct.

Who loves a garden, loves a greenhouse too,

Unconscious of a less propitious clime

There blooms exotic beauty, warm and snug,

While the winds whistle and the snows descend.

*William Cowper*

# NYMANS

I N 1890 Ludwig Messel decided to design a garden around the home he had bought at Handcross. He could not have chosen his friends more wisely. Amongst them were some of the greatest horticultural names of the day, and they encouraged and advised him. There was Gertrude Jekyll, who designed one of her beloved herbaceous borders for the garden. William Robinson's passion for the wild garden would have ensured the informal planting of trees and shrubs, and the advice of the greatest rhododendron breeder of the day, Sir Edmund Loder, would have been useful in the planting of the rhododendrons, azaleas and camellias for which the garden is now world famous. Ludwig's brother Alfred was an architect and so he designed the Temple, and Ellen Willmott would no doubt have influenced the planting of the rose garden.

Nymans sounds like a garden of bits and pieces, and that is exactly what it is. There is no slavish adherence to a single school of gardening – instead it is a superb collection of formal and informal gardens on 12 hectares of fertile, acid soil in West Sussex.

Ludwig Messel had knowledgeable and willing friends but there is no doubt that the overall plan was his. The practical side was looked after by James Comber, the head gardener at Nymans for over 60 years. Ludwig's son Leonard was an even more distinguished horticulturalist and he carried on with the work at Nymans when his father died in 1915. In the gardens as well as in many nurserymen's catalogues you will find *Magnolia* 'Leonard Messel' and *Camellia* 'Leonard Messel' as well as *Eucryphia* 'Nymansay'.

## It is a superb collection of formal and informal gardens

Now to the present. The Wall Garden was the first part to be created by Ludwig Messel, and here you will find the herbaceous borders, topiary, an Italian

> A little garden square and
> wall'd;
>
> And in it throve an
> ancient evergreen,
>
> A yew tree, and all round
> it ran a walk
>
> Of shingle, and a walk
> divided it.
>
> *Alfred Lord Tennyson*

fountain and many attractive shrubs. Near the entrance is the Pinetum where some of the oldest trees in the garden are to be found. Look at the rarities there and then take the Victorian Laurel Walk to the Sunk Garden with its collection of flowering shrubs and bedding plants.

The number of gardens is quite bewildering. There is the Rose Garden which contains an excellent collection of old-fashioned shrub and climbing roses. There are the Heather Garden and a Rock Garden as well as the Tasmania Garden, which contains plants from that country.

Nymans is obviously a very busy garden crowded with plants, but that is only part of the story. It is the only garden where the dovecote is crowded but the house is deserted. In 1947 a fire destroyed Messel's home, but the empty shell was not pulled down – the ruin now forms a picturesque

screen for tender plants and a unique support for climbing plants. By the side of the house are the lawns, and this tranquil scene of uninterrupted grassland and the gaunt ruin of the house is in marked contrast to the massed plantings and rainbow colours of the various gardens.

Nymans was once described as a home garden on a grand scale rather than a grand garden on a small scale. There are a Wild Garden and Rhododendron Wood – splendid versions of the shrubbery you might have at home, and there are common-or-garden bedding plants and a wide variety of roses. The lawn is there and so is the rock garden, but there are no terraces, grand vistas nor lakes stretching into the distance.

---

## Nymans was once described as a home garden on a grand scale rather than a grand garden on a small scale

---

In 1949 the idea was put forward that the National Trust should administer outstanding gardens which were worthy of preservation in their own right, and not just as gardens which were linked with some historic house. The first three gardens considered worthy enough to be accepted by the National Trust were Bodnant, Hidcote ... and Nymans. Go to Nymans and see why.

# SHEFFIELD PARK

S HEFFIELD PARK provides a pleasant day's outing for people who live close to London. It is situated in East Sussex, close to Uckfield, and each year more than 100,000 people walk along the paths of this National Trust property. They do not go to see fountains, statues, garden buildings, flower beds, rolling lawns or any other of the grand sights we associate with the stately home garden. Every day apart from the Christmas holidays they go to see the trees, shrubs and lakes, for that is all you will find at Sheffield Park.

But what trees and shrubs they are! Pick a fine and dry day in late October and go there, because this garden was designed to show the full range and brilliance of the hues of many of our trees and shrubs when their leaves change colour in the autumn. You will see the brilliant scarlets and crimsons of the maples, fothergillas and Snowy mespilus. The Swamp cypresses turn to bronze and the birches turn to yellow but the star of the show is the Tupelo tree (*Nyssa sylvatica*). Tupelos are planted along the lakeside, and their autumn leaves look like burnished gold as their reflection twinkles in the water.

This description of Sheffield Park makes it sound like a place for people who like unusual Latin names. This, of course, is true – there is a comprehensive guide book which talks about plants and not about history and stone like the guide books of so many other gardens. You will find many trees and shrubs you may never have seen before – *Eucryphia*, *Nothofagus*, *Embothrium* and so on, but Sheffield Park is not a museum nor a botanical garden. Its clever planting provides a series of stunning, picture-postcard views which make a visit worthwhile even if you can't tell an oak from an apple.

Nor is autumn the only time to see this garden. In spring there are the silver birches with their white-washed trunks standing above carpets of bluebells; in May and June you can see the massed plantings of rhododendrons and azaleas in bloom. All year round there are the stately conifers – you will see Wellingtonias, Canadian redwoods, Incense cedars and Monterey pines towering above the garden.

## You will find many trees and shrubs you may never have seen before

This popular showplace provided a very different scene a hundred years ago. In 1775 the owner, the 1st Lord Sheffield, employed Capability Brown to landscape the estate. Brown created a couple of lakes in his usual style and planted clumps of trees on the grass-covered slopes.

> All gardeners know better than other gardeners.
>
> *Chinese Proverb*

Humphry Repton modified the Capability Brown garden, more lakes were added, but the tree garden we know today was not started until 1909. In that year the 3rd Earl of Sheffield died and the new owner, Arthur G. Soames, set about from that year until his death in 1934 to create one of Britain's first arboreta. One or two, such as the Hillier Arboretum and Westonbirt, may have more species but none can rival the autumn display at Sheffield Park.

The site purchased by Soames was ideal for the purpose – 55 hectares with 5 lakes, each one falling into the next. Trees were selected to provide contrasts in shape and colour – dark and sombre conifers form a backcloth for showy flowering trees and shrubs such as *Eucryphia glutinosa* and *Cornus florida*. Some trees were planted in large groups, others as isolated specimens so that their size, flowers or autumn foliage colours could be seen to their best effect.

There are better places to go if you want a day out with the children – there is no house to visit and picnics are forbidden. If, however, you want to see the full beauty of trees reflected in a lake studded with water lilies, Sheffield Park should be added to your list of places to go.

# STOURHEAD

HORACE WALPOLE was captivated by the new garden he had seen at Stourhead. Writing in the 18th century, he described it as 'one of the most picturesque scenes in the world'. Many authors and artists have agreed with him over the years, and today it is the finest example you will ever see of the Landscape or English garden.

You will be disappointed if you go there and expect to see lots of interesting roses and flowers – you would do better to visit your local park. Stourhead is a living painting, like the ones produced by Poussin and Claude, showing idealised countryside in which is set a series of temples and grottoes. Note that it is *idealised* countryside – it is certainly not a piece of downland on which a few mock Roman buildings have been placed here and there. It is man-made – the lakes, the pathways, the careful selection of trees were the work of clever landscape architects and gardeners.

Surprisingly, not one of the legendary creators of the Landscape garden laid a finger on Stourhead. The genius of this garden was not Kent, Repton or Capability Brown – it was Henry Hoare of the famous banking family, who in 1741 inherited the house set in a bare Wiltshire valley. Damming the stream turned the small fishponds into an impressive, three-fingered lake covering 8 hectares. Hoare wanted to create a scene from the writings of Virgil or Pliny (he had been collecting paintings in Italy at the time of his mother's death in 1741) and the classical temples and grotto were built during his lifetime.

Trees were set out around the lake and hills at this time, but the main plantings of deciduous trees and the creation of the pathways were the work of his grandson, Richard Colt Hoare. Later generations added more trees – the conifers in the middle of the 19th century and the massed

planting of rhododendrons and azaleas about 50 years later, but there has been no attempt to change or 'improve' its character. It is an 18th century garden frozen in time – go in the spring to see the rhododendrons ablaze with colour or wait until the autumn for the beautiful hues of the foliage.

Start your tour at the well-photographed stone bridge – the winding pathway will lead you on a one hour stroll around the garden. Your first stop will be at the Temple of Flora with its pillars and portico. Later you will pass the Grotto, and here you should go down the steps into the underground room. You will see the statue of a nymph on a couch over which water is flowing – this is one of the springs from which the River Stour (hence 'Stourhead') arises.

Continuing on your tour there is the Rustic Cottage and then the largest building, which is perhaps the symbol of Stourhead – the Pantheon. This miniature version of the Pantheon in Rome houses a number of classical statues and after a visit inside you should follow the path to the final building – the Temple of the Sun.

And so back to the bridge once more. As a keen gardener you can remember the beautiful trees you have seen – the maples, nyssas, taxodiums, horse chestnuts, oaks, willows and so on, or as a lover of beauty you can remember the classical scene. If on the other hand you are a thirsty and rather tired tourist, you can retire to the Spread Eagle, an inn built centuries ago for people just like you.

# VAUX-LE-VICOMTE

NICOLAS FOUQUET, Finance Minister of France, had heard about the gardener Le Nôtre from his artist friend Le Brun. The year was 1653 and Fouquet had decided to build a fine house and garden at a spot between Paris and Fontainebleau.

Young Fouquet was a character who could have stepped straight out of the pages of a historical novel. Not yet 30, he was already Chancellor to the Sun King, Louis XIV – a wilful teenager who was in the early years of his long and eventful reign. Fouquet had already amassed a personal fortune but it was not enough –

he wanted more money and more power, because he was a connoisseur of fine art and fine women.

## Long avenues were lined with closely-clipped yews and elaborate statues

The gentle 40 year old Le Nôtre seems to have been a strange choice for such a man. As his life story on page 34 reveals, Le Nôtre had done little to inspire great confidence. He had redesigned part of the

Tuileries and showed a liking for long, wide avenues but he had never designed a great garden from scratch. It is probable that Fouquet was more interested in having a fine house than a spectacular garden.

There is no evidence that Fouquet wished to set a new standard in garden splendour, but he had not reckoned on the latent genius of Le Nôtre. The result was to give Fouquet his proudest day and then a prison cell for the rest of his life. Such was the strange story of Vaux-le-Vicomte.

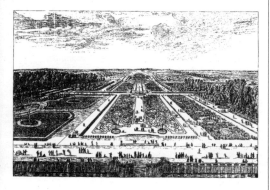

The gardens were started in 1656 and completed in 1661. On August 17 Fouquet arranged a grand gala to open his new garden and to impress and delight the King and his courtiers. The gates opened to reveal more than just a new garden – they opened to reveal a new style of gardening which was destined to dominate the whole of Europe for a century. Here was the vast central vista stretching from the house to the distant horizon – the hallmark of the Le Nôtre style. The

parterres were embroidered in complex designs with dwarf box hedges and the spaces between were filled with powdered brick. Long avenues were lined with closely-clipped yews and elaborate statues stood everywhere.

The King watched a play by Molière and then a ballet. The garden was designed as a vast outdoor palace for entertaining – another feature of the Le Nôtre style. The guests moved further into the garden to see the colonnaded grotto and then the most spectacular sight of all – the Great Canal or *théâtre d'eau* with its many sumptuous fountains and large fire-spouting whale.

At the end of the night-long fête King Louis had little to say. He had never seen a garden like it – his own estates had not yet had the Le Nôtre touch. Fouquet interpreted the King's silence as unqualified admiration, but in reality it was anger and envy. The Finance Minister was imprisoned and never released, dying in jail 19 years later. Louis' reasoning was simple. Fouquet must have been embezzling money to have created such a garden. In a strange demonstration of his own 'honesty', the King stole Fouquet's liberty, his gardener and most of the statues and trees from Vaux-le-Vicomte. The gardens have been restored to something like their former glory, but we cannot really imagine what the effect of seeing the first Le Nôtre garden must have had on the guests at that ill-fated gathering on August 17, 1661.

# WISLEY

V ISITS TO Wisley are like peanuts at a cocktail party – if you have a taste for them, then you will not be satisfied with just one. The Wisley devotees go there in early spring to see the daffodils and in late spring to see the azaleas and rhododendrons in full bloom. All year round there are countless features of interest, and for these people Wisley is Britain's favourite garden.

## Wisley is a working garden which fulfils a vital role in British horticulture

It is not everybody's favourite. There is no overall spectacular plan as you will find around the ancestral home of the aristocrat – instead of a stately home of pillars and porticos you will find an odd collection of lecture rooms, offices and laboratories. This lack of outstanding architecture or garden design has been unfairly criticised by some writers – after all, Wisley is a *working* garden which fulfils a vital role in British horticulture.

Behind the scenes it carries out experiments on a wide range of gardening topics and it also trains young horticulturalists. In the gardens there are trials on new varieties of fruit, vegetables and flowers – the best of them receive First Class Certificates and Awards of Merit.

The trials in Portsmouth Field are a popular attraction, but the main function of Wisley which interests the visitor is the provision of a comprehensive collection of garden plants. Here you will find everything from tiny alpines just peeping above the ground to forest giants soaring into the sky.

Some of these plants are in demonstration areas – there are the Model Fruit

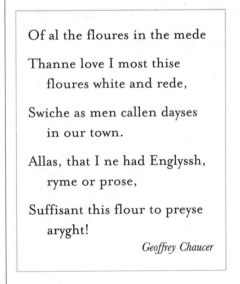

Of al the floures in the mede

Thanne love I most thise
    floures white and rede,

Swiche as men callen dayses
    in our town.

Allas, that I ne had Englyssh,
    ryme or prose,

Suffisant this flour to preyse
    aryght!

*Geoffrey Chaucer*

> The purpose of a garden
> is to give happiness and
> repose of mind, which is
> more often enjoyed in
> the contemplation of the
> homely border ... than in
> any of those great gardens
> where the flowers lose their
> identity, and with it their
> hold of the human heart.
>
> *Gertrude Jekyll*

Garden, Model Vegetable Garden and the Model Suburban Gardens. Look at these plots if you want to see how to garden rather than what to grow. There are regular demonstrations throughout the year and you will find the forthcoming programme in *The Garden*, the monthly magazine of the R.H.S.

After the lessons learnt in the Model Gardens and at the demonstrations there is the joy of the plants in the various sections of the garden. The favourite feature for photographers is the Alpine Meadow – go in early April when Hoop Petticoat daffodils clothe the turf in a yellow blanket. It is only a short walk to the world-famous Rock Garden with its bridges and streams and vast collection of alpines. Rockery plants, however, are not to everybody's taste and many prefer the azaleas, rhododendrons, camellias and magnolias which cover Battleston Hill. Another popular area for the tree and shrub lover is Seven Acres – around its large pond you will find woody varieties in all shapes and sizes. The Heather Garden here is a colourful sight throughout the year.

There is a Pinetum with its collection of conifers and the greenhouses with tropical flowers, exotic succulents and tender plants of every description. The long herbaceous borders provide some of the best examples you will find anywhere in the world. Things continue to appear – the new glasshouse, the Bonsai garden etc.

The Wisley story began in 1878 when G. F. Wilson bought a small plot of derelict land near Ripley in Surrey. He developed and extended the site into an attractive Woodland Garden and on his death in 1902 the garden was purchased by Sir Thomas Hanbury. This distinguished horticulturalist presented the 24 hectare garden to the R.H.S. in the following year, and the outdoor home of the Society moved from Chiswick to Wisley.

The R.H.S. Gardens now cover nearly 80 hectares. Go there if you love flowers and you are near to London. It is open all year round and admission is free if you are a member of the R.H.S.

# LOOKING BACK

'OH, YOUR British gardens are wonderful!' When visitors from overseas pay us this compliment we accept it without question. We feel they are right – where else in the world can you find gardens to visit in such numbers and variety, and where else do over 80 per cent of the population have a garden of their own?

Row upon row of colourful and carefully-tended gardens – each with its lawn, borders, beds, shrubs and trees. The visitor believes it must always have been so, and so do we if we rely on memory alone. Surely it was the British who taught the world how to garden …

Looking back through the eyes of history rather than memory we see a very different picture. Gardening began far from our shores about 4000 years ago – in Egypt and in China. In Egypt thousands of slaves tended the gardens at Thebes and Luxor, and in China the parks of the first emperors were landscaped with steps, terraces and walkways. From these two centres the delight in decorating a plot of land and growing plants for pleasure spread outwards over the centuries.

From the Nile it moved to Babylon which had its Hanging Gardens (page 136) over 2000 years ago, and to Greece where the first gardening book appeared before the birth of Christ (page 138). In some of these Western civilisations the major fascination was with the garden itself, as in Persia and Moorish Spain, whilst in other lands there was a passion for a particular plant – the lotus in Egypt, the violet in Greece and the rose in Rome (page 163).

So gardens and gardening flowered early in many lands, but not in Britain. Throughout the troubled Middle Ages our gardens remained poor imitations of the elegant and flowery enclosures found in Italy and France. For us it was a time for fighting and not flowers, and the small plots found in monastery and castle were used for growing herbs and as grassy refuges from the smells of indoor living.

Then came Henry VIII at the start of the 16th century with his revolutionary ideas on marriage, religion … and gardening. A garden was now a place to be adorned and admired, and the artificial mound he built with a quarter of a million bricks at Hampton Court was the foundation stone of the Grand Garden in Britain.

But we still had little to offer the rest of the world, and nothing changed until we created the closely-cut, regularly-shorn lawn in the 17th century (page 152) and the landscape garden (page 14) in the 18th century. By 1750 we were at last the garden masters – the velvet lawn and *le jardin anglais* were the envy of the world, but that was less than 250 years ago in a 4000 year history.

> ## Find out what plants grow well … and plant a lot of them.
> *2nd Lord Aberconway*

Our Grand Gardens have been a fascinating section of British gardening but they are not the whole story. We owe the survival of our garden flowers to the cottage garden (page 166) and the backyards of industrial workers (page 178). In early Victorian times the middle-class villa garden arrived (page 172), and for the first time flowers became a vital feature in the large as well as the cottage garden.

This 'gardenesque' approach we owe to Loudon and his wife (page 140) and their ideas have influenced the pattern of the small suburban garden of today. The Victorian garden is recent enough to show its relics everywhere, and the style has a strange fascination – we either love it or detest it. It was a time for carpet bedding (page 134), flower sellers (page 169) and ostentation on the grand scale (page 146). Looking back to Victorian times and beyond teaches us one major lesson – the garden you are looking at outside your back door is a very recent innovation.

# 'DEAR SIR'

## THE STRANGE STORY OF THE READERS' PAGES IN THE 19TH CENTURY MAGAZINES

A N IMPORTANT feature of a gardening magazine is the contribution from its readers. The 'Dear Sir' page contains letters on all sorts of subjects – there are bouquets 'I've been a regular reader for 37 years and never missed an issue …', brickbats 'Why do you *never* write about iresines …', and interesting snippets 'The enclosed photograph shows a tomato I've grown which bears a striking resemblance to Winston Churchill …'

In the gardening magazines of the 19th century the 'Dear Sir' pages were of far greater importance than they are today and they filled much of the journal. These contributions were articles rather than chatty letters and hundreds or even thousands of words were used to describe new discoveries, profound opinions, favourite techniques and so on. No one would have dreamt of sending in a tomato which looked like Winston Churchill, for gardening was a serious business. So in the early days of magazines we find page upon page of rather solemn discourses on a wide collection of topics. A random selection from the *Gardener's Magazine* (1826–1842) reveals

'HISTORICAL NOTICES ON THE RISE & PROGRESS OF GARDENING IN BAVARIA'

'ON THE PHILOSOPHY OF MANURES'

'ON THE CEMETRIES OF EDINBURGH AND LEITH'

'OUTLINES OF HORTICULTURAL CHEMISTRY'

The contributors were the keen horticulturalists and professional scientists of the day, well supported by noted nurserymen and the inevitable 'Regular Reader'. The founder of the first popular

magazine also wanted to hear from the people who actually did the work, as his well-meaning if somewhat patronising note in the first issue clearly spelt out:

> 'We especially invite practical gardeners to come forward and support a work calculated for their own honour and advantage. Let them not make excuses as to being unaccustomed to write, want of style, etc., but fix on a subject and begin at once, and write straight on to the end, regardless of anything but the correctness of their statements. This done once or twice, a good style will come of itself.'
>
> *Gardener's Magazine (1826)*

There was some response to this appeal, but in a time of low wages and poor conditions it is not surprising that it was their lot rather than their plants which featured in the letters. Rather more surprising, perhaps, was the complaint from the Head Gardener who was forced by his master to sleep in the house next to the chambermaids rather than in the garden where he felt that he rightfully belonged.

The contributors remained a mixed bunch. There were distinguished figures of the horticultural world and sometimes the literary world who were invited by the 'conductor' (editor) to write an article or series of articles. There were the keen gardeners who wanted to see their name in print, the philanthropists who gave 'sound'

advice on how cottagers with eight children could cope quite happily by means of good husbandry and there were the scientists with their theories.

Even in the earliest days of gardening magazines there were also the disgruntled:

> From **Disappointed Lancashire Farmer**: 'I wish to know whether I cannot recover damages, either of you or the author of the articles on the Cow Cabbage ... I am now a ruined man, beset with duns on every side.'
>
> *Gardener's Magazine (1832)*

> From **Well Wisher**: 'We have had constant tirades against gentlemen for not yielding more and better accommodation to their gardeners ... but every man knows that labour is a marketable commodity just worth, as Butler writes, what it will bring. Where a vacancy occurs, the numerous applications permit the master to pick and choose at his own price. Is this the employer's fault?'
>
> *Gardener's Magazine (1830)*

It was not always the reader who took the magazine to task – occasionally the conductor would add a critical footnote to the contribution by a reader:

> 'Our Correspondent mentions gossip as one of the products of tea; but why should not the cottager's wife have her gossip as well as the wife of the

landlord? Neither man nor woman can go on for any length of time without relaxation; nay, even dissipation.'

*Gardener's Magazine (1830)*

The grumblers and the gardeners, the scientists and the scholars combined to play a part in directing the future of horticulture through the pages of the 19th century magazines. As the century progressed the importance of these reader contributions declined and the content written by staff and commissioned writers increased towards the present level, where the 'Dear Sir' page is an entertaining diversion from rather more serious matters.

The 'Problems' page is rather different – it is part of the more serious matter. For many years common and not-so-common queries have been printed with detailed answers set out below. In this way all readers have been given the benefit of the information and of course this approach is not unique to gardening magazines. You will find it in women's magazines where the questions are often more unusual and even more interesting, but it did not occur to the early editors to follow this obvious approach.

For most of the 19th century the policy was to print either the question without the answer or the answer without the question. In either case the reader who had not asked the question was left partly or completely in the dark, and it is amazing that this unsatisfactory state of affairs continued for about 60 years.

At first the practice was to print the question and leave it to other readers to provide a reply which could be printed in a future issue:

From **G.M.**: 'I should like to know the best time of year to strike cuttings of *Thunbergia alata*, and how to ripen its seed.'

*Gardener's Magazine (1830)*

As the magazine was published quarterly poor G.M. had to wait many months for an answer to his problem. The answers provided in this way were often sound, but not all the queries were answered and some of the replies were distinctly odd:

From **J.N.**: 'The reason why earthing-up potatoes should not be done is quite simple – it retards the growth of the tubers and keeps them small.'

*Cottage Gardener (1850)*

It soon became obvious that the magazine had to provide the answer and not leave it to the reader, but unfortunately when this happened the editors did not bother to print the question. So we find a shoal of meaningless replies:

To **J.W.**: 'Many thanks; it is in hand.'

To **J.B.**: 'Yes, it is the same.'

*Gardener's Chronicle (1890)*

To **Onion**: 'You are doing quite right.'

*Amateur Gardening (1894)*

Not all replies were meaningless – it was often quite easy to guess the question from the reply, and here we see one of the most amazing facets of 19th century journalism. The editor regarded himself as the Principal of a learned institution – a College of Print – and appears to have been offended when one of his flock asked a question which was unworthy of the reader or the magazine. Look for the Victorian Headmaster attitude which glowers through these replies to the poor unfortunate readers:

To **W.S.**: 'How can you imagine for a moment that we can tell the name of a dahlia from seeing a single petal?'
*Cottage Gardener (1850)*

To **T.S.M.**: 'We cannot tell you how much tobacco would be required to destroy the greenfly and black thrip in a Vinery 33 ft long and 15 ft broad. You should be the best judge of that yourself.' *Gardener's Chronicle (1870)*

To **A.F.**: 'Read your Gardener's Chronicle! The Currant-bud Mite has been figured and described repeatedly!'
*Gardener's Chronicle (1888)*

To **Flower**: 'Your question is not so easily solved as you seem to imagine, and we regret that more important work will not permit us to go into it.'
*Amateur Gardening (1892)*

To **A.B.C.**: 'You ask us to give you some idea of the nature of peat. Any description will be less effectual than your asking any florist in your neighbourhood to show you some.'
*Cottage Gardener (1851)*

To **W.T.**: 'We do not recognise it. When your plant is larger perhaps you will send a *good* specimen, and say from what *part* of America it comes. To say that a plant comes from America is like saying that it comes from *anywhere*!'
*Gardener's Chronicle (1850)*

It is a pity that magazine editor George William Johnson did not read this admonition, as he gave the following advice to a reader 3 years later:

To **Y.Z.**: 'Peat is valuable to all American plants ...'
*Cottage Gardener (1853)*

These replies and countless others give the distinct impression that the early editors did not feel it was their job to answer straightforward queries from the people who bought their magazines. They acted like learned scientists being asked to give the answer to 3 times 5, and we do know from a rather bad-tempered editorial by John Loudon in the *Gardener's Magazine* that this was indeed the attitude of the day:

'If we were to comply with the requests which are frequently made by readers who, without meaning the slightest disrespect for them may be included under the designation *Amateur Gardeners* or *Babes in Floriculture* it would be merely to reprint books which they may purchase. The Magazine is not intended to assist in matters which are already treated in popular works on gardening.'

*Gardener's Magazine (1831)*

*Amateur Gardening* began in 1884, and on its 'Doubts and Difficulties' pages both questions *and* answers were given. At last the reader knew exactly what was going on and simple queries were answered – the early idea that a Magazine was not intended to assist in matters which could be found in a textbook had been dropped. Much of the advice is of course out of date for today's gardener but some is as applicable as ever:

From **J.R. Luton**: 'I have some lilac bushes which have thrown up suckers from the roots. Should any or all be removed?' Answer – Remove the suckers at once.

*Amateur Gardening (1894)*

> I have banished all worldly care from my garden; it is a clean and open spot.
> *Hsieh Ling-yin (A.D. 410)*

The magazines were now serving the readers rather than preaching to them, but not *all* the bad temper had gone. One poor reader who suggested that the queries could be put in alphabetical order was asked just how much more than the present mine of information plus coloured plate he was entitled to expect for just one penny. And of course the ideas were strictly Victorian – Tilory Jones asked *Amateur Gardening* (1891) for a cure for her very pale complexion, and was told that 'If you were a young gentleman we should advise you to reside in the country and garden energetically ...'

The last word must go to the conductor of the *Gardener's Chronicle* in September 1850. Perhaps it was at the end of a long and weary day reading queries from 'Babes in Floriculture' that he penned the following reply:

To **C.E.**: 'If you have £30 at your command, do emigrate by all means.'

# CARPET BEDDING

CARPET BEDDING is sometimes put forward as a good example of Victorian bad taste. The plants were regimented into complex patterns, the colours were sometimes garish and the overall effect was totally unnatural. It is, however, strange that people can admire the artistry involved in creating the two-dimensional designs in a piece of tapestry or embroidery and yet hold up their hands in horror at the mention of carpet bedding.

Extensive carpet bedding schemes in the 19th century villa gardens were a symbol of wealth as a hand-made Turkish carpet in the living room would be today. There was usually a series of beds, each one being a geometrical shape and being

part of a strictly symmetrical whole. Symmetry was the key word, and it applied to the arrangement of the plants within the bed. The varieties chosen were dwarf-growing with colourful leaves – the aim was to create a two-dimensional design in which the colours were derived from foliage and not from flowers.

With these simple tools – grass-fringed beds of soil and a range of dwarf plants, the gardener set out to create an intricate pattern. It is often said that he attempted to produce designs which were reminiscent of an Oriental carpet, but contemporary paintings and photographs show little Eastern influence. Inner boundaries were marked out with fine sand, and silver-leaved plants were sometimes used to mark these boundary lines. Holes were dug with a narrow trowel or with the fingers and everywhere the plants were tightly packed together to hide the soil below. That was only the start of the work for the gardener and his staff – at regular intervals the tops of the plants had to be pinched out to prevent flowering or spreading. Obviously the cost was high, which explains the association of carpet bedding with wealth.

The plants used were not the popular bedding plants of today – *Salvia, Tagetes,*

*Alyssum, Nemesia, Ageratum* and so on. These rely on their flowers for their colourful display and would be most disappointing if kept at a height of less than 5 cm. *Alternanthera* was a favourite with its green, red and orange leaves – *Calocephalus* was another popular carpet-bedder and so was the silver-leaved *Antennaria* – how many people would recognise them today?

The plants mentioned above are old-fashioned, garden perennials – in addition two other groups were used which we would not consider to be bedding-out plants. Dwarf succulents were a vital part of every carpet-bedding scheme, and they were occasionally allowed to flower. The rosette-forming *Echeveria* was used for edgings and divisional lines – popular varieties included the bronzy-leaved *E. gibbiflora metallica* and the blue-leaved *E. glauca*. Other succulents widely used in these Victorian schemes were *Sempervivum* and *Sedum*.

In addition to the succulents a number of lawn weeds and lawn weed relatives were used. This is not as surprising as it may seem at first glance – lawn weeds

survive because they are able to flourish even when trimmed at regular intervals – a vital property for a carpet-bedding plant. Pearlwort and its yellow-leaved relative were used for filling in large spaces, the chickweed-related *Stellaria graminea aurea* was employed for dividing lines and another carpet-bedder *Cerastium tomentosum* (Snow-in-summer) is closely related to Mouse-ear chickweed.

Carpet bedding is now a thing of the past for the home gardener – the costs of material and labour would be prohibitive. But it does survive in some of our parks where floral clocks are decorated and coats of arms are created in dwarf foliage plants. More common are modified carpet bedding schemes where the plants used are taller than the Victorian rules permitted – *Coleus*, Wax begonia, *Santolina* etc., together with tall dot plants such as *Abutilon*, standard *Fuchsia, Fatsia, Cordyline* or *Yucca* to provide a pillar standing above the carpet.

Please speak softly when next you criticise carpet bedding – it would be a pity if the last museum pieces which are created in the parks were to disappear.

# FACT OR FICTION?

## The Hanging Gardens of Babylon

NEBUCHADNEZZAR ruled Babylonia for more than 40 years, from 604 to 562 B.C. In that time he restored the country to its former glory and the Greek historian, Herodotus, wrote that its capital Babylon 'surpassed in splendour any city of the known world.'

He had power over everyone. In the fertile valley which is now southern Iraq he could put to death his enemies or his slaves but he did not, it seemed, have the power to make his young wife happy. The home of Queen Amytis was far-off Media, a long-vanished kingdom in what is now north-western Iran. She had grown up among green and wooded hills and she was homesick as she walked the corridors of her palace. Outside lay the flat and uninteresting valley of the Euphrates – the mighty King Nebuchadnezzar could move people, but he could not move mountains.

So he decided to create one. In a corner of the royal palace he built a huge, stepped pyramid which towered 50 m into the sky. Along its shady pathways and between its trees his wife could walk and climb as she had done as a girl in Media – he had brought the mountain to Queen Amytis.

The classical authors described the Hanging Gardens in great detail. The site covered about a hectare and each tier consisted of a wide terrace supported by a series of pillars. Stairs and paths connected each terrace. The Babylonians did not have stone and so these 1 m wide columns were built of sun-baked brick. The hollow pillars were filled with earth, which allowed large trees to be planted directly above them. Here, then, was the world's first large-scale use of container planting.

The 5 m wide terraces were lined with wood, lead and tiles before being filled with soil and then planted with trees, vines, shrubs and flowers. We know little of the actual varieties grown – the early writers were much more concerned with building details than with plant lists.

Watering obviously was a problem, but this was overcome by using slaves to turn a chain or spiral pump which carried water from the Euphrates to the various tiers of the wedding cake-like structure.

The effect of this towering mountain of flowers and greenery must have been tremendously impressive to the people of the plains, and the Hanging Gardens of

# GARDENS OF DELIGHT

by Ruth Cobb

Eastern Gardens

Babylon were one of the Seven Wonders of the World. But the question remains – did they *really* exist? Just because the classical authors described them in great detail does not make them factual – the mythical country of Atlantis was described in great detail by Plato, and many legendary beasts were written about in graphic style. A German archaeologist, Robert Koldewey, made a discovery at the beginning of the 20th century which helped to move the Hanging Gardens story from an Atlantis-like legend to a probable historical fact. Whilst excavating the main palace of Nebuchadnezzar at Babylon, he located a peculiar structure in the north-eastern corner. A massive series of chambers and vaults were found, with the upper portion covered with a thick layer of earth and a three-shafted well in one of the vaults. The foundations revealed by his spade and trowel fitted closely to the account of the fabulous garden in the sky which the Greeks had recorded so many years ago.

# THE FIRST
# GARDENING BOOK

IT MUST BE nice to be remembered by posterity as the Father of some particular subject – to Theophrastus goes the distinction of not one but three subjects. He was the Father of Ecology, the Father of Botany and the Father of Gardening Books.

Theophrastus was born in 372 B.C. His home was at Eresus in Greece, and after a spell as a pupil of Plato he moved to the colonnaded grove at the Lyceum where he became a disciple of Aristotle. On the death of the great philosopher all his manuscripts passed to Theophrastus who took over as head of the school. His work rate must have been phenomenal – more than 2000 pupils came to learn from him and he wrote more than 200 books before his death in 287 B.C.

Only two books have survived and on these his reputation as the Father of Botany and Gardening Books has been built. The nine-volumed *Enquiry into Plants* and the six-volumed *Etiology of Plants* contain his observations and teachings on the nature and care of plants, and in 1916 the *Enquiry into Plants* was translated into English.

More than 450 plants out of the 3000 native species in Greece were recorded, and his words on them and on plant growth were taken as unchallengeable truths until the 15th century. Obviously, as the first recorder of botanical observation he must have got some things right, but it is amazing that his more glaring errors were not questioned for more than 1500 years. The work was of course unscientific by today's standards, but it was a start – the first gardening book and some of its concepts have stood the test of time.

Friends of Theophrastus point to the section on roses as an indication of his horticultural soundness, and it certainly is valid advice – 'As the plant comes slowly from seed, they make cuttings at the stem, as has been said, and plant them. If the bush is burnt or cut over, it bears better flowers, for if left to itself, it grows luxuriantly and makes too much wood.'

> Begin now buying those Garden Books you intend giving away for Christmas; in the meantime you can read them.
>
> *Richardson Wright*

The reference to 'burning' puzzles rose experts but the general instruction sounds quite modern, as does the complaint by Theophrastus that roses are no longer as fragrant as they used to be!

Plant feeding with dilute liquid manure is described along with the soil-warming properties of dung. Theophrastus told his readers that if they dug in fresh manure then the harvesting of crops could be speeded up by about three weeks. The pre-war gardener was well aware of the hot-bed technique but the gardener of today is much less aware of the soil-heating properties of undecomposed organic matter. One up to Theophrastus.

Theophrastus is equally sound on the subject of tree planting. His book stresses the need for the hole to be large enough to accommodate the root ball without bending or damaging the roots. The need is also stressed for the soil in the planting hole to be similar in composition to the soil making up the root ball. Two up for Theophrastus – many container-grown plants fail to establish properly because the plant is grown in a peaty compost and the garden is low in organic matter. Adding some organic matter to the planting hole would help greatly, but Theophrastus already knew that.

> One of the things that never cease to astonish me about colours in gardening is the amazing description that nurserymen give them in their catalogues. You read of 'deep crimson tipped with mauve', and when the thing flowers it's simply purple.
>
> *J. F. Leeming*

It would be silly to claim that *Enquiry into Plants* is a 'good' gardening book – its ideas were far too primitive to warrant such a description. The information on pests was meagre and the nature of disease was misunderstood. The cures proposed did not even contain the urine and sulphur treatments which we know the ancients employed. Plants were divided into trees, shrubs and undershrubs – a rather valueless classification – and the belief is expressed that plants are made pregnant by their own sap in the wintertime and so produce buds in spring. Not the last word on gardening then, but it was the first.

# THE FIRST POPULAR
# GARDENING MAGAZINE

*ANUARY 1826 was a milestone in the history of gardening. In that month the first popular gardening magazine was launched and at last horticulture had a platform from which it could speak. The word 'editor' was not in general use at the time – its conductor was John Loudon and through the pages of the *Gardener's Magazine* news, discoveries and opinions were disseminated. Readers ranging from noted scientists to working gardeners expressed their views or recorded their findings – 'The Setting of the Fruit of Granadilla' rubbed shoulders with 'The present state of Gardening in Ireland' and 'Observations on the Effects of Green Vegetable Manure.'*

*The January 1826 issue was small (20 x 13 cm) and thick (96 pages) ... and deadly dull by today's standards. It was a learned journal and it certainly was designed neither to entertain nor to cater for novices as you would expect from a modern magazine. There were few illustrations and its criticisms were sometimes bitter. But it did give horticulture a voice and the debt the gardening world owes to it is incalculable.*

JOHN CLAUDIUS LOUDON was 43 years old when he published the first issue of the *Gardener's Magazine* at the start of 1826. He was a shining example of the Great Victorian Era which was soon to dawn – incredibly industrious, highly knowledgeable, serious-minded and devoted to the new technology.

In the preface of this first issue he set out the purpose of the magazine – 'We had two grave objects in view: to dis-seminate new and important information on all topics connected with horticulture, and to raise the intellect and the character of those engaged in the art.' Viewed through present-day eyes this objective to improve both the intellect and character of the reader sounds pompous in the extreme, but things looked different at the start of the Victorian age.

Gardening was then a scientific study for the master and a noble profession for the worker. A sad letter in this first issue from Alexander McNaughton, a jobbing gardener who had fallen on hard times, illustrates this point better than any garden history book: '… my wife is dead, and if the disease which shall carry me off be a lingering one, I have no other prospect than the workhouse … but I consider it would be degrading to the profession to which I belong if I were to become a publican.'

Mr McNaughton, despite his poverty and lowly position, would have been offended if the new magazine had the modern mixture of colour, simple features and answers to run-of-the-mill queries. Thus it is not true that the *Gardener's Magazine* showed the emerging middle classes how to garden – that task was performed by the popular books on

gardening to which Loudon and his wife contributed with such works as *Suburban Gardens* (1838) and *Suburban Horticulturist* (1842).

With this in mind, the stance of the conductor of the *Gardener's Magazine* becomes much less strange. He set out to provide new and important information, and each issue was devoted to Original Articles from readers, Book Reviews, Transactions of the Horticultural Society and Intelligence from Home and Overseas. The volume of news provided greatly exceeded anything you will find in all the modern popular magazines put together, but the reluctance to give simple advice was apparent from the first issue, which stated 'M M'Dougal's secret for killing slugs is well known, but we do not mention it because most people make light of things which cost nothing.'

The man was no less fascinating than the magazine. Born in Lanarkshire in 1783, John Loudon trained as a gardener during the daytime and stayed up two nights a week to learn French and Italian. At 20 he moved to London where his first article was published and at 23 he was struck down by rheumatic fever. Henceforth he was permanently disabled with a period of drug addiction in early life and bouts of great pain until the day he died, but his thirst for knowledge and his obsession for work never wavered.

In 1822 he published *An Encyclopaedia of Gardening* which transcended the standard work, Philip Miller's *Gardener's Dictionary*. This monumental work by Loudon was directed at the emerging Industrial class

rather than the estate-owning gentry. His main concern was with the home garden of the middle classes and the public parks for the poorer people. He was keenly interested in improving the lot of the professional gardener, and these and other interests appeared in the features he wrote in the magazine he founded in 1826.

The *Gardener's Magazine* was produced quarterly and it was his life's work – he remained its conductor until his death in 1843. There were, however, other interests. In 1828 he met the author of a book he had warmly reviewed – instead of the elderly scribe he expected he found the writer to be a girl of twenty. He married Jane Webb in 1830 and she remained his constant collaborator, companion and secretary throughout his lifetime.

In 1838 came his *magnum opus*, the eight-volumed *Arboretum et Fruticetum Britannicum*,

which to this day remains one of the classics on trees. Biographers of Loudon point out that he was not an active garden designer, but he did create the first purpose-built public park in a British town – the Derby Arboretum. Winding paths climbed small hillocks on which a wide variety of clearly-labelled trees were planted for the instruction of the visitor – it was always Loudon the Educator.

His pressure resulted in great improvements being made in London's parks and his magazine had highlighted the poor wages of the working gardener. His books and ideas were responsible for bringing gardening to the masses, but it brought him little leisure and even less money. He worked for 20 hours a day and died deeply in debt – but he is one of gardening's immortals who gave us our first popular horticultural magazine.

Other magazines followed – *The Horticultural Register* (1831) and *Paxton's Magazine of Botany* (1834), but the next major advance was the launch of the *Gardener's Chronicle* in 1841. This was different to Loudon's magazine as it was a weekly paper and carried advertisements, but the same high tone was there – 'A weekly record of everything that bears upon horticulture

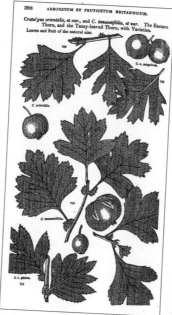

and garden botany'. The *Gardener's Chronicle* provides an unbroken record of horticulture from 1841 to the late 20th century, ending as a magazine for the gardening trade. Through its pages you can follow the emergence of our present-day ideas from the Victorian seeds.

The *Cottage Gardener* (1848) was a pleasant magazine and *The Garden*, founded by William Robinson in 1871, was a vehicle for the promotion of his ideas on informal and wild gardens. But the 20th century was approaching and what was needed was a magazine designed to entertain as well as to enlighten, to instruct as well as to preach. *Amateur Gardening* began on 2 May 1884, and its editorial sums up the new approach: 'We shall therefore only promise to endeavour to make ourselves generally useful, our principal object being to smooth the path and delight the life of the lovers of the garden.' At last the magazine and not the editor became the important thing, but even in this promising editorial the old Victorian work ethic was there – 'This paper is not for idlers of any class; we forbid them to read it'!

# THE FLORAL CODE

THE FLORAL CODE, it seems, began in the Ottoman Empire hundreds of years ago – it was cultivated in the harems where there was little else to do. A young suitor knew that an iris meant *no* and a grape hyacinth *yes* when worn or carried by his loved one. In a culture where the sexes could not speak freely it was left to flowers to do the talking.

Lady Mary Wortley Montague was intrigued and in 1718 sent a letter from Constantinople to a friend in England with the details. Her letters were published the year after her death and the concept of a language of flowers caught the imagination of the limited circle who read her correspondence.

---

## In a culture where the sexes could not speak freely it was left to flowers to do the talking

---

It was not until 1820, however, that the Floral Code was established in Europe with the publication of *The Language of Flowers*. It was followed by other floral dictionaries and the idea could not have come at a better time. As the 19th century progressed young women were looking for accomplishments other than household skills – learning the Floral Code and the recognition of all of the plants involved offered such a challenge. In addition it

## THE LANGUAGE OF FLOWERS

| | |
|---|---|
| **Alyssum** | Worth beyond beauty |
| **Anemone** | Forsaken |
| **Bluebell** | Constancy |
| **Buttercup** | Ingratitude |
| **Gladiolus** | Ready armed |
| **Heather** | Solitude |
| **Hyacinth** | Play |
| **Lilac** | First love |
| **Lobelia** | Malevolence |
| **Lupin** | Voraciousness |
| **Marigold** | Grief |
| **Nasturtium** | Patriotism |
| **Pink** | Boldness |
| **Poppy** | Consolation |
| **Rose** | Love |
| **Stock** | Lasting beauty |
| **Tulip (red)** | I love you |
| **Wallflower** | Fidelity in adversity |

> Some persons may think that Flowers are of no use, that they are nonsensical things ... I hesitate not a moment to prefer the plant of a fine carnation to a gold watch set with diamonds.
>
> *William Cobbett*

provided a method of passing secret messages in an age when the chaperone system was in operation and the telephone had not been invented.

The code worked by the giving or receiving of a posy or single flower. The recipient answered *yes* by touching the flowers with her lips and *no* by pulling off a petal. Another way of signifying *no* was by giving a snapdragon. Some popular flowers had a simple and clear-cut meaning. A double red rose meant *love*, a white lily signified *purity* and sweet violets denoted *modesty*. Tulips were a declaration of love, but not all flowers carried messages of love, respect or kindness. Narcissi accused the recipient of *conceit*, hydrangeas meant *boasting* and foxgloves *insincerity*. You could be told off by a bunch of flowers!

The language was complex and often confusing as not all the dictionaries agreed over the interpretation of a particular flower. Take lavender as an example – according to which book was read it could mean *distrust* or *pleasant memories*. The peony meant *shyness* in one dictionary and *shame* in another. Even when there was common agreement amongst the experts, the need for botanical skill was present. A rose is a rose is a rose certainly did not apply – a Sweet briar meant *I wound to heal*, a Musk rose signified *capricious beauty* and Moss rose *voluptuousness*. The chance of error was great and the number of mistakes must have been many. Unfortunately they have not been recorded, and it does seem a golden opportunity for a historical novelist who is looking for a plot with a strong flavour of misunderstanding.

## During its heyday the language of flowers had become incredibly extensive

Such a writer could choose any period within a span of nearly a century, for the Floral Code did not die out until World War I. During its heyday the language of flowers had become incredibly extensive – dictionaries included hundreds of species, including the Fly orchid, Nutmeg geranium and Queen's rocket. There were precise instructions to bend the flower to the right to indicate *I* and to the left to denote *thou*. Obviously the freedom and gaiety of the Twenties could have no place for a language born out of the intrigues and silence of the medieval Ottoman Empire.

# THE GREAT VICTORIAN GLASS PALACES

*HE GREENHOUSE* has a long history. The first ones were made by the Romans, but the heated room for plants did not become a feature of the British garden until the 17th century. At first they were used exclusively as orangeries – only later were they employed for the year-round cultivation of exotic tender plants.

These early greenhouses were poor structures. The amount of glass was often small and badly sited, and the source of heat was a stove or fire within the room. It was not until the 19th century that two events combined to make possible the erection of truly effective greenhouses.

In 1816 the piped hot-water system was introduced into Britain – the stove was now on the outside and so were the plant-damaging fumes. About 20 years later sheet glass was invented and the production of large plates was now possible. The way was clear to create a Victorian Glass Palace.

THE FRIENDSHIP of Joseph Paxton and the Duke of Devonshire is one of the most fascinating stories in the world of horticulture. The two men could hardly have had more dissimilar backgrounds. William George Spencer Cavendish was born in 1790 and at the age of 21 became the 6th Duke of Devonshire. He belonged to one of the most important families in the land, and a meeting in the grounds of the Horticultural Society's gardens brought him in contact with young Joseph Paxton.

Paxton was born in 1803 on a small farm in Bedfordshire. He received little formal education and after working as a gardener's boy he moved to the London gardens of the Horticultural Society at Chiswick in 1823. His industry and ability were soon brought to the attention of the Duke and in 1825 he was appointed Head Gardener for the Duke's estate at Chatsworth in Derbyshire.

The 23 year old Paxton arrived at Chatsworth on May 9, 1826, and the account of his first day is an oft-repeated story in gardening history books. 'Arrived at 4.30 a.m. ... climbed over the wall, looked around grounds. Set the men to work at 6.00 a.m. Ordered all the water works to be switched on ... had breakfast and fell in love with the housekeeper's niece [who was to be the future Mrs. Paxton] before 9.00 a.m.'

So began the association between the humble gardener and the aristocrat which lasted until the death of the Duke in 1858. For 32 years he was the Duke's gardener, garden teacher, travelling companion, confidant and closest friend. 'To me he was a friend, if ever man had one', wrote the Duke.

In return Paxton received immense support and the opportunity to rise from a Bedfordshire cottage to the Houses of Parliament and a knighthood before his death in 1865. Even in death the two men remained close – they are both buried in the small churchyard at Edensor.

## The Great Conservatory took 4 years to build

The story of Paxton's work at Chatsworth is told on page 102, but if you visit that garden you will not be able to see Paxton's most famous triumph – the Great Conservatory. It was the largest greenhouse in the world when it was built but only fragments of the walls now remain.

A few statistics. The Great Conservatory took 4 years to build (1836–1840) and covered over 3 hectares. It was 70 m long, 35 m wide and 20 m high and the

Now everybody knew the name of Paxton and he set about designing the biggest building in the world for the Great Exhibition of 1851. He had mastered the use of glass and iron, and the removal of the tax on glass in 1845 had stimulated interest in the material. The result was the Crystal Palace – an immense structure covering over 7 hectares. Its construction was brilliant – after the exhibition in Hyde Park it was dismantled and then re-erected on Sydenham Hill in South London.

The reputation of Paxton has not dimmed over the years but his glass palaces have not been so fortunate. The 9th Duke of Devonshire blew up the Great Conservatory in 1919 after many of the plants had died as a result of the fuel shortage and the Crystal Palace was destroyed by fire in 1936.

doors at each end were large enough for the entry of the Duke's carriage. It became one of the wonders of the age – a corner of the tropics transplanted into Britain.

The greatest achievement of Paxton's glass palace at Chatsworth was the cultivation there of the Great Water lily (*Victoria regia*). Discovered in 1837, in British Guiana, its seeds came to England with the legend that the leaves were large enough to support the weight of a child. Horti-culturalists in Britain desperately wanted to produce a full-grown flowering specimen of the plant which had been named in honour of the young Queen. Only Paxton succeeded in the vast Lily House he had constructed at Chatsworth – the 2 m wide leaves supported his small daughter and in 1849 the first flowers appeared.

## THE LARGEST BUILDING EVER CONSTRUCTED

Sir Joseph Paxton's Crystal Palace was erected in Hyde Park for the Great Exhibition of 1851. It was 650 m long and 120 m wide – at the time the largest building ever constructed. Paxton had learnt his architecture by designing the Great Conservatory and other glasshouses at Chatsworth and he based the iron tracery of Crystal Palace on the leaf veins of the Great Water lily. It was this gardener's design which was the forerunner of the steel-framed and prefabricated buildings of today.

# HERBALS AND HERBALISM

FOR CONSUMPTION take 30 snails and 30 earthworms of middling size. Bruise the snails and wash them and the worms in clean water. Cut the worms into pieces. Boil these in a quart of spring water and reduce to a pint. Pour it boiling on to 2 ounces of candied Eringo root sliced thin. When cool strain through a fine flannel bag. Take ¼ pint of it warm with an equal quantity of cow's milk, at twilight. Continue till well.

*Old Herbal Recipe*

THE ROOTS of herbalism are buried deep in time. The grave of a Neanderthal man buried about 60,000 years ago was found to contain a variety of medicinal plants and the first herbal was written in Sumeria about 5000 years ago. The title of Father of Herbalism goes to the Greek doctor Dioscorides who in the 1st century A.D. listed 600 plants with curative properties.

This ancient book remained the source of herbal knowledge for many hundreds of years, and the early European herbalists of the 16th century used a great deal of its information in their own works. There was Brunfels who busily copied from contemporary and classical herbalists, and Bock, who stated on the front of his herbal that 'Having read everything there is to read', proceeded to copy some of the

NICHOLAS            CULPEPER

words and pictures he had seen. These herbalists of the Renaissance were an argumentative, sometimes brilliant and often naive group who set the stamp on herbalism for centuries to come.

Nicholas Culpeper was cast in the same mould. Born in 1616, he had a sincere belief in the power of herbs. English herbs, that is, as he made quite clear in the preface to his herbal *The English Physician* – 'Man may preserve his body in Health, or cure himself, being Sick, for Three-pence Charge, with such Things only as grow in England, they being most fit for English Bodies.' He seems to have fought against everybody – against his contemporary horticulturalists like Gerard and Parkinson ('Neither ever gave one wise reason for

> Come, my spade. There is no ancient gentlemen but gardeners, ditchers and grave-makers; they hold up Adam's profession.
>
> *Hamlet (William Shakespeare)*

what they wrote') and against the College of Physicians ('A company of proud, insulting, domineering doctors') whom he offended by translating their Latin pharmacopoeia into English. He fought against Charles I in the Civil War but he lost to Fate – his herbal contained several cures for the Consumption, but he died of tuberculosis at the age of 38.

Culpeper's book remained the herbal bible for over a century. Up to the 18th century there was no division between doctors and herbalists – doctors *were* herbalists. With the advance of science and the Industrial Revolution more extracts and tinctures were used and the cult of using fresh herbs declined, except in rural areas. The modern revival in herbalism is mainly due to Mrs Leyel who opened Culpeper House in London in 1927, and interest has grown steadily in this form of alternative medicine.

Is there anything in it? Many of the remedies were based on superstition and were quite worthless. Others were based on astrological links and were equally

useless. A large number of plants listed in the herbals owed their so-called powers to the Doctrine of Signatures. The Swiss doctor Paracelsus (1493–1541) developed the idea that Providence had put a sign or signature on all living things for the guidance of man, and by looking at a plant and studying its growth habit it is possible to tell its healing properties from this signature.

The brain-like form of the walnut meant that it would cure headaches, and the eye-like form of the flowers of Eyebright would sooth inflamed eyes. Hairy roots would prevent baldness, rock-splitting roots such as saxifrage would remove kidney stones and the ear-like leaves of *Cyclamen* would relieve earache. The list of signatures is vast – the yellow-flowered broom for jaundice, the lobe-leaved liverwort for liver complaints and so on.

Nonsense, of course, but at the beginning of this century about half the cures prescribed by doctors were to be found in the herbals. Buried in these books were some sound remedies which have stood the test of time. It was the herbalists who first discovered the medicinal properties of *Digitalis, Rauwolfia, Aconitum, Aloe, Ephedra,* Peruvian bark, senna, liquorice, peppermint and many others – only later did scientists isolate the chemicals responsible for the effects.

You may wish to try some of the simpler herbal remedies for minor ailments or as a

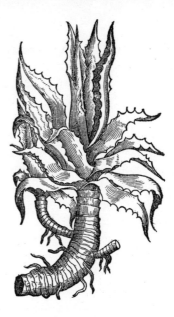

pick-me-up. Pour boiling water over rosemary leaves and allow the brew to stand for an hour. Strain the liquid and use as a hair rinse. It will brighten dull hair and prevent baldness … perhaps. Substitute pot marigold flowers for rosemary leaves and you will have a tonic which will help the heart and circulation. If on the other hand a bad cough is the problem, you can use coltsfoot flowers to make an age-old infusion for bronchitis and asthma. Southernwood tea is a general pick-me-up with eradication of worms, freedom from rheumatism and prevention of baldness on its list of claims.

A word of warning – do not experiment and do avoid the more complex and outlandish recipes. And do go to a doctor if the symptoms are serious – do not rely on a nature cure or a do-it-yourself diagnosis.

# HOW GRANDFATHER
# CUT THE LAWN

THE CARTOON from *Punch* on page 153 shows that the small hand mower was not too different a hundred years ago. The lawn mower had the grassbox, spirally-bladed cylinder, small front roller and large back roller with which we are all familiar. Grandfather (and perhaps great-great-grandfather) cut the lawn exactly as we did before the petrol- and electrically-driven models came along to make our lives easier.

Going back a little further in time we see a very different picture – fifty years before the *Punch* cartoon there were no

lawn mowers at all. Before then the closely-cut lawn was a luxury restricted to the wealthy – the scythe was the only cutting tool available, and it took three skilled scythemen a whole day to cut an acre of turf. Behind them followed the lawn women to brush and gather up the shorn grass. For ordinary people such a laborious operation was unthinkable, so the cottage garden was a place for flowers, fruit, herbs and vegetables but not grass.

For the leisured classes, however, a lawn was an essential feature. The idea began long, long ago, perhaps with Sir Francis Bacon who wrote in 1625 that 'nothing is more pleasant to the eye than green grass closely shorn'. In the 17th and 18th centuries visitors from overseas marvelled at the English lawn and it became our first contribution to the world of gardening.

The Industrial Revolution, the onset of the Victorian Age and the mushrooming of countless small villa gardens changed the face of gardening in the early 19th century. The work involved in scything and constant rolling meant that the lawn would have had no place around the suburban villa if it had not been for the invention by an obscure foreman working in a textile factory in Stroud.

Edwin Budding was the illegitimate son of an illegitimate father ... and we know very little more about him. While maintaining the machines which trimmed the pile of the cloth produced in the factory, he had the idea that the same principle could be applied to cutting a lawn. His patent was granted in 1830 and the first factory-produced cylinder mowers were introduced by Ransomes of Ipswich in 1832. The small model at 7 guineas was 'for a gentleman who wishes to use it himself' and a larger 10 guineas version was available 'preferably for workmen'. For the first time cutting the grass became an unskilled and relatively speedy job which Budding claimed to be 'an amusing, useful and healthy exercise'. His work made the modern-day lawn possible but he received very little financial reward and no honour for his invention.

## For the leisured classes a lawn was an essential feature

A stream of improvements, new ideas and patents now appeared. It was unfortunate that the internal combustion engine had not been invented when Budding had his brain-wave, which meant that horse-power was the only practical answer for the large mowers. In 1842 the first pony-driven model appeared and in the early 1850s the 30 in. and 40 in. models pulled by leather-booted horses became very popular.

The steam-driven lawn mower arrived in 1893, but it was the petrol engine which provided the next breakthrough. At the beginning of the 20th century the first motor mowers were introduced, but for grandfather and the rest of the small home gardeners it was still the heavy, hand-pushed, cylinder mowers which were used – the inexpensive motorised mower is a relatively recent innovation.

We know that grandfather took longer to cut his lawn than we do with our power-driven and rotary-bladed models, but the quality of the cut was equal to and often better than we get today. Looking back further, we shall never know how good a job his ancestors did with their scythes. There are glowing descriptions of 'pieces of green cloth' by some early writers but perhaps Budding was closer when he noted in his patent that the scythe resulted in 'circular scars, irregularities and bare patches ... which continue visible for several days.'

# HOW PLANTS
# CROSSED THE OCEAN

THE AGE OF Exploration opened up new frontiers and revealed plants which amazed European eyes. Pressed specimens of flowers were collected and seeds were sent back, but the life expectancy of living plants transported on the sailing ships was almost nil. It has been estimated that only one plant in a thousand survived the long voyage from Australia to England. Orchids earned their 'luxury' image because of the inability to import living specimens in any quantity.

Early plant hunters tried various methods to get living specimens back to

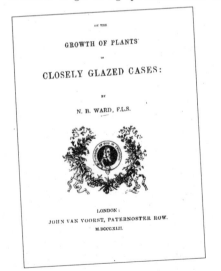

ON THE

GROWTH OF PLANTS

IN

CLOSELY GLAZED CASES:

BY

N. B. WARD, F.L.S.

LONDON:
JOHN VAN VOORST, PATERNOSTER ROW.
M.DCCC.XLII.

Europe. The first of the American plant hunters, John Bartram, enclosed in an ox bladder the roots of each new discovery which he then carried in his saddle bag to his farm in Philadelphia. There he planted the trees or shrubs in large wooden boxes which he shipped to England. The start of container growing, perhaps, but it did not solve the problems of serious losses at sea.

The answer was found in a wide-mouthed glass jar. In 1829 a London doctor, Dr. Nathaniel Bagshaw Ward, placed a chrysalis in damp soil in a jar and sealed the top. He observed the emergence of the moth but was much more interested in the grass and fern seedlings which appeared. The plants continued to grow for four years without addition of water, and Dr. Ward believed that he had discovered the way to transport plants safely by sea.

At the time, the practice of transporting plants over the ocean was to keep specimens in slatted boxes on the deck. There they had to withstand wide variations in temperature, irregular watering, shortage of light inside the box, the killing effect of sea spray and the gnawing effect of hungry rats. Dr. Ward's grass and fern had survived for years in his sealed jar and he reasoned that a plant in a sealed glass container on board ship would be protected from all the perils and would receive sufficient light through the glazed panels. In 1833 he placed ferns in the damp soil at the bottom of two miniature sealed greenhouses (Wardian Cases) which he had constructed. They were shipped to Sydney and his theory was correct – they arrived safely.

Now for the return trip. Native Australian plants were put into the Wardian Cases and they arrived back 'in the most healthy and vigorous condition'. Ward continued his experiments, and in 1842 published *On the Growth of Plants in Closely Glazed Cases*. The horticultural world saw at once their possibilities and the Wardian Case was quickly put into use. Robert Fortune was able to send 20,000 tea plants from Shanghai to the Himalayas by this method and so start the Indian tea industry. Rubber and quinine plants were sent from South America to Kew and then on to the Far East. Before the invention of the Wardian Case the attempts by the Duke of Devonshire to introduce plants from the East Indies to Chatsworth in Derbyshire had proved disappointing. Later he was able to write to Dr. Ward 'Whereas I formerly used to lose 19 out of 20 of the plants I imported during the voyage, 19 out of 20 is now the average number that survive.'

The Wardian Case allowed plants from South America, China, Australia, India, Africa and other far-off lands to travel safely to Europe. It was not all one-way traffic – Dr. Ward's 'closely glazed cases' were also used to transport new crop plants from English botanical gardens to tropical countries where they could found new industries.

The Wardian Case was also put to good use at home. Dr. Ward's original observation had been in the grimy East End of London, and the fern *Dryopteris felixmas* growing in the jar would not have survived for long in the smoke-filled atmosphere outside the case. Loudon popularised the Wardian Case in his *Gardener's Magazine* as a way of growing delicate plants in the home, and it soon became a familiar sight in the Victorian drawing room. After the start of the 20th century its popularity declined, but the modern-day bottle gardens and terraria (page 231) have revived the method of growing plants which began in the little jar on Dr. Ward's shelf in 1829.

# LOOKING BACK AT CHELSEA

The Chelsea Flower Show held in late May is the Mecca of the gardening world. Each year people flock to the Show Grounds at the Royal Hospital in Chelsea. This is the Great Spring Show of the Royal Horticultural Society – and there is nothing quite like it anywhere else in the world.

On the last Monday in April the South Grounds of the Hospital are leased to the R.H.S. for 40 days. During this time the vast Show is created and later dismantled, returning the site to its pre-show state of lawns and gardens. The highlight of all this work is, of course, the Show itself.

Monday is the day of the Royal Visit, and Tuesday and Wednesday are reserved for Members – they are called the 'Private View' days but the crowds belie the name. Thursday, Friday and Saturday are for everyone. Not quite everyone – children under five are not admitted.

> If the 'Private' view of the Chelsea Flower Show is privacy, Trafalgar Square on New Year's Eve is glorious isolation.
>
> *Alan Melville*

Chelsea has its critics. It is extremely crowded, but if you take some of the finest horticultural displays in the world and place them under rather cramped conditions in the capital of a nation of gardeners, then overcrowding is inevitable. For many years the Showpiece was the Grand Marquee – with 1.5 hectares of covered space it was claimed to be the largest tented area in the world. The criticism that Chelsea is 'a show for Londoners' is not fair – more than 60 per cent of the visitors travel to London especially for the Show.

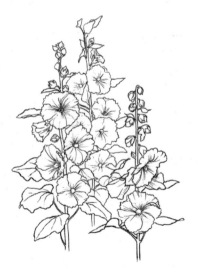

The first annual Royal Horticultural Society Shows were not held at Chelsea. The Horticultural Society of London began in 1804 (it did not become 'Royal' until 1861) and its first Horticultural Fete was held at Chiswick in 1827. In 1861 the Society moved to its new Gardens in Kensington and some shows were held there, but the concept of an annual Spring Show began with the Temple Show held in 1888 in the Embankment Gardens of the Inner Temple.

Interest in gardening continued to flourish and by the early years of the 20th century the Embankment Gardens were too small. In 1913 the first R.H.S. Chelsea Flower Show was held and has never looked back. From that day to this the Chelsea Flower Show has been an important date in the gardening calendar, and it has been held annually apart from breaks during the two World Wars.

## 1866

When the Royal Horticultural Society's Gardens moved in 1861 from Chiswick to Kensington the membership increased and more money was available. Many flower shows were held in the new and sumptuous surroundings and the most important was the International Horticultural and Botanical Exhibition in 1866. But the R.H.S. was never really happy there and later moved out. In May 1888 the annual Temple Shows in the Embankment Gardens began. Marquees, garden and exotic plants, military bands ... the style for the Chelsea of the future was set.

## Pre-World War I

In May 1912 the Royal International Horticultural Exhibition was staged in the grounds of the Royal Hospital in Chelsea. This eight-day show covered 11 hectares and was a great success. There had never been a horticultural show like it – over 1000 exhibitors applied for space, there were large displays of topiary, orchids, banks of flowers, exotic gardens, rockeries, gardening sundries ... and nearly 200,000 people flocked to see it. The R.H.S. had provided financial support for the venture and the Society decided to hold its next

Great Spring Show at the same site. On May 20th in 1913 the Royal Horticultural Society Chelsea tradition was born.

The second Chelsea Flower Show was even more successful than the first. The weather was perfect, and the 'garden party' atmosphere of the Opening Day became a feature of the early years of Chelsea – an occasion for the society set to meet and look at the flowers. The Show carried on for part of World War I but it was cancelled in 1917 and 1918.

## Between the Wars

Chelsea was resumed in 1919 and was never to be quite the same again. The exhibits became more extensive and lavish, and during the 1920s the Opening Day was a time when the large garden owner and his staff came to order plants – it was no longer just a social occasion. The public days which followed were extremely popular with hordes of garden enthusiasts having their day out in the sun.

## Post-World War II

The Chelsea Flower Show was one of the casualties of World War II and was not staged between 1940 and 1946. In May 1947 Chelsea was back and there were alterations. Flower arranging became an additional feature and the Show had to cater for the change in society. Exhibitors had to appeal to the people with semi-detached gardens who now had buying power. People thronged the sundries stands along Eastern Avenue as well as gathering around the Show gardens.

## The 1980s

Chelsea had continued to evolve. With the rise of the garden centre the number of people ordering shrubs had declined and a new type of exhibitor had appeared. Now there were many overseas and educational exhibits, displays by park departments and a new emphasis on conservation. There was perhaps more to learn and less need to buy, but the old magic which began in 1913 remained. There were gold, silver and bronze medals to be won by the exhibitors and new varieties for the visitor to admire.

## 2008

Thirty years had passed by, but the boundaries had not changed. Within the showground, however, there were many new features. There were now two 'Private View' days (Tuesday and Wednesday), and the public days now included Saturday. Wheelchairs were at last permitted, and a Charity Gala Preview had been introduced. Gone was the Grand Marquee – in its place stood the 12,000 sq.m Grand Pavilion. About 160,000 visitors came to see the Show – millions more watched the nightly T.V. broadcasts.

# OLDE GARDENING TOOLS

THE STUDY of gardening tools contains one major surprise. Our basic armoury today is quite small compared with the vast array of equipment which was marketed between the two World Wars. Old catalogues listed scores of knives and scissors, dozens of hoe designs and a bewildering array of other equipment. Clearly there was a belief that good gardening required a large range of tools in various shapes and sizes in the same way that a good cabinet maker used a variety of wood-working tools.

This approach to gardening tools was not a product of the Industrial Revolution nor the result of the growth in home gardening in Victorian times. John Evelyn in his *Elysium Britannicum* illustrated the tools which a keen gardener would have needed in 1659. Well over a hundred pieces of equipment appear in the picture

– knives, sickles, dibbers, sieves, carts, rakes, tampers, forks, etc., etc. Thus, we have gone backwards and not forwards in the number of tools we keep in the garden shed. There are several reasons – the use of lightweight materials means that we no longer have to turn to the smallest piece of equipment for minor jobs – you really would not want to carry a forged iron spade from Tudor days around the garden to dig a small hole. Today's spade is light enough to be an all-purpose tool. Also, mass production has removed regional variations and the need to have tools tailor-made by local craftsmen.

It all began with the bone mattocks and digging sticks with which Stone Age man broke up the earth for his seeds. The flat-bladed mattock, which is swung by the arms into the soil, became a basic piece of agricultural and horticultural equipment –

from it came the adze, a large-bladed chopping hoe which the farmers of today's developing countries and the gardeners of yesterday's Britain used to break up the soil. The digging stick, like the mattock, has not evolved into a basic part of the modern gardener's tool kit.

It is really an instrument for sandy soil, and its last vestige today is the dibber.

Our basic item is the spade, and in a number of museums you will see the heavy iron models left by the Romans. In the medieval garden wooden spades edged with iron were used and a variety of regional types developed over the centuries. By Victorian times there was a clear-cut pattern of D-gripped handles in the South, T-gripped handles in the North and long-handled West Country spades with triangular shovel-like blades. The pointed shovel is no longer used as a garden spade, but the pattern persists in the United States.

The three-tined garden fork was once widely used for digging as well as for 'spreading and disposing of Dung upon the Beds – a Gardner cannot be without it'. The modern fork has grown an extra tine and there are both flat-tined and narrow-tined versions.

The hoe is a cultivator which is dragged through or pushed over the soil. It may be chopped into the ground but unlike the adze it is not designed to be swung from the shoulders. The history of gardening has seen the development of many hundreds of hoe designs – Loudon's *Encyclopaedia of Gardening* in the early 19th century described more than twenty. One of the most popular types in the early days of gardening was the breast plough, a badly-named piece of equipment as the wide blade was pushed through the ground by the lower abdomen and not the chest. Like so many other hoe styles it has died out, and we are left with two basic types with numerous variations – the draw hoe which you pull backward and the dutch hoe which you push forward.

Spades, forks, hoes … tools as old as gardening itself in England. But the trowel is of much more recent origin – it first appeared in the 17th century and was developed from the more complex transplanter of earlier times. The trowel's companion, the small hand fork, seems to have been of even more recent origin.

The Romans were clever enough to use ladders for picking fruit and sieves for producing fine soil to cover seed drills, but they did not develop a wheelbarrow. They used baskets for small loads and carts for heavy work – the one-wheeled wheelbarrow did not appear until the 14th century.

The pictures of water carts in garden history books are a reminder that there was a time when watering the lawn was not just a matter of turning on the tap, and even today we have to get the water from the tap to the garden. The watering can has a long and interesting history – the clay pots of the 15th century were replaced by metal cans in the 18th century and the watering can rose did not become commonplace until the start of the Victorian era. For watering large areas the watering pot or can was impractical then as it is now – at first jointed metal tubes were used which were followed by canvas tubing, and then by rubber tubing which dramatically improved the ease of watering large areas.

Garden shears and pruners began with the Romans and reached their zenith in Victorian times – how they would have loved our electric hedge clippers for their topiary! Hand-powered clippers were used in the 19th century, but in earlier times a skilfully-wielded sickle was used where we would often use shears today.

Many of the 'olde' garden tools have gone. Until the advent of weedkillers the two-pronged daisy grubber was popular and glass bell jars were used to protect tender plants before the tent-like cloche appeared. The displanter has gone, and so has the rolling stone and the beetle. But they did know a thing or two which we have perhaps forgotten. Straw 'panniers' were widely used to protect plants in winter and hollow-bottomed pots were sunk into the ground around shrubs to facilitate watering. The advent of mains water has allowed us to forget how to do the job properly!

The changes in the gardener's tool kit over the years reflect the rise and fall of successive gardening styles. Equipment to keep gravel paths smooth and weed-free were once important, but such items have no place today. Instead we have an array of lawn care tools, as turf has taken over from gravel the role of the outdoor carpet.

> A gardener is never rich, yet he is ever raking together. There is no man who has more beds than he, but never a one worth lying on.
>
> *Wye Saltonstall (1635)*

# ROSE MANIA IN ROME

THE BRITISH love of roses is well-known throughout the world – four out of every five gardens have some and there are ten times more roses than people on this island. Yet this appreciation of our national flower pales in comparison with the Rose Mania which gripped Ancient Rome during its heyday and declining years.

The Greeks grew roses and the Ancient Egyptians offered the flowers to their gods, but it was the Romans who adored them in a way which has never been rivalled. The wealthy citizens walked on them, slept on them, made love on them. Pillows were filled with them and rose water gushed from the fountains.

An inch-thick layer of rose petals was used to carpet the floors of banqueting halls, and the thickness of this floral floor-covering became a status symbol. Nero topped them all – at one royal banquet the cascade of petals which descended from the ceiling covered the guests below and suffocated several of them!

Rose petals garlanded the heads of the worthy Romans, floated in their wine, and acted as a medicine when they were ill. There were rose honey, rose wine, rose puddings … burnt roses were used as mascara and fresh roses were used as an aphrodisiac.

There was nothing effeminate about this rose cult – soldiers went into battle wearing wreaths of roses and the victorious chariots were bedecked with the flowers when they returned to Rome. Obviously, the need for more and more blooms was a problem, and the gardens of Rome could not cope. Olive groves and fruit orchards were neglected and cereal fields reduced as farmers turned to the cultivation of this flower.

In winter when the bushes are bare our love for rose blooms around the house declines, but it did not for the Romans. They grew roses in steam-heated greenhouses – a novel idea which was not to be seen again until modern times. Vast quantities were imported from Egypt. They also brought them from Rhodes – an island which is supposed to owe its name to the red roses which were grown there for the Roman market.

The collapse of Rome meant the death of this love of roses, and the early Christian Church rejected the flower as a symbol of the decadence of the Roman Empire. But the rose was far too beautiful a flower to remain banished for long, and the flower which had been associated with Venus soon became one of the symbols of the Virgin Mary.

# THE SHOCKING STORY
# OF GERARD'S HERBALL

⟨≈⊙≈⟩

LET US BEGIN with the standard version of the story concerning John Gerard and his *Herball*. Gerard was born in Nantwich in 1545 and came to London to seek his fortune. He qualified as a barber-surgeon but took up an appointment as Superintendent of the magnificent gardens at Theobalds in Hertfordshire. In this position he was able to travel to Europe and meet the distinguished horticulturalists of the day, but he would have been long forgotten if he had not put together his slim *Catalogue* in 1596.

Gerard cultivated about 1000 plants in his own garden at Holborn in London and he listed them, many for the first time, in his 24-page *Catalogue*. Even to this day it is taken as the date of introduction for many of our garden plants.

Greater success was to follow. In 1597 his *Herball*, or *Generall Historie of Plantes* appeared and met with instant acclaim. It appealed to scholars and housewives alike and remained immensely popular for centuries. Nearly 100 new plants were mentioned and the style was lively – who could fail to be amused by the statement that 'The root of Solomon's seal, stamped while it is fresh and green, takes away in one night or two at the most any bruise, black or blue spots gotten by falls or women's willfulness in stumbling in their hasty husbands' fists …'

But Gerard's *Herball* is not really an amusing story – it is a shocking one even for the Renaissance era when honesty amongst writers was not a common quality. It began when a London printer, John Norton, asked Dr. Priest to translate the new Latin herbal *Stirpium historiae pemptades* into English. The *Pemptades* had been written by the distinguished Flemish botanist Rembert Dodoens, and was obviously destined to make a great impact on the horticultural world.

Unfortunately Dr. Priest died before the translation was finished and the printer commissioned Gerard to complete it. That was his mistake and Gerard's opportunity. The barber surgeon-turned-gardener completed the work and added a poor translation of some of the writings of L'Obel, another distinguished Continental botanist. Mrs. Gerard now entered the picture – she added passages for women to widen its appeal and they bought a job-lot of illustrations from a printer who had produced an earlier herbal in Germany.

This quaint stew was put together under Gerard's name with no acknowledgement at all to the real author and illustrator, and the book became an outstanding success. Scientific authors stealing each other's work in the 16th century was not unknown, and without other deceits it would have been a sad but not unusual story for the times. But the story did not end there.

Not surprisingly, Matthias de l'Obel was angry that his work should have been misused in this way and that Gerard should have become famous as a result. Illustrations had been put into the wrong place and the Latin translation was often inaccurate. Gerard defended himself by claiming that L'Obel's knowledge of English was at fault and that the book was correct – Gerard set out to denigrate the reputation of his former friend, the man who had advised him and helped him with his *Catalogue*. The Frenchman could do nothing and described Gerard as 'a hard man' – today we might use stronger language. James Garett and L'Obel made some improvements in later editions but it was not until 1633 that Thomas Johnson produced the corrected edition. It had been 'Enlarged and Amended' according to the frontispiece.

So Gerard stole the text and illustrations for his immortal *Herball* and blackened the character of the innocent and able scientist who tried to defend himself. That should have been enough, but there is evidence that Gerard planted peony seeds so that he could claim discovery of 'a new English wild flower'. Like all fields of human activity, horticulture has had its share of sinners as well as saints.

# THE STORY OF THE
# COTTAGE GARDEN

*O*NE OF the joys for a city dweller passing through a rural area is the sight of a long-established cottage garden in full bloom. It seems to be a living piece of nostalgia – old-fashioned plants all crowded together with scent and butterflies filling the air.

At first glance it would appear that such a sleepy jumble of plants could have nothing to do with the evolution of the modern suburban garden or the flower-filled grand garden. Yet a number of the flowers we grow and some of the gardening styles we adopt owe their existence to the long and unbroken heritage of the cottage garden. During the past few hundred years the trend-setters and fashionable people have sneered either at the presence of flowers or the lack of design and straight lines in these humble plots. But in the end we have adopted the multicoloured and informal grouping of flowers as the mainstay of the garden of today and consigned many of the once-fashionable gardening concepts to the dustbin.

WE SHALL never know the date when the first cottage gardens began to appear but we do know that their development increased greatly in the settled and prosperous Elizabethan age. Manor houses were built by the wealthy merchants and nobility, and around them clusters of cottages were erected. Gardens were created and tended, and a writer in 1677 noted that 'There is scarce a cottage in most of the southern parts of England but has its proportionable garden, so great a delight do most men take of it.'

At this stage all of the basic features of the cottage garden were laid down, and it is essential to consider these features if you are to understand the unique role that this style of gardening has played in the history of horticulture. First of all, the size is generally small and it is enclosed by hedges or walls – the cottage garden was not designed for the pleasure of the passer-by. As space is short the plants are crowded together to leave little or no exposed earth.

Planting takes place when a bare hole appears, and the introductions are rarely if ever bought. Cuttings, plants from neighbours, seedlings from elsewhere in the garden, a scattering of seeds … the nurseryman's catalogue has little place in the cottage garden.

The plants chosen are a veritable hotch-potch. Once aromatic flowers and culinary herbs were all-important and dominated the garden – now they are less important but you will still find lavender and honeysuckle, rosemary and pinks scenting the air. Colourful plants abound now we are less concerned with growing our own herbs – you will find hollyhocks, sunflowers, gypsophila, forget-me-nots, pansies, cornflowers, marigolds, Michaelmas daisies and so on.

Vegetables grow among and alongside the flowers – a line of beans, a clump of cabbages or a cluster of onions. Fruit has always been a feature, and the accent these days is more on soft fruit than the apples, pears and plums which once had the dominant place. Now currants, gooseberries and raspberries grow together to the delight of the children and the birds.

What a jumble! Pots and old sinks overflowing with flowers, winding narrow paths, bits of lawn, maybe a chicken or two, a water-butt and perhaps a seat or two. Every inch seems to be covered – roses or Virginia creepers cover the high walls and ferns, stonecrops and wallflowers grow between the stones of the low walls.

In the 17th century the French garden arrived in England, and the fashionable set with large houses began to create miniature and watered-down versions of Versailles or Vaux-le-Vicomte. The Dutch style came later, smaller and fussier, but all of this had no impact on the cottage garden – no straight lines, sculptured trees or rectangular ponds for them.

Which is just as well, because in about 1730 the Landscape garden arrived and for the next hundred years all straight lines were outlawed by the fashionable. This, however, did not make the cottage garden any more acceptable to the horticultural high-priests – flowers were also outlawed.

One of the biggest mistakes of all in some gardening history books is the statement that as a result of Capability Brown and others, flowers were no longer grown in the English gardens of the 18th century. This is a gross oversimplification – many of the grand estates did indeed destroy their flowers and French-style formal layouts, but the vast majority of British gardens, which were the cottage

gardens, took no notice. Nothing changed.

Some of the flowers and shrubs thrown out from the grand gardens by the new school of landscape designers were taken by the country folk and planted in front of their cottages. Our floral heritage was preserved, and if it was not for the cottage garden many of our flowers could well have disappeared. Here was our repository for roses, our home for hollyhocks, waiting for a time when they would once again be appreciated.

Before Queen Victoria's accession to the throne flowers and formalism came back, and towards the end of her reign the cottage garden was set to make its second great contribution. William Robinson, the Father of the Modern Garden, drew much of his inspiration from the cottage garden. In *The English Flower Garden* he wrote 'Those who look at sea or sky or wood see beauty that no art can show; but among the things made by man nothing is prettier than an English cottage garden.' Here he found a lack of planning, a lack of regimented planting and an environment where the plant was all-important. And the plants knew no class barriers – trees, shrubs, perennials, annuals and vegetables all grew happily together.

Robinson passionately believed he had found the key and developed his ideas of the informal flower garden through his books and magazines. Gertrude Jekyll was captivated by his ideas and the memory of the cottage gardens she had seen and loved in the Surrey countryside when she was a child. In her role as a garden designer as well as an author she did not abhor straight lines but the plantings within the borders and beds had to be gay and informal.

Great modern gardens such as Sissinghurst have drawn their inspiration from these pioneers who were influenced by the lowly cottage garden. The herbaceous border was conceived by Robinson and Jekyll as a hardy perennial form of the cottage garden jumble.

The original flower-laden plots remain unchanged, although their numbers have been reduced as cottages give way to roads, rebuilding and modern developments. Garden fashions have come and gone but they have had no effect on the *real* English garden. In recent times it has helped to mother a style of its own, but it still remains the same as it did when Drake played bowls on Plymouth Hoe – unplanned, unsophisticated and unspoilt.

# STREET SELLERS
# OF YESTERYEAR

'Come buy my fine roses,
My myrtles and stocks
My sweet-smelling blossoms
And close-growing box.
Here's my fine rosemary, sage and thyme,
Come buy my ground ivy,
Here feverfew, gillyflowers and rue,
Come buy my knotted marjoram, too!
Here's your sweet lavender,
Sixteen sprigs a penny,
Which you will find, my ladies,
Will smell as sweet as any.'

Old London Street Cries

THE STREET SELLERS of today are alive and well and living in every town and city. You will find their barrows and stalls crowded with blooms – daffodils, roses, carnations, chrysanthemums or tulips depending on the season. These street sellers of flowers are maintaining an age-old tradition, but both the method of selling and the plants have changed over the years.

There seem to be three phases in the story, but there are no clear-cut lines between the chapters. We do not even know when this story of selling plants in the streets began, but the first phase was well-established in Tudor and Elizabethan times. In those days the housewife bought plants for their fragrance rather than their beauty. The role of the sweet-smelling herbs which were bought in the streets was a strictly practical one – the lavender, basil, rosemary, gillyflowers (carnations), mignonette, violets, thyme and so on were used to make pot-pourri, toilet water or nosegays (bundles of flowers held under the nose to mask unpleasant smells and to protect the carrier from 'unhealthy airs

> My love is like a red, red rose
>
> That's newly sprung in June,
>
> My love is like the melodie
>
> That's sweetly play'd in tune.
>
> *Robert Burns*

and vapours'). Flowers were spread on floors, in cupboards and over clothes but the artistic flower arrangement was unknown.

The flower girls who sold the aromatic plants carried them in large baskets on their heads or arms – they were pedlars, carrying their wares as they moved from place to place, and not hawkers, who use some form of transport. Walking from street to street the girls 'called' their wares – 'Sweet primroses, four bunches a penny, primroses' or 'Come buy my mint, my fine green mint'. It is claimed that they recited verses as set down on page 169 as well as simple phrases to describe their wares, but we shall never know.

In the 17th and 18th centuries the second phase began. The range of plants sold in the streets was extended to include some of the recent introductions from overseas – phlox, lupin, Michaelmas daisies, etc. – as well as a wide range of English flowers – hollyhocks, snapdragons, stocks and so on. There was now more interest in attractive flowers for decoration and not just herbs for fragrance. Fruit such as oranges and apples were sold, and vegetables like watercress were offered. The range depended on the time of the

## THE ONION-SELLER

If you are middle-aged or elderly you will probably remember him. The Breton onion-seller from northern France was once a familiar sight in city streets with his beret, bicycle and strings of onions. But these days he has become a museum piece as only a handful now cross the Channel to sell their wares.

The trade began at the start of the reign of Queen Victoria and by the time of her death more than 2000 'Johnny Onions' came over each year with their plaited onion strings. It must have been hard work – they would sell about 1000 onions each day and yet they were noted for their cheerfulness. How strange that in these European Union days this pre-war symbol of international trade should have faded away. It seems that the picturesque onion-seller could not survive against import regulations, increased transport costs and a decline in the popularity of the mild and pink-fleshed Breton onion.

year, and winter-cut flowers were still a thing of the far-off future.

The picture of the flower girl calling her wares is a romantic one, but in reality it must have been a hard and dreary life. Some turned to prostitution during the flowerless days of winter and a few rose to fame if not fortune – Nell Gwyn became the mistress of Charles II and 'Nosegay Fan' Barton of Vinegar Yard became the famous 18th century actress Mrs. Abington of Drury Lane.

## The flower girls who sold the aromatic plants carried them in large baskets on their heads or arms

Several writers including Henry Mayhew, the energetic chronicler of the London poor, have given us a clear picture of the street seller in the middle of the 19th century. Covent Garden Market was their magnet, and more than 3000 men and women would buy their stock in the early morning and then tie the flowers into halfpenny and penny bunches. Violets were a favourite flower, but primroses, roses, lavender and bedding plants were also sold. Baskets laden, they moved off into the streets. Some walked, others sat on the steps of public buildings – a scene illustrated by Eliza Doolittle in the musical *My Fair Lady*. But not all these flower sellers were attractive young ladies like Eliza –

some were only seven years old. Walking or sitting, they called their wares – 'Flowers all a-blowing, all a-growing', 'Sweet vi-lits, penny a bunch' and 'Two bundles a penny, primroses'.

Today's street trader represents the third and final phase. The baskets have gone and the wares are hawked and no longer peddled. The emphasis is on bunches of long-stemmed blooms for flower arranging rather than short-stemmed ones for posies and buttonholes. Out-of-season flowers are the main attraction, and winter is no longer a period of inactivity. The cries handed down from mother to daughter have disappeared, but the flowers these days are beautiful enough to speak for themselves.

The tradition of walking from street to street is not quite dead. The gypsy who thrusts a purple sprig at you with 'Buy a bunch of lucky heather' is maintaining a way of selling flowers which began before Columbus set sail for America.

# THE VICTORIAN GARDEN

QUEEN VICTORIA came to the throne in 1837 and died in 1901, and throughout her reign the Victorian style of gardening flourished. This statement over-simplifies a complex picture – the Victorian style began before her Coronation and its demolition began well before her death through the work of William Robinson and others. The strict formality and the geometrical bedding schemes of the 1800s were swept away as the fashionable form of gardening before the end of the century, but they did not entirely disappear. Signs of horticultural Victoriana are clearly seen to this day in

back gardens as well as in well-tended public parks throughout the land.

Another complexity is that there was no such thing as a set Victorian style of garden design. It was instead a period of history when people set out to establish their status in the gardens around their homes. The spirit of the age demanded that the most ornate designs and the most exotic plants should be judged as the most praiseworthy, and each household took features from a number of gardening styles and movements to establish its Victorian garden.

Personal preference played a role, of course, but the styles chosen were largely dictated by the wealth of the owner. The rich demanded that the Neo-Italianate style should play a prominent part in their estates. The style was introduced in about 1830 and featured stone terraces linked by steps and decorated with vases, balustrades, fountains and sculpture. Sir Charles Barry was the arch-priest of the style and he created many masterpieces in the grand Victorian style – today you can see his work at Harewood House (York-shire), Trentham Gardens (Staffordshire), Shrubland Park (Suffolk) and Holkham Hall (Norfolk). The Neo-Italianate style spread to the middle-class villa garden by the middle of Victoria's reign, but it could have none of the dominance there that it enjoyed in the grand garden.

The Rustic movement was a great leveller. The craze to use tree trunks and branches for garden ornamentation affected rich and poor alike – the wealthy built rustic garden houses and temples whilst the not-so-wealthy had their rustic pergola or bark-covered flower box. Cast-iron seats were produced in the leafy branch pattern and some remain today alongside the rustic trellis to remind us of a style which has never quite disappeared.

The common link between Victorian gardens of all sizes was the adoption of the Gardenesque style. Its arch-priest J. C. Loudon (page 140) had begun to popularise the concept when Victoria was only a little girl and it really is the essence of the 19th century garden. Loudon defined it as a design 'best calculated to display the individual beauty of trees, shrubs and plants; the smoothness and greenness of lawns; and the smooth surfaces, curved directions, dryness and firmness of gravel walks; in short it is calculated for displaying the art of the gardener.'

Gone were the days when the garden was meant to look like a piece of idealised countryside and unborn was the idea that fashionable gardens should be oases of restrained good taste in an informal setting. Loudon put his finger on the Victorian pulse when he said that the garden should be a place where you used plants to display your art ... or the art of the regiment of gardeners you employed.

To show off their art the Victorians adopted two basic approaches. The geometrical bed cut in the lawn became the display area and this was filled with a patchwork of brightly-coloured annuals. Zinnias, lobelias, dahlias, fuchsias, pelargoniums and so on filled the tapestry of squares, circles, diamonds, butterflies and cornucopiae in the lawn, and the concept of 'tenderness' was important. The use of hardy cottage-garden plants was scorned – only frost-sensitive plants displayed 'the art of the gardener'. The labour requirement was enormous – a large country house would have a staff of 60 gardeners or more to tend the rows of greenhouses needed for bedding plant production, to look after the display houses with their exotics, to maintain the flower beds and borders, to grow the vegetables and to care for the rose gardens, rockeries, ponds, fountains, lawns and shrubberies.

If the garish flower beds were one pillar of the Victorian garden, then the shrubbery was certainly the other. Surprisingly the shrub border in the average villa garden was a plain affair. There was no attempt to mirror the colourful beds – the aim was to produce a sombre green wall of privet, yew, holly and laurel. There was no shortage of flowering trees and shrubs – a flood of exciting discoveries from America, China, India, Africa, Australia and elsewhere was pouring into the country – but the middle-class shrubbery was not considered the place for such 'far-fetched' plants. Exotic trees were used as isolated specimens in the villa garden, but the choice was usually restricted to a stately species which was destined to create problems in a small garden for a future generation – the Deodar cedar, the Monkey puzzle tree or the Wellingtonia.

The situation was quite different in the grand garden – here there was an insatiable thirst for novelties and the latest introductions. Catalogues were combed, exhibitions were visited and head gardeners sent off to Europe to find new trees and shrubs. These were planted in the arboretum, and such collections of trees and shrubs became an important feature of many large 19th century gardens.

The Victorians have been criticised for forgetting to look at the garden as a whole and for their obsession with formality, fussiness and novelty. Yet they evolved the concept of massed flower colour to brighten up grimy cities and it was their desire for out-of-the-way varieties which stimulated both plant exploration and plant breeding. Whether they should be criticised or praised is up to you to decide.

# A WOMAN'S PLACE

T HE WOMAN'S place in gardening is a complex and sometimes confusing story. It has fluctuated greatly over the years – in the 1st century Pliny pronounced that 'garden work is women's work' but in the middle of the 19th century Mrs Loudon wrote in her *Gardening for Ladies* that 'It must be confessed that digging at first sight appears to be a very laborious employment, one peculiarly unfitted to the delicately formed hands and feet of a woman.' There has obviously been a change over the years, but it was not a simple slide from complete involvement in Ancient times to complete inactivity in the 19th century – the story has been a complex, sometimes confusing but always fascinating one.

## In early times gardening around the ordinary house was a way of raising food and herbs

At least the modern-day picture is straightforward – men and women share the work in the garden. On average men spend about seven hours a week working outdoors and women about six. In one third of our gardens the woman is in charge and in about a quarter the responsibility is shared equally – these figures clearly illustrate that the garden of today is usually a partnership in which the female partner does half the work.

The division of labour, however, does vary. Only 20 per cent of gardening women are responsible for digging and cutting hedges, and only 30 per cent are responsible for the lawn. In about half the gardens it is the woman who is in charge of planting, watering and tidying up and in two-thirds of them she has to do most of the weeding.

An interesting feature of this division of labour is that the concept of 'woman's work' does not vary with social class. In the richest group with the biggest houses 20 per cent of the gardens are dug by the

housewife and the figure is the same at the lowest end of the economic scale. It is the same for all the other tasks – the woman's place in the garden of today is utterly classless.

It was not always so, and that makes the picture confusing. For much of our history the garden was a place where peasant women worked and gentlewomen walked or picked the flowers and herbs. Before the modern era you cannot generalise about the woman's place without stating which level of society you have in mind.

In early times gardening around the ordinary house was a way of raising food and herbs, and like today it was a shared activity. Thomas Tusser, writing in 1577, noted that 'In March and April, from morning to night, in sowing and setting,

good housewives delight.' At about the same time the weeder women worked in the grand gardens of the nobility – Hampton Court, Woburn, etc. – where they weeded and watered for threepence a day.

This pattern continued through the great ages of gardening. The country housewife cultivated her herbs and flowers around the cottage, nuns grew herbs in the convent gardens and gave lessons on their cultivation and use, peasant women worked in the gardens of the wealthy and the gentlewomen walked in their gardens, sat in the bowers and perhaps gathered flowers. The plain landscape garden popularised by Capability Brown meant that the labouring role for women decreased, but paintings do reveal that moving the shorn grass was their responsibility.

The influence of women as creators and trend-setters was hardly apparent before the mid 19th century, but it should still not be underrated – their influence was sometimes present behind the scenes. Mary, Duchess of Beaufort (1630–1714) introduced many plants from overseas into her garden at Badminton – these exotics included the Zonal pelargonium. Princess Augusta (1719–1772) was the patron of William Kent and her garden at Kew became the nucleus of the Royal Botanic Garden. Queen Charlotte (1744–1818) was an active patron of Kew and the contribution by Empress Josephine (1763–1814) is recorded on page 25. This long tradition of Royal horticulturalists was maintained by Queen Elizabeth, the late Queen Mother.

At the beginning of the 19th century it had become a social necessity for young ladies to be well versed in botany and the natural sciences.

Textbooks were written by women (for example *Botanical Dialogues for use in Schools* by Mrs. Maria Jackson) and plants were collected by them – Countess Amherst brought *Clematis montana* to England from India in 1826. Country housewives worked in their cottage gardens but gardening as a career was strictly a man's world. And nobody considered working in the garden as a suitable recreation for ladies of quality.

Jane Loudon pioneered the change which has led to today's equal partnership in the garden, as outlined in the surveys described on page 175. In 1840 she wrote *Gardening for Ladies*, and in it she said that the flower garden 'was pre-eminently a woman's department'. Other books for the new middle classes appeared – *Every Lady Her Own Flower Gardener* (1840) by Miss Louisa Johnson and *The Ladies Companion to the Flower Garden* (1841) by Jane and John Loudon. Gardening became a family activity and women began to emerge amongst the ranks of distinguished horticulturalists. There were landscape designers, like Gertrude Jekyll, patrons like Ellen Willmott and writers such as Mrs. Earle. As the 20th century advanced the numbers increased – Vita Sackville-West and Marjory Fish, Mairi Sawyer and Beatrix Havergal, Eleanour Sinclair Rohde and Frances Perry.

Although Jane Loudon opened the door to gardening as a hobby for women, the door to professional horticulture remained closed for many years – it was not until 1895 that Kew employed its first female gardeners. In 1902 Swanley College became the first horticultural training centre for women and in 1910 Studley Horticultural College for Women was founded. Waterperry started in 1932 and has become internationally famous as a training ground for women determined to prove that horticulture is no longer just a man's world.

---

## It was not until 1895 that Kew employed its first female gardeners

---

According to the old Greek philosopher Democritus, 'the growth of greenstuff is checked by contact with a woman'. These days we are much more enlightened – on the professional gardening side the role of women matches the part played by men in garden writing, broadcasting, design and landscaping.

# WORKING-CLASS PLANTS

⟨⟨⟩⟩

ANY OF the everyday objects around us give an indication of our social status or class. The large detached house, the Rolls Royce and the Afghan Hound are indicators of wealth or importance, but one of the pleasures of garden plants is that they are classless. The African violet and the Flowering cherry may be found in either castle or cottage, and they are equally at home in both places.

It was not always so. About 200 years ago the gentry began to reject some of the simple cottage-garden plants and these were taken up by the new working classes in the Midlands, Lancashire, Yorkshire and Scotland. The lowly plants became a passion for the weavers, miners and labourers – breeding new varieties, exhibiting them in public houses and caring for their prized stock like a mother with her children. To the middle classes, these once-loved cottage-garden plants were now regarded as 'mechanic's flowers' and no 'genteel' house would grow them.

THE INDUSTRIAL Revolution spawned a new breed – the working class. Farm labourers left the flowers and crops of the countryside to work in the mines, mills and factories, but they did not forget their roots. Gardening on the grand scale was of course impossible around their tiny terrace houses, but they wanted something to grow to remind them of what they had left behind.

The new exotic species of flowers and shrubs which were being introduced into Britain were too delicate or too expensive for them. They turned instead to those old-established favourites of the cottage garden which were compact enough to be grown in pots. These were the 'florist's flowers'. The list is quite a short one – anemone, auricula,

carnation, hyacinth, pinks, polyanthus and ranunculus. Tulips became a working-class flower when the price of bulbs fell in the 19th century, and the latecomers were sweet william and pansy. These, then, were the flowers for the labourer, miner and the mill-hand, and a guide printed in 1824 warned the estate gardener against plants which had 'degenerated' in such a way.

There were no strict geographical boundaries between these working-class flowers. Auriculas, pinks and carnations were grown in most urban areas, but there was some specialisation. The ranunculus had been brought over to Britain by the Flemish weavers in the reign of Elizabeth and it was grown by the descendants of the original Huguenot settlers. The Lancashire cotton weavers raised the finest auriculas and the Paisley weavers bred the laced pink.

It is surprising that several features of modern gardening arose from these humble beginnings. Let us start with the Horticultural Societies of today, which had their origin in the Florist Clubs. Here the men would meet to discuss the cultivation of their chosen favourite. These clubs were not regarded as a place for womenfolk and they were certainly not the place to give away treasured secrets to other 'florists' – feeding recipes, techniques and plant stocks were jealously guarded. Most of these Florist Clubs have now disappeared, but a few do remain.

At regular intervals the Florist Club Shows were held, and these were the birthplace of the Horticultural Exhibition. It is strange to think that Chelsea, the National Dahlia Show, the R.H.S. Spring Flower Show and all the other shows, large and small, began at these tiny gatherings. In church halls or public houses the pots of auriculas or pinks were put on display. They were painstakingly judged, and the lucky grower of the most meritorious was awarded a trowel or a two-shilling piece. Competition was intense and interest was high – it has been stated that the Florist Club magazine sold about 10,000 copies per issue at a time when money was scarce and literacy was low.

So it was the town-dwelling 'florists' and not the estate owners who gave us our societies and shows. It was a visit to a Nottingham miners' flower show which inspired Dean Hole to found the National Rose Society. Perhaps even more important was the contribution to our ideas about plant breeding. These people showed that new varieties could be raised by amateurs with few facilities for such work. The Lancashire mill-hands developed magnificent new auriculas but the crowning achievement was the breeding of the laced pink by the Paisley weavers. The creation of intricate patterns was part of their trade, and they bred a race of pinks which bore a lacy coloured edging to the petals.

---

## The crowning achievement was the breeding of the laced pink by the Paisley weavers

---

By 1860 the popularity of the Florist Clubs had begun to wane. No longer were their beloved plants regarded as working-class flowers – they had moved into the villas of the middle classes. The mantle was taken up by the gooseberry and the leek – growing the largest berry or heaviest leek was the new quest and today the tradition is maintained in northeastern England at the many Pot Leek Clubs. Here you will find all the ingredients you would have found in a Lancashire Auricula Club in 1800 – fierce rivalry, secret techniques, specially bred plants, painstaking cultivation and a desire to win the first prize at the show.

# THE WORSHIPFUL
# COMPANY OF
# GARDENERS

THE GARDENERS COMPANY is steeped in more than 650 years of tradition – it first appears in the history books in 1345 when a 'fellowship' of Gardeners of the Earls, Barons, Bishops and Citizens of the City of London petitioned the Lord Mayor. Their request was to be allowed to continue to sell their produce in front of the Church of St. Austin – a clear indication that even in the Good Old Days there were Planning Regulations.

This fellowship of gardeners received its Royal Charter in 1605 and the Guild became increasingly powerful. Its basic role was to control the 'trade, crafte or misterie of gardening; planting, grafting, setting, sowing, cutting, arboring, rocking, mounting, covering, fencing and removing of plantes, herbes, seedes, fruites, trees, stocks, setts, and of contryving the conveyances of the same belonging.' Eleven years after its Royal Charter the Guild was empowered to search for and destroy defective plants, fruits and vegetables in 'the City of London and within six miles thereof'.

Obviously Trading Standards are nothing new, and neither is the closed shop – in 1632 the Guild received the protection it had always wanted from the Recorder of London – any person using the trade of gardening in contempt of the Company's Charters would in future be arrested.

The amateur gardening which took place in and around London in the 17th and 18th centuries did not seriously concern the Guild. This consisted of cottagers tending their small plots of herbs, fruit, vegetables and flowers where the 'trade, crafte or misterie of gardening' was not considered to be involved. The Guild was concerned with the market gardener and the craftsman who worked as a gardener for others, and for these people the Guild set the standards and granted them permission to practise. In those early days The Worshipful Company of Gardeners was much more than a group involved in charities and the maintenance of traditions.

The 19th century saw a great change in gardening in and around London and this resulted in a transformation in the

IN·THE·SWEAT·OF THY·BROWS·SHALT THOW·EATE·THY·BREAD

Gardeners Company. Urban development swept away the multitude of market gardens clustered around the City, and the new army of middle-class amateur gardeners was catered for by the Horticultural (later Royal Horticultural) Society. The power of the Gardeners Company dwindled and its role in setting standards ceased. As a result it moved into charitable work – in 1892 it instituted its first scholarship and in 1895 gave its first pension to a retired gardener. The Guild however preserved its strong sense of ceremony – in 1911 the Company presented Queen Mary with her Coronation bouquet and continues year by year to provide replicas of the Coronation bouquet for Her Majesty the Queen. In 1923 it continued the privilege of providing the bridal bouquet for a Royal marriage – Lady Elizabeth Bowes-Lyon (the late Queen Mother) carried this flowery tribute, and similar bouquets were presented to Princess Marina (1934), the Duchess of Gloucester (1935), Queen Elizabeth (1947), Princess Margaret (1960), the Duchess of Kent (1961) and the Princess of Wales (1981). The Company provided a floral set piece for the wedding breakfast of Princess Anne (1973) and continues with an important role in ceremonial events in the City.

The Gardeners Company increasingly attracts key members of the horticultural world into its livery. Membership of this 'club' is prized as it is restricted to 250. However, the modern Gardeners Company is now focused on charitable works, maintaining traditions and promoting horticulture in the City of London. There are at least three Court Dinners with distinguished guests each year. The grades of membership – Livery-man, Freeman, Patrimony Candidate, Apprentice plus the officers of power, (Spade bearer, Renter warden, Upper warden, Master, Clerk and Stewards) – all have the ring of a bygone age.

The Worshipful Company of Gardeners, from its offices in Luke Street, London, also involves itself in many ways in the garden scene of today. It runs the Flowers in the City campaign which manages competitions for the best window box, garden, courtyard and horticultural features in the City. A number of London and horticultural charities and colleges are supported and its extensive gardening library in the Guildhall is open to all.

And the Worshipful Company does keep up with the times, even if it is rather delayed on occasions. In 1974 it agreed to accept ladies into the Livery, and the first female Liveryman (not Liveryperson) was Princess Alice. Women have long been associated with gardening and it was therefore fitting that the Gardeners Company should have provided London with its first Lady Lord Mayor – Dame Mary Donaldson. Recently the Company elected its first female Master (not Mistress).

The modern Gardeners Company is effectively an exclusive fraternity of those who share a passionate interest in horticulture and gardening. They work together, using their expertise, charitable giving and influence to promote gardening in the City and elsewhere whilst enjoying each other's company and upholding the traditions of an ancient craft guild which is nearly 500 years older than the Royal Horticultural Society.

# THE YEAR HOLLAND WENT TULIP MAD

*THERE WAS a time when you would have gladly given a month's salary for a tulip bulb. This may sound like madness, but Tulip Mania gripped a whole nation and lasted for more than three years.*

THE AUSTRIAN Ambassador in Turkey, Ogier Ghislain de Busbecq, saw drifts of strange plants growing between Adrianople and Constantinople. In 1544 he sent some of the bulbs to Vienna and they were planted in the Imperial Gardens. Plants from later shipments were grown in the gardens of Austrian merchants.

In 1577 the first tulips arrived in Britain. Thirty years later they were growing in France but they created little interest in Europe – there was no sign of the madness which was to appear later. The flowers were plain, in shades of white, yellow, purple or dull red – the spectacular feathered types did not exist in those early days. The history books usually illustrate this lack of interest with the story of the Antwerp merchant. He fried and ate a consignment of tulip bulbs because he didn't know where he could sell them – a consignment which would have made him a fortune 50 years later.

Nobody can give the exact date when the tulip caught the imagination or when the craze to own unusual varieties began. We do know it began in France between 1610 and 1620 and prices rocketed, but it was in Holland in 1634 that Tulip Mania broke out.

Possessions of all sorts were sold to buy bulbs – a rare type could cost the price of a farm, house or coach and horses. Of course there were not enough bulbs to go round and so Tulip Mania became a paper

speculation. These buyers and sellers of Tulip Notes met at the home of the van der Beurse family in Bruges, and the French word *bourse* for Stock Exchange passed into the language.

---

## In April 1637 the Dutch Government decreed that all Tulip Notes had to be honoured and the bulbs supplied

---

Dutchmen from every walk of life bought and sold these Tulip Notes – it was no longer a matter of *owning* a bulb, it was a matter of making money. Peasants became millionaires in a matter of months,

and the value of the Notes which promised to supply a stated number of bulbs continued to increase as they were sold from one investor to another.

Then it happened. In April 1637 the Dutch Government decreed that all Tulip Notes had to be honoured and the bulbs supplied. The market crashed – Tulip Mania was over and the harvest was a bitter one. Rich men became paupers overnight and suicides were commonplace.

Although other countries had not been caught up in this madness, the value of tulips remained high. They were much admired in Britain and remained expensive until the 19th century, when they became a flower 'for shopkeepers and workers'. The first flood of cheap bulbs was from America, but Holland became the centre for growing tulips. Each year more than 1000 million bulbs are exported – the mania may have gone but the love for this garden flower certainly remains.

> I have caught hold of the earth, to use a gardener's phrase, and neither my friends nor my enemies will find it an easy matter to transplant me again.
>
> *Lord Bolingbroke*

# WILDLIFE IN
# THE GARDEN

SITTING IN THE garden on a summer afternoon you might feel that you are all alone apart from the bird singing in the tree and the butterflies flitting above the buddleia. Actually the garden is teeming with wildlife and you are certainly not alone.

Your fellow residents vary widely in both size and numbers, from a solitary fox skulking amongst the dustbins to the thousand million bacteria which occur in a single gram of soil. A couple of spadefuls will contain about a million tiny creatures – springtails, nematodes, bristletails, mites and so on, but we can leave these lowly members of the biomass to the scientist. Our interest in wildlife usually centres around the animals we can see.

The mammals are the largest of the garden residents but they are not the most evident. The hedgehog (page 195) and the bat (page 187) are garden friends but they are creatures of the night. The mole (page 197) is quite definitely not a friend and spends most of its life underground. The rabbit is another garden foe. The fox

(page 215) has become a regular visitor to many town gardens, but nature has taught it to keep out of sight as much as it can. The wood mouse (page 191), vole and tiny shrew are all timid creatures and only the squirrel (page 213) comes into the open to romp during the day. You will see the squirrel, but you will have to listen for the grunt of the hedgehog, the squeak of the shrew and the scream of the vixen.

Birds are much more obvious than mammals. Some of them, such as the bullfinch (page 189) can be destructive, but a garden without birds would be a sorry place. The robin (page 209) is the least afraid of humans and the tits (page 193) are the most amusing to watch. A wide variety of birds will pass through the average-sized garden during the course of a year – watch for wrens, swifts, swallows, house martins, thrushes, blackbirds, sparrows, fieldfares, starlings, warblers, dunnocks, crows, wood pigeons and owls.

Frogs and toads (page 199) are not as numerous as they used to be and the butterfly population has declined in recent years (page 204). The caterpillars feeding on your flowers and shrubs are the larvae of moths and not butterflies, and gardeners generally feel quite unsentimental about these relatives of the butterfly. Earthworms (page 207) may or may not be plentiful, depending on how much organic matter is present in the soil; slugs and snails (page 211) may also be plentiful, but their stimulus is wet weather, together with decaying vegetable matter and adequate places to hide.

The rest of the small creatures which are visible to the naked eye are usually referred to as 'insects', but this is often incorrect. A true insect has six legs and a body divided into three distinct segments. Butterflies and moths belong here, and so do the beetles, flies, ants, gnats, ladybirds and wasps. The bees (page 202) are insects but the spiders are not. The commonest one, the orb spider, spins a web so fine that a band of it circling the equator would weigh less than 250 g.

There is much talk these days about the threat to garden wildlife from chemicals, air pollution and so on and it is hard to get an unbiased picture which is coloured neither by the defenders of uncontrolled technology nor the back-to-nature school. Perhaps the best plan is to look at a few basic facts. The starting point is that wildlife is *not* dying out, even in the centre of cities. Changes in the balance do occur but this is not new and there is no single or simple cause. Some species become more frequent and others decline over the years, and factors such as the weather, presence of cats, and design of the garden have an influence alongside pesticide sprays, increased urbanisation, modern farming practice, etc. Secondly, many of our popular garden flowers, shrubs and trees are just as attractive to birds, bees and butterflies as our native flora.

It is vital to remember that only a tiny fraction of the wildlife population are enemies – a much larger number are beneficial and the remainder neither help nor harm the garden. There are times when some of the potentially crippling foes such as greenflies, caterpillars or slugs get out of hand, and then treatment may be necessary. The situation is different with minor pests which cause little damage – these can often be picked off or ignored.

Your objective should never be to turn your garden into an insect-free reserve; with increased urbanisation it is essential that gardens become a refuge rather than a no-go area for much of our wildlife. Plant berry-forming shrubs to attract birds, make a shallow pond for frogs and newts, grow fragrant bushes for butterflies and provide a well-stocked bird table (page 210). You have the right to defend all your hard work against the ravages of a pest, but you do not have the right to try to destroy all the wildlife which lives in your garden. In fact, you have the duty to improve the lot of the multitude who are indifferent or beneficial to your plants.

# BATS

⟴

*B*ATS ARE mysterious creatures, flitting over the garden at dusk and swooping to
pick up moths and other insects on the wing. They are also frightening
creatures to some people, but they need not be. All the European species are insect-
eaters and will certainly not attack man or animals. Nor will they fly into your hair
– their 'radar' is far too effective to allow them to do such a clumsy thing.

There are 14 different species of bats in Britain but only a few inhabit gardens.
The one you are most likely to see is the smallest of all – the pipistrelle. It is about
5 cm long with a 20 cm wingspan. Its flight is fast and jerky and it emits squeaking
sounds. The serotine is sometimes seen – a larger but slower-moving bat. Quickest
of all the garden bats is the golden-brown noctule. All of them should be made
welcome, for each one devours thousands of flying insects each night.

## HOW CAN I GET
## RID OF BATS?

You really mustn't think about killing bats
if they frighten you or if they are roosting
in your house. All species are protected and
it is an offence to kill, injure or harm one.

Drastic measures are very rarely called
for as they will never harm you and can be
useful in destroying woodworm. Occasionally a large group will congregate in the loft
or behind woodwork and both their
droppings and squeaking can be a
nuisance. In times gone by the answer was
to seal off their entrance holes once they
had moved off to their winter quarters in
autumn. It is now an offence to block off

access – consult the Bat Conservation
Trust for advice. Do remember that bats
are part of our endangered wildlife.

## WHERE DO BATS LIVE?

During the day bats cling to an object in a
dark place and hang upside-down. The

catch in flight, although they occasionally swoop down to pick up an insect moving on the ground or resting on a leaf.

A large moth can be more than a mouthful, so the bat bends its tail forward and forms a 'feeding bowl' in which it holds its prey whilst it is being eaten.

## How do Bats Fly at Night without Bumping into Things?

Some bats have good eyesight and so the expression 'as blind as a bat' is not strictly true. However, they use a 'radar' system and not their eyes for navigation purposes. A high-pitched noise is emitted 50 times a second and the strength of the echo bouncing back from nearby objects guides them in their flight. They avoid static objects with unerring skill and they can detect and catch flying insects with amazing accuracy.

For the technically-minded it is not a radar system at all. Radar depends on radio waves – the bat uses sound waves, so it is a sonar or echo-location system.

roosting place which is chosen depends on the species and the sort of living quarters available. The pipistrelle favours the loft of a house, a barn or an ivy-covered hollow tree; other bats like church steeples. Although hundreds may congregate there is no social life within the roost. It is not true that bats like old houses – they prefer buildings which are new, clean and free from draughts.

The winter hibernation quarters may be miles away from the roosting place. Thousands of bats may congregate in a cave, barn, cellar or steeple and remain there in a deep sleep from October until April.

## What do Bats Eat?

Tropical bats have a varied diet. They eat fruit and fish, and the vampire bat of S. America really does lap up the blood of the animal it has attacked. Our small bats are much gentler creatures – their diet consists of moths and beetles which they

> Not God! In gardens! When the eve is cool?
>
> Nay, but I have a sign;
>
> 'Tis very sure God walks in mine.
>
> *T. E. Brown*

# GARDEN FINCHES

---

*T*HE FINCHES are basically woodland birds which live on seeds – put out wild bird food if you want to attract them. They are generally handsome and often brightly coloured with a wave-like flight path. Over the years some of the finches have spread onto farmland and then into urban areas – four of them are now common garden birds.

You cannot generalise about the garden finches. The aggressive and solitary chaffinch guards its territory whereas the others are social birds – the greenfinch helps to make up mixed flocks of 5000 or more. The bullfinch has been a farm pest for centuries and now has moved its activity into the garden, yet the chaffinch is positively beneficial in the spring when it gathers insects for its young. The female chaffinch is as plain as a sparrow – the gaudy male goldfinch was a popular cage-bird in Victorian times.

## ARE BULLFINCHES A SERIOUS PEST?

The bullfinch has always been hated by fruit growers, and with good reason. When other food is short a couple of bullfinches will strip one bud per second from a gooseberry bush or pear tree.

Until recently this bird did not move far away from its woodland haunt, but during the past 50 years it has spread into town gardens where it now breeds. If the seeds of ash, bramble and birch are plentiful in autumn the ravages in the following spring are generally slight. But if the seed crop

has been poor then the buds on all sorts of garden shrubs and trees may be attacked. Prevention is difficult – the fruit cage is the answer where practical, but black thread between the branches is frowned upon and chemical bird repellents are ineffective when alternative food is short.

## WHERE DO GARDEN FINCHES LIVE?

Trees and shrubs are the nesting sites for finches and each type has its favourite. The neat nests of the chaffinch, made of moss and grass and lined with hair, are built in hedgerows or shrubs. The goldfinch prefers something much higher and builds its nest in the upper branches of trees. The greenfinch builds its nest in a bush, and you will sometimes find several nests made by these birds in the same shrub. The bullfinch, like the other social finches, meets its mate in the winter flock and the pair later fly off to a hedgerow to create a nest and start their family. The nest is made of twigs and moss with a lining of small roots.

## How do You Tell the Garden Finches Apart?

The **Goldfinch** is unmistakable – a black, white and red head plus black and yellow wings make it stand out in a crowd. The **Greenfinch** has rather more muted colours – olive green with yellow wing-bars – and the **Chaffinch** is equally attractive with its slate-blue head and its pinkish-brown chest. The **Bullfinch** is the one you ought to learn to recognise, because it spells trouble in spring. It is easy to recognise – powerful beak, black head, red breast and a back of grey, black and white.

## What do Garden Finches Eat?

Goldfinches and greenfinches are straightforward seed-eaters. Thistles and dandelions are the goldfinches' favourites – grasses are sought by greenfinches and so are the peanuts provided by some kindly gardener. The remaining two finches are seed-eaters with variations. The chaffinch feeds almost entirely on the ground, looking for the seeds of grasses, cereals and many other plants. At breeding time its diet changes – now the hunt is for aphids and caterpillars to feed the young chicks. The bullfinch also spends most of the year eating seeds and in the spring looks for tree seeds. When they are in short supply the buds of many trees and shrubs are devoured.

# GARDEN MICE

THE MOUSE you are most likely to see in the garden is a pretty little creature, golden brown in colour with a pinkish underside. It is the wood mouse and its favourite diet is garden produce. The wood mouse shuns daylight – it doesn't even like a full moon when it is foraging for food. It is just as well that you are not likely to come across it when gardening – this mouse has the disturbing habit of leaping about a metre into the air when disturbed.

Other species of mice do invade gardens but the wood mouse is the commonest. It is not a solitary creature – each one belongs to a super-family which extends over several acres and is ruled by a male leader.

## HOW CAN I GET
## RID OF MICE?

An active cat is, of course, an effective mouse controller, but you cannot expect it to eradicate a large outdoor population of wood mice. You can use traps indoors, placed close to and at right angles to skirting boards, but you may find this control method unpleasant. Several proprietary mouse baits are available, and these newer poisons are much safer than the chemicals which used to be sold. But you must still read the label carefully and follow both the instructions and the precautions.

The prevention of damage without killing the mice is difficult. Delay planting

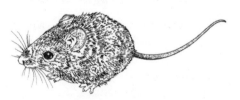

peas and beans or place prickly twigs over them, put mothballs around the crocuses and make your fruit store mouse-proof … if you can!

## WHICH MICE LIVE
## IN THE GARDEN?

The **Wood Mouse** is the basic garden type but you will occasionally find its close relative, the **Yellow-necked Field Mouse**. This species has a bright yellow patch on its chest and doesn't burrow into the ground like the wood mouse. The only other type you are likely to see in the garden is the ordinary **House Mouse** – mousy grey in colour and with a shorter tail than its outdoor-living cousins. It is never really at home in such an exposed situation where its natural enemies abound.

Man and his combine harvester have been the greatest enemy of the **Harvest Mouse** and this species has started to move into the allotment for refuge. The **Dormouse**, beloved by Victorian children, is now rare.

## WHERE DO GARDEN MICE LIVE?

The home of wood mice is a series of underground tunnels which they burrow below hedges or under outdoor buildings. These tunnels may be 60 cm below the surface, and here they breed (up to 4 litters during the summer months), sleep and store their food. Unlike dormice they do not hibernate, and your house may be used as their winter quarters. The usual points

of entry are the eaves, which they reach by climbing up shrubs and trellis on the walls of the house. You can't keep them out but they will not enter if a family of house mice is already in residence.

## DO MICE DO ANY HARM?

Stored vegetables, fruit and bulbs are the prime targets. The smell of apples neatly wrapped and boxed is irresistible to the wood mouse, and all the produce may be fouled even though little is eaten.

Stored potatoes and carrots are nibbled, crocus and hyacinth bulbs are damaged and large seeds are scraped out of their drills and devoured. Strawberries are pulled off the plants and both trees and bushes are scaled in the quest for fruit and nuts. Wood mice must therefore be regarded as serious garden pests, although most people are prepared to live with them provided they stay out of the house.

# GARDEN TITS

⟨⟩

*THE TWO* favourite garden birds are the robins and the tits – the robins for their friendliness and the tits for their antics. Both are most noticeable in the winter when so much of the garden is still, and the place to watch the tits is at the bird table. Hang up a string bag or wire tube filled with peanuts, or suspend a piece of wire with a lump of fat at the end, and watch them swing upside-down as they feed.

The two commonest garden tits are the blue tit and the great tit. Many hundreds may pass through the garden during the year but only a few are present at one time. During the spring and summer a vast quantity of insect pests are devoured – about 10,000 caterpillars are taken back to feed the young in a single nest. Tits are certainly birds to be encouraged!

## SHOULD NESTING BOXES BE PROVIDED?

Throughout the winter, tits look for holes in walls and trees which could make satisfactory nesting sites in the spring. Nesting boxes are available for hanging up in the garden – you may be able to buy one at your garden shop or you can make one by following the rules laid down by the Royal Society for the Protection of Birds. The entrance hole must be 3 cm across, there must be no perch outside the hole and the box should be placed at least 2 m above the ground.

It does seem a great kindness to provide such a nesting box but it may not be so. Caterpillars are much less common in gardens than in woodland, and the chick deaths in a garden nesting box are many times greater than in a natural nest in the countryside. Maybe our job should be to provide food in winter and not a nest in spring.

## What do Garden Tits Eat?

Tits occasionally eat fruit buds and berries, but their main diet consists of aphids, beetles, caterpillars, spiders and slugs. In autumn they search for seeds – the great tit can break open a hazelnut. In winter food is scarce, and they will readily descend on a well-stocked bird table.

The great tit is aggressive and noisy, driving other birds away from the fat or cheese on the table. The blue tit is also quarrelsome, but is more willing to move off to a hanging feeder where it can eat in peace. Feeding all year round is now the accepted recommendation, but during the breeding season young chicks need grubs, not cheese.

(11 cm) has a bright blue crown and a black eye-stripe – the **Great Tit** (14 cm) has a black and white head and a black stripe down its chest. The **Coal Tit** (11 cm) is less common and is quite different – the body is grey and buff.

## When did Tits first Learn to Drink Milk from the Bottle?

Nobody knows for certain when the first tit learnt to drink the cream from the milk bottle on a doorstep. The first recorded instance of a tit tearing off the cardboard top was in Southampton in 1921 – many hundreds of sightings were reported in 1949 and today it is a commonplace occurrence. Tits are active and inquisitive and tearing away a cardboard cap to get to food below is perhaps not surprising – tits tear bark to get to the hidden insects. The introduction of the foil top made cream-stealing even easier, and the technique would have been quickly learnt and spread by other tits watching the milk-drinking pioneer.

## How do You Tell the Garden Tits Apart?

The two commonest garden tits are rather similar, with yellow breasts and blue wings. Look closely at their heads – the **Blue Tit**

# THE HEDGEHOG

ITTING OUT on a summer evening you may hear grunting noises coming from the herbaceous border or from beneath the shrubs. A hedgehog is at work, and occasionally it will stray on to the lawn in daytime, much to the delight of the children.

But hedgehogs are creatures of the night, and they prefer untidy gardens to neat ones. Between dusk and dawn they rummage amongst fallen leaves and debris searching for food, relying on a keen sense of smell to detect their prey.

They are inoffensive creatures with surprising habits. They can climb walls and trees and then drop to the ground as a rolled-up ball. They anoint themselves with their own spittle and occasionally run around in circles for hours … and nobody knows why. Their eyesight is poor and they become immobile when frightened – the dead ones on our roads show that the poor hedgehog was not designed for the motor car age, and so does not always live out its normal life-span of about seven years.

## ARE HEDGEHOGS FRIENDS OR FOES?

Our ancestors were in no doubt – hedgehogs were pests. In the 16th century a price was put on their heads and up to the last century they were killed on sight. It was believed that they ate eggs (which is occasionally true) and attacked chickens (which is false). The most serious charge was that they milked cows, which is also false. Wet teats may be licked and it seems that beetles crawling on the teats and udders may be eaten, as tiny teeth marks are occasionally found.

These days the hedgehog is known as the gardener's friend, devouring slugs,

cutworms, beetles, caterpillars and mice. It can also kill an adder – a remarkable feat for our apparently inoffensive garden hedgehog!

## Can Hedgehogs be Kept as Pets?

They are not suitable as pets to fondle or to keep in a confined space – hedgehogs are infested with fleas and can carry the bacteria responsible for food poisoning. Their wanderings each night can stretch for miles and they are not territorial – their paths can cross without leading to serious conflict.

Because of their pest-destroying activity it is a good idea to put yourself on the night-calling route – a pet for the garden if not for you. If you see or hear one, put out a saucer of water or some tinned pet food in the evening. It will soon learn to call and will resume the habit after hibernation.

## Where do Hedgehogs Go in the Wintertime?

In October the hedgehog looks for a place to hibernate. The favourite spot is in a pile of leaves under a hedge and there it will stay, hardly breathing, until March or April when it will resume active life once again.

Before going into its deep winter sleep it is essential for the hedgehog to build up its reserves. For this reason late summer is a time of intense activity, and this is the time when you are most likely to see them feeding during the daytime. Feeding may continue until early December if the weather is mild but by midwinter they are all fast asleep. When you are working in the garden at this time you may hear the characteristic snore of the hibernating hedgehog. Do not disturb or the creature will wake and wander off to find a new home, and its vital energy reserves may be exhausted as a result.

## What are the Spines for?

Self-protection is an obvious purpose. When a hedgehog is at peace with the world the spines lie flat on its back. When disturbed the spines become erect, a sharp deterrent against a would-be attacker. Hedgehogs sometimes jump upwards when touched, but a much more usual response to real danger is for the animal to roll into a tight ball for protection – a spiky but not completely protected mouthful.

Spines also have a less obvious function – they provide a soft blanket to deaden the fall when hedgehogs drop to the ground. They are fearless climbers and have been known to fall more than 6 m without injury.

> How fair is a garden amid the trials and passions of existence.
>
> *Benjamin Disraeli*

# THE MOLE

———◦————

IT IS hard to believe that a creature so small could cause so much trouble. The mole is about 20 cm long, covered in black velvety fur and bearing powerful, shovel-like front feet. Just one of them straying on to your lawn in spring can turn it into an eyesore in a week or two.

The mole is not blind and it occasionally comes to the surface, but it spends most of its life underground hunting for worms. An underground larder is created to store food for a rainy day and its appetite is enormous. It hunts throughout the day and night with only short periods of rest – a solitary animal which hates its fellow moles almost as much as we hate them.

## WHAT DAMAGE IS CAUSED BY MOLES?

A mole will disturb the plants in beds and borders but the most serious damage is to lawns. It tunnels below the surface to create feeding runs and its speed of excavation is amazing – it can move 14 kg of earth in an hour.

The earth is forced to the surface and there forms a molehill. If the tunnel is close to the surface an extra problem arises – a ridge is formed in the lawn directly above the tunnel, and this ridge can collapse. If the soil is rich in worms the creation of tunnels and molehills may stop after a few days.

The mole moves along its tunnel system looking for worms – excess ones are stored after their heads have been bitten off to prevent escape. Occasionally a mole will come to the surface – in the morning you will find the shallow trench it has gouged out in the turf.

## WHY ARE SOME GARDENS ATTACKED WHILE OTHERS ESCAPE?

Moles thrive in woods and grassland where the soil is undisturbed – if your garden borders such an area you can expect trouble. The mole's diet consists mainly of earthworms with a sprinkling of slugs and leatherjackets. Obviously lawns with a high worm population are a prime target

whereas poor, acid soils are rarely invaded by moles.

Small gardens are usually avoided because moles are deterred by above-ground activity, such as people walking on the lawn or along nearby paths. Their favourite garden home is an extensive lawn with an adjacent orchard or shrubbery.

## How can I get Rid of Moles?

Once the tell-tale signs of mole activity have appeared it would seem a simple matter to get rid of the underground pest. After all, you can see the area of activity and it can't be all that far below the surface.

In fact, it is extremely difficult to drive off or kill a mole. There are mole smokes which you can light and insert below the hills and along the runs. All sorts of concoctions have been recommended – burning rags, disinfectant, creosote, old kippers and so on, but they are of little or no use. Buying a cat is claimed to be an effective method – the sound and smell of a cat scratching above the tunnels seems to have driven off moles in a few cases. The most effective device is the battery-operated sonic deterrent. This is inserted into the mole run and the vibration it produces is claimed to drive the pests away.

Undoubtedly the best method is to set out to kill the offending creature. Mole traps are available, and it is a good idea to use a trained mole catcher for this job … provided you can find one! If you decide to use poison then you should certainly call in an expert.

> What would become of the garden if the gardener treated all the weeds and slugs and birds and trespassers as he would like to be treated?
>
> *T. H. Huxley*

# THE SECRET LIFE OF
# FROGS AND TOADS

*O*NCE FROGS were plentiful and now they are not. At the beginning of the last century they were a common sight in both country areas and urban gardens, and each spring innumerable ponds were choked with spawn. Then the population began to decrease steadily and by 1950 frogs had disappeared from many areas.

It has always been a hard life for frogs and toads. Only a small percentage of tadpoles escape the effects of predators such as fish, birds and water insects. The survivors become frogs or toads which then have to face up to the danger from hedgehogs, rats, birds, snakes and so on. To maintain some sort of balance they have a prodigious breeding rate (a female frog lays about 2000 eggs in spring) and have evolved various defence mechanisms (skin which can change colour, the poisonous warts of the toad, etc.). As a result there has been a fairly constant population over the ages. It is the increased activity of humans in recent years which has changed the balance and has threatened their survival.

## WHERE DO FROGS AND TOADS COME FROM?

In summer the small frogs and toads leave the ponds in which they were born. At first they do not move far away from the water, but later they may wander to gardens which are well away from pools or streams. They mature slowly – a frog is three years old before it starts to breed.

In October they prepare for hibernation. Frogs choose the mud at the bottom of ponds or ditches; toads prefer to hide in

holes in the earth or under a pile of leaves. When they awaken in early spring the call of the water is irresistible, and nobody has ever discovered the magnet which draws them to the ponds or pools where mating takes place. Frogs are content to move to shallow pools or ditches, but toads require deeper water. Once in the water the frogs and toads find their voice, calling out to make it quite clear to which sex they belong.

Eggs are laid with a jelly-like covering. Large shapeless masses of these eggs are produced by frogs; toads lay long ribbons of jelly-coated eggs. In May or June the tadpoles emerge. The garden pond these days has become an important breeding ground – the main enemy here is the goldfish. Some vegetation must be present for survival, and a series of changes (metamorphoses) transform the tadpoles into frogs or toads. The complex life cycle has been completed and the 1 cm frogs hop on to the bank in July to face a hostile world.

## What is the Difference Between a Frog and a Toad?

### Common Frog

- 8 cm long
- Various skin colours, marbled black or brown
- Other frog species are much less common in gardens
- You may see the edible frog
- Smooth, moist skin
- Angular body
- Dark marking behind the eye
- Moves in a series of leaps, up to 15 cm in length
- Tadpoles have a pointed tip
- Long and powerful hind legs

### Common Toad

- 8 cm long
- Skin colour brown, olive or grey
- Other toad species are much less common in gardens
- You may see the midwife toad
- Warty, dry skin
- Squat, rounded body
- No dark marking behind the eye
- Moves with a clumsy, ambling gait, hops are very feeble
- Tadpoles have a rounded tip
- Hind legs shorter and less powerful

## WHERE HAVE ALL THE FROGS GONE?

Countless ponds which used to provide children with frog spawn in the spring are now quite bare. The sudden disappearance of frogs in so many places has been due to the effects of modern farming practices and increased urbanisation. Field drainage has increased and much natural water is now managed. Watercourses may be polluted – the favourite reason given by conservationists – but there is evidence that the early decrease in the frog population before World War II may have been due to another reason. The spawn-collecting forays by every school and college to obtain specimens for teaching and laboratory purposes seriously reduced frog numbers.

## WHAT DO FROGS AND TOADS EAT?

Their diet changes with age. Feeding tadpoles eat tiny water fleas, and young frogs live on greenfly. The adult frog flicks out its long and sticky tongue to catch flies or snails. If a worm is caught, the frog rubs off the dirt with its fingers as it is being swallowed. Frogs usually look upwards for their food but toads stalk their prey on the ground – a spider or woodlouse is caught by the toad's agile tongue and swallowed whole in a fraction of a second. Because slugs, snails and greenfly are part of the frog's diet, it is usually regarded as the gardener's friend. Obviously it must be of some help in keeping down the pest population, but the numbers eaten are far too small to have any real effect.

> Give a man the secure possession of a bleak rock, and he will turn it into a garden; give him a nine years' lease of a garden, and he will convert it into a desert.
>
> *Arthur Young*

# THE SECRET LIFE
# OF THE GARDEN BEE

BEES DO nothing but good in the garden … which is not always true. Bees will sting you for no reason at all … which is never true. Obviously the bees in the garden have their secrets.

The two types of bee you are most likely to see are the honey bee and the bumble (or humble) bee. They both help the gardener by taking pollen from one plant to another, but the heavy bumble bee can sometimes damage delicate flowers which may make it a pest for the exhibitor.

Both of these familiar insects are known as social bees because they live in organised communities. Two other garden types are referred to as solitary bees because each individual lives in its own tunnel in the ground, hollow stem or crevice. They pollinate flowers, like other bees, but they are pests – the leaf-cutter bee cuts pieces out of the leaves of roses, rhododendrons etc. and the mining bee lives in the lawn, raising conical piles of earth.

## WHY DO BEES STING?

A bee will only sting you if it is provoked. It will not attack if you are standing close, but bees are irritated when you swing your arms wildly to drive them off. If you are frightened, just walk away. Honey bees are most easily provoked when a thunderstorm is threatening.

The sting from a worker honey bee is a case of 'this hurts me more than it hurts you'. The sting remains in the flesh and the bee dies soon afterwards. Obviously this

defensive mechanism was evolved to protect the hive and not the individual.

# Honey Bee

The usual home is a nearby hive, but there may be a nest in a tree. Colonies are usually large – average 50,000 bees of which the vast majority are workers.

**Queen**
fertile female – lays eggs. More than 1,000 eggs may be laid in a single day. Usual life span is a year.

**Worker**
sterile female – collects food, builds honeycomb, cares for larvae. This is the type you see in the garden.
**Drone**
male – fertilises queen. Reared only when food is plentiful. Driven out to die at the end of the season.

# Bumble Bee

The usual home is in grassland. Colonies are small – average 30–150 bees.

## How do Honey Bees Talk to Each Other?

The returning messenger bee performs a dance against the face of the honeycomb which is then decoded by the other worker bees which fly off in the direction indicated.

| Figure-of-eight dance | Body moves upwards during the 'waggle' part of the dance | Figure-of-eight dance is at an angle of 20° | Scent on the body of the messenger bee |
|---|---|---|---|
|  |  |  |  |
| *'I have found a fresh source of food more than 90 m away'* | *'The source of food is towards the sun'* | *'The source of food is 20° to the right of the sun'* | *'Only pick up nectar with the scent I have brought back'* |
| Note: If the food is closer than 90 m, the dance is a circular one. | Note: The duration of the body movements indicates the distance of the food source. | | |

# THE SECRET LIFE OF THE GARDEN BUTTERFLY

*W*E ALL have a soft spot for butterflies and remember the warm summer days of our childhood when we watched them flit from flower to flower. They were so much more abundant then … or were they? This controversial subject is discussed on page 206, but most other facts about butterflies are firmly established, if somewhat surprising.

Their antennae, for instance, are not 'feelers' at all – they are organs of smell. The coiled proboscis under the butterfly's head is unwound at feeding time – drinking in nectar from flowers in spring and summer. Some types drink the juice from rotting apples and pears in autumn, and they *do* get drunk on the fermented brew!

Surprise follows surprise. Butterflies can be remarkably long-lived, despite the 'one day of life' legend. If not killed by birds, mice, wasps, spiders or human collectors they survive for ten days to ten months, depending on the species. There are about 70 species classed as British, although some travel here in summer. The Monarch comes all the way from America, and nobody is certain how it gets here.

## HOW DO YOU TELL THE GARDEN BUTTERFLIES APART?

About a dozen species are commonly seen in gardens, although a much larger number may drift in occasionally from surrounding fields or woodland. The male butterfly is generally the one illustrated for identification purposes, as he usually has the bolder colours and is sometimes the one which gave rise to the common name. For instance, the female of the Common Blue is brown – it is the male which is shining blue.

The adults of the **Brimstone** hibernate in the leaves of evergreens over winter, emerging in the early spring. Eggs are laid on buckthorn. **Cabbage Whites** are the only butterflies which are not welcome in

the garden. There are three species, fluttering in the garden in May and August and laying their eggs on members of the cabbage family in the vegetable patch and nasturtiums in the flower bed. The **Comma** hibernates over winter and appears in the spring. Later broods are seen in June and August, the caterpillars eating nettles, elms and hops. The **Common Blue** is a small butterfly which you may see in early or late summer. The **Holly Blue** is a more frequent visitor to the garden, but you probably won't be able to tell the difference. It lays its eggs on holly and ivy. The **Orange Tip** is a familiar visitor in May, flitting amongst the spring blossoms. The caterpillars feed on weeds belonging to the cabbage family. The **Painted Lady** is one of our larger bright butterflies. It arrives from N. Africa in May and lays its eggs on nettles or thistles. They are most numerous in August and a buddleia is the

## WHAT IS THE DIFFERENCE BETWEEN A GARDEN BUTTERFLY AND A GARDEN MOTH?

Butterflies and moths are separated from all other insects by having scales on their wings. They have many similarities, especially in their life cycle, but there are enough points of difference to enable you to tell them apart.

### Garden Butterfly

- Each antenna ends in a small knob
- All fly in the daytime
- Wings are usually brightly coloured
- Wings are nearly always held vertically when at rest

### Garden Moth

- Each antenna ends in a sharp point or fine 'feathers'
- Nearly all fly at night
- Wings are usually dull
- Wings are nearly always held horizontally when at rest

place to see them. The **Peacock** is equally showy with its large eye-markings on each wing. It hibernates over winter and emerges in March. Eggs are laid on nettles. The **Red Admiral** is another garden favourite, arriving from S. Europe in May but not becoming abundant until August or September. The **Small Copper** may not be as big or pretty as some other garden butterflies but it is certainly faster as it races from flower to flower. The **Small Tortoiseshell** wins the 'early bird' prize – it wakes from hibernation in January if the weather is mild. The **Wall Brown** is recognised by its eye-markings on each wing. The caterpillars feed on grasses.

## DO GARDEN CATERPILLARS TURN INTO BUTTERFLIES?

The green caterpillars on cabbages turn into Cabbage Whites, but practically all of the rest of the caterpillars in the garden turn into moths. Butterflies and moths don't just lay their eggs anywhere – they pick specific plants which provide acceptable food for the caterpillars. Butterflies choose plants in the countryside, and leaving a patch of nettles in the garden does not provide a lure. The eggs hatch to produce caterpillars, which after eating their fill pupate to produce a chrysalis or pupa. This case is usually hung from the plant or other support by silken threads, and from it the butterfly emerges.

You can attract butterflies by planting nectar-providing plants. The vital four are buddleia, Michaelmas daisy, *Sedum* and lavender – in addition there are scores of others: honesty, thyme, alyssum, primrose and so on. The reduction of weeds on our farms means that butterflies must rely more and more on gardens for their nectar.

## WHERE HAVE ALL THE BUTTERFLIES GONE?

The butterfly population has declined in some of our recent summers but naturalists argue over the cause. Modern farming is blamed by some – pesticides, hedge removal and so on are cited but these techniques may have played only a minor role in reducing the number of butterflies.

Butterflies are sun-worshippers and Britain is almost on the northern edge of their ability to survive. For some there is a reluctance to travel north of Birmingham, and only in fine summers do we see an abundance of butterflies, especially in the northern counties. Unfortunately we have had a succession of poor summers and that could be the main cause of the drop in numbers. We all remember the masses of butterflies of our youth, but psychologists tell us that we only remember fine summers.

# THE SECRET LIFE OF THE GARDEN EARTHWORM

'*I*T MAY be doubted whether there are any other animals which have played such an important part in the history of the world as these lowly organised creatures.' *The Formation of Vegetable Mould through the Action of Worms* (**Charles Darwin, 1881**)

Darwin was the first naturalist to demonstrate the invaluable role of earthworms in dragging plant remains below the soil surface, bringing organic-rich soil up to the surface and improving aeration and drainage by the creation of tunnels.

He was right — earthworms are a great help. About **90** per cent of the fallen leaves in an orchard are dragged into the soil by worms, but Darwin had an over-simple view of the role of these 'lowly organised creatures' in the creation of fertility. It is bacteria which turn raw plant remains into humus — fertile soil produces an abundance of earthworms rather than the other way round. Still, they are a vital part of the story and should be treated as friends in bed or border.

One sq. metre of fertile soil will contain more than **100** worms. Most of them will be in the upper **20** cm, but the common earthworm may have its permanent burrow a metre below the surface. It feeds underground but may come to the surface on a damp mild night, leaving its tail end firmly attached to the tunnel entrance. Light or vibrations will send it back quickly — with birds, hedgehogs, beetles and slugs to guard against. Nature has taught it to be cautious.

## CAN WORMS BE CUT IN HALF AND SURVIVE?

When worms are cut in half during digging, both pieces wriggle quite actively and many gardeners assume that the ends heal and the two halves survive. This is not so – the two halves generally die.

When the tail end of a worm is severed, new segments are formed and the worm is soon as good as new. When the head end is removed the injured worm stays immobile for about a couple of months, by which time a new head is regenerated. It then wriggles away – a born-again worm!

# How do Worms Move?

Each segment of the worm's body bears minute, hooked bristles. With these bristles the worm anchors its rear end and then pushes its front forward. In soft soil it moves between the crevices; in hard soil it eats its way through. The body becomes stretched; the worm then anchors its head end by means of its bristles and draws up its tail. In this way the worm tunnels through the soil, depositing the earth and organic matter which has passed through its body in coiled heaps known as casts. A couple of species eject these casts on the surface – the rest accumulate them in the burrows.

## How do Worms Reproduce?

Each worm bears male and female organs. It is indeed an odd creature, but self-fertilisation rarely takes place. Two worms come together, on the soil surface or underground depending on the species, and lie head to tail, covering themselves in mucus. There is an exchange of sperms after which they separate. Eggs are laid by each worm and these are collected in a membrane formed by the saddle-like clitellum. This membrane then begins to slip away, picking up the sperms as it moves over the worm's body. Once it is free, fertilisation of the eggs takes place. The membrane around the fertilised eggs forms a protective cocoon, and after a few months the baby worms emerge.

## Should Lawn Worms be Killed?

The cast-forming species in the lawn are not efficient soil aerators and the harm caused by the mounds of coiled sticky earth which they produce far outweighs any benefits. These worm casts are an eyesore when numerous but the hidden dangers are much more serious. The lawn surface is rendered uneven and fine grasses are stifled. The muddy surface is open to weed invasion. To avoid this problem, remove clippings after mowing and use a fertilizer containing sulphate of ammonia in the spring. Scatter worm casts with a besom before you mow.

I would not enter on my
   list of friends
(Though graced with polish'd
   manners and fine sense,
Yet wanting sensibility)
   the man
Who needlessly sets foot upon
   a worm.

*William Cowper*

# THE SECRET LIFE
# OF THE ROBIN

⸻ ⸺ ⸻

A NATIONWIDE SURVEY revealed that the robin is our favourite bird, and the reason is not difficult to find. When many of our songsters have deserted the garden in winter the robin is still there, resplendent in its red waistcoat and hopping jauntily in the snow. It sings almost all year round – a plaintive warbling song which is most welcome when other birds are silent.

And it is *our* robin, as the bird you see in your garden is as territorial about the area as you are. It is his (or her) garden too, and there is a special relationship between the gardener and the bird. When digging or hoeing the robin stands close by – hopping around your feet to pick up the worms and insects which are exposed, or standing on top of your spade.

Before the age of gardening the robin was a shy woodland bird. It has remained so over much of Europe, but in Britain it has become almost tame – if you buy some mealworms from the local pet shop it may feed from your hand. Bold and fearless in many ways, it is still at heart a woodland bird and does not like to venture too far away from trees and shrubs.

## IS THE ROBIN AS FRIENDLY AS IT SEEMS?

The robin enjoys human company more than any other wild bird, and it will accompany you in the garden, knock at the window and even venture through the door. It is a friendship of convenience, as people are regarded as food providers. Once it was cattle and deer which were followed for the insects exposed by their hooves – now it is people with their spades, hoes and bird tables.

This friendliness does not extend to its relatives – the robin is the most territorial and one of the most aggressive of all birds. Both males and females adopt territories which can extend up to an acre, and any red-breasted robin entering this territory will be threatened and attacked if need be – and it can be a fight to the death. Juveniles without red breasts are exempted and so are partners at breeding-time, but rival robins must stay away. Its pretty song is not an outpouring of joy – it is a warning that the territory will be defended.

Birds other than robins may be tolerated or attacked, and our red-breasted friends are generally a nuisance at a bird table – driving away other species which are trying to feed. It is a good idea to feed a robin away from the bird table. Obviously, the robin is *not* as friendly as it seems.

## DO ROBINS HAVE A NORMAL FAMILY LIFE?

Robins certainly do not have the typical family life of the British bird – the hen plays a most unusual role. She is the liberated woman of the bird world.

Both sexes look alike and the female, like the male, sings for most of the year to warn off intruders and she will fight to defend her territory. At the beginning of the year the cock robin sings to inform the females in the area that he is available, and it is the females who leave their territories to look for a suitable mate. Once paired it is the male's job to provide the food and both nest-building and incubation are left to the female.

Nests are built in sheds, garages, trees or hedges, and discarded objects may be used – kettles, biscuit tins, old boots, etc. Breeding begins as early as March or as late as June, depending on the location. About five eggs are laid and there are two or three broods a year.

## FEEDING GARDEN BIRDS

These days the advice is to feed all year round, not just in winter. Continue when you start – the birds will come to rely on you. Many food types are available – obtain a copy of a bird care catalogue from your garden centre. A mixed diet is best – each bird type has its own preferences.

On the bird table spread out food so that a number of birds can feed at the same time. Provide bacon fat, proprietary wild bird food and nuts, worms and cheese – avoid salted peanuts, white bread and uncooked meat. Some birds, such as thrushes, robins and dunnocks, prefer to feed at ground level.

# SLUGS AND SNAILS

$S$NAILS CAME first – somewhere along the evolutionary path certain types lost their shells and became slugs. The slug has very few friends – even if it was not a pest its slimy body would make it repulsive to many people. The fact that it is so destructive in the vegetable garden brands it as Enemy Number One to most gardeners.

Snails are rather less common and do not occur at all on soils with a high sand content. Both slugs and snails move by means of powerful muscles on the foot, and progress is eased by secretion of mucus. This mucus when dry forms the familiar slime trail. Neither can stand dryness nor extremes of temperature – the snail retreats into its shell and seals up its trapdoor, the slug hides under debris or burrows into the soil. They are simple souls – there is no internal skeleton and both male and female organs are present. Beetles, hedgehogs and frogs seek them for food and thrushes crack open the shells of snails. We are fond of their close relatives, the sea shells, but in the garden they are outcasts.

## WHERE DO SLUGS AND SNAILS LIVE?

Most slugs and snails are surface feeders, crawling over the ground when it is mild and damp but hiding under rubbish, stones, wood, etc. when it is dry. Nearly all species shelter in the nearest suitable spot when conditions are unfavourable, but the garden snail has a home to which it returns after feeding. Some slugs, such as *Milax*, spend most of their lives underground and are a menace in the potato patch.

## Do they all Harm Plants?

About 30 species of slugs and snails are found in gardens but not all of them are pests. Some of the snails are carnivorous, eating worms and insects, and others eat dead vegetable matter and fungi. A few snails, however, are a nuisance. The **Common Snail** with its tortoiseshell cover is the most widespread and the smaller **Strawberry Snail** with its appetite for nearly all garden plants is the least welcome. The **Banded Snail** cannot make up its mind – it usually eats weeds and grass but will turn to the lettuces for variety.

The slugs with small shells on their tails live on earthworms. The **Great Grey Slug** grows up to 20 cm long but is harmless to

plants, and the **Large Black Slug** eats decaying vegetable matter as its first choice and does not do a great deal of harm. It is the smaller slugs you have to worry about – the 2.5 cm **Netted Slug**, coloured white and pale brown, is a menace and the 2.5 cm **Garden Slug**, dark grey with an orange foot, attacks vegetables both above and below ground.

## How do Slugs and Snails Eat?

On the underside of its head the slug or snail bears a rasp-like tongue. This carries rows of tiny, claw-like teeth and this organ, the radula, is used to scrape away at leaves, stems, fruit, tubers, worms or other food sources. The teeth wear out but the radula continues to grow.

## How do I get Rid of Them?

Everybody agrees that you should clear away rubbish such as broken pots, old wood, etc. If hiding places like these do occur near to susceptible plants, turn them over on a dry day and kill the pests sheltering underneath.

Not everybody agrees that you should remove dead vegetable leaves – some naturalists believe that attacks on garden plants are worse when there is an absence of decaying vegetation. To get rid of slugs and snails you can sink jam jars of beer into the soil or go slug hunting with a flashlight and pointed stick at night. Some gardeners scatter slug pellets around the plants to be protected. If you do use pellets then read the instructions and precautions, and remember to spread them very thinly and not in mounds.

# THE SQUIRREL

NEIGHBOURS FALL out over squirrels. To some people the grey squirrels romping on the lawn or leaping through the trees are the most likeable of all garden animals. They are tempted with titbits to come to the back door and even feed from the hand ... and they are treated like pets.

You mustn't try to keep a squirrel as a pet – you would be breaking the law. It has no friends in high places and it is classed as a serious pest. So your neighbour who doesn't like them is right to some extent, although in the average garden they do little harm. People who enjoy watching them remain in the majority and as there is no prolonged period of hibernation they can be seen during any month of the year. But the population of squirrels continues to increase, and soon we may have to regard them a little less kindly.

## WHERE HAVE THE RED SQUIRRELS GONE?

Until quite recently there were only red squirrels in Britain. In 1876 the grey squirrel was introduced to the London area from America, and within a century this species had spread to nearly every part of the country.

Now the grey squirrel is a familiar sight and the native red one is rare – you will have to go to the coniferous forests to find it. The idea that the aggressive grey squirrel simply killed off the weaker red squirrel is not correct. The reds were declining due to disease before the grey arrived and the much more adaptable greys simply took over their feeding places. Once the greys were established the reds were not allowed back, and so they have

had to content themselves with the pine forests – grey squirrels cannot thrive on cones alone.

## Are Squirrels Really a Nuisance?

Rather sadly, the squirrel is a pest. About 70 years ago foresters began to realise that the grey squirrel was damaging tree plantations and today large areas of beech, sycamore and pine are attacked. The list of troubles caused by squirrels is a depressingly long one – bulbs dug up, soft fruit eaten, tree bark damaged, herbaceous plants stripped, bird tables robbed and so on.

You can obtain advice on the various legal ways of killing them as unlike bats they are not protected animals, but it would be sad indeed if gardeners felt that there should be no more romping squirrels to amuse the children.

## What do Squirrels Eat?

Squirrels live in a tree nest called a drey. Around this area they may not like visitors, but they are not aggressively territorial – they quite happily share feeding areas. They move several hundred yards away from the drey in search of nuts and other items of diet – the favourite foods are acorns, beechmasts, chestnuts, hazelnuts, fungi, eggs and fruit when they can find it.

Many books talk about squirrels collecting nuts in autumn for the winter to

come. It seems that squirrels are not really that intelligent as they bury food if it is plentiful at any time of the year. Nuts are most abundant in the autumn and that is why caches of them are created shortly before winter.

## How does a Squirrel Use its Tail?

The grey squirrel can beat its red-coloured relative at most things, but not in the quality of its tail. The red squirrel's tail is much bushier, and there are three basic uses for this part of the squirrel's anatomy. It is used by the red squirrel for heat regulation (a warm fur wrap in winter and an insulating blanket in summer) and it is used by all squirrels as a balancing rod.

The third use is a signalling device. At the first sign of danger the tail is raised and if it threatens another squirrel the tail is moved about rapidly. Hairs are bristled to signify aggression.

> If we had a keen vision of all that is ordinary in human life, it would be like hearing the grass grow or the squirrel's heart beat.
>
> *George Eliot*

# URBAN FOXES

THE FOX was once solely an animal of the countryside and did not concern the town gardener. It was associated with hunting, with chicken stealing and with children's fables. It has, quite suddenly, become an urban animal in Britain – a phenomenon which has not occurred in the same way in the U.S. or on the Continent. Over the last 50 years the fox population in the country as a whole has hardly changed, but there has been a dramatic increase in the number of urban foxes which roam city streets at night. Quite simply, the fox has come to live in the town garden which has become a place to raise its cubs.

In London a fox has been seen in Trafalgar Square and you may have seen one in your garden – so we have a new gardening question to ask. Do foxes cause any harm?

## How do I Know if a Fox is Living in my Garden?

If a vixen is in residence in winter you will certainly be in no doubt – her blood-curdling scream at night is quite terrifying if you have not heard it before! The dog fox barks but the cubs which appear in spring are silent.

Disturbed dustbins and torn refuse bags are tell-tale clues. So is a strong, musky smell, but not all people can detect it. If you are really curious to know whether you have a fox-sensitive nose, go to the wolf cage at the zoo – it's the same smell. The favourite spot for a fox's earth is at the back

of a garden shed and your first sighting may be cubs playing in the sunshine in April or May.

## Do Foxes Cause any Harm?

Foxes have a varied diet – they eat chickens, rabbits, rats, mice, squirrels and hedgehogs. They are excellent hunters, stalking their prey at night and using their highly developed senses of sight, smell and hearing.

Despite their reputation, they do not kill cats. A fox will only attack a very young or infirm cat – a healthy adult would be a dangerous opponent. The nuisance caused by a fox is nothing to do with damage to plants – it is you they disturb with their noise at night and by scattering the contents of the dustbin.

## WHY HAVE FOXES COME INTO TOWN?

The drastic reduction of the rural rabbit population by disease some years ago forced the fox to look for another source of food. Rats and mice are highly acceptable, and so foxes began to choose railway embankments as a place to build their earths. They followed the lines of the tracks to towns where mice were plentiful.

In the towns there was another food source – the household dustbin. It seems we are throwing away more scraps than ever, and the amount put into refuse bags, bins etc. has been sufficient to persuade the fox to come and live amongst us. But this animal is not really becoming domesticated – large gardens are preferred where the scent of human beings is not strong.

## HOW CAN I GET RID OF A FOX?

Once a fox and its family have decided that your garden is a good place to live, it is very difficult to persuade them to go. Merely filling up the tunnel of the earth and sprinkling an evil-smelling deterrent over it will be of very little use. A fox has an acute sense of smell and will easily pick up the scent of its old home. In a single night the soil you have added will be removed and the tunnel restored.

---

The favourite spot for a fox's earth is at the back of a garden shed

---

If the earth is in the open garden you can plant prickly shrubs such as *Berberis* over the area. It is more likely that the fox's earth is under the garden shed – you can try laying paving stones over the filled-in entrance.

# THINGS TO DO INDOORS

THINGS FOR the plant lover to do indoors when the weather is cold and the soil is waterlogged usually centre around house plants. This is as it should be, and many beautiful specimens are grown with loving care. But it is a shame that the design sense we use to group shrubs, flowers or roses together to produce a pleasing bed or border outdoors seems to evaporate when we turn our hand to indoor gardening. Pots are placed singly on windowsills, sideboards, table tops and in room corners without any attempt to create an indoor garden.

Pot plants are more attractive and certainly less trouble when they are grouped together. You can do this by setting the pots in a large planter but there are other ways. You can create a pot-et-fleur (page 229) which incorporates cut flowers or you can make a bromeliad tree by wiring small bare-rooted specimens (*Cryptanthus, Vriesia* etc.) to an old dead branch or piece of driftwood. If you want to cut down on watering and at the same time increase the chance of success with delicate varieties, then try a terrarium (page 231). Your indoor gardening need not be restricted to purely decorative plants – salad pots made from margarine tubs can supply saladings and herbs on the windowsill (page 225) when the vegetable plot outdoors is snowbound.

For some keen gardeners the winter months are the interval between one season's enjoyment and the next. House plants and flower hobbies are not for them – instead winter is a time for preparation – there are tools to mend or buy, catalogues to study (page 242), geraniums to over-winter (page 226), greenhouse crops to care for and seeds to order. For the flower arranger, however, the winter months involve the same activity as the summer season – there are attractive floral displays to create. The supply of material from the garden is limited once the growing season is over, so a supply of glycerine-preserved foliage (page 240), skeletonised leaves (page 222) and dried flowers (page 223) should be produced before the cold weather comes. A novelty to try at any time of the year is the vein-dyeing of pastel flowers with bright colours (page 224).

The normal course of events outdoors is to watch the flower buds swell, admire the open blooms, cut a few for the house if they are sufficiently attractive and then, once the season is over, wait until the cycle starts again next year. Roses form buds, bloom for our delight and then are dead-headed for the compost heap. This pattern is not inevitable as there are other things we can do with the flowers  and some of the leaves from the ornamental garden. A few of these flower hobbies and crafts may appeal but some will certainly not – it would be odd indeed if you wanted to try *all* the ideas described in this section!

First of all, you can put your plants to a practical use. They can be turned into food or drink – there are flower wines (page 236) which are easy to make and you can crystallise petals (page 221) for use on cakes or desserts. For the adventurous there are recipes using flowers (page 247) and weeds (page 219). This may sound odd, but nettles and ground elder were being cooked and eaten when tomatoes were still regarded as a poisonous fruit. Just one word of warning: do not cook and eat flowers, leaves or fruits which you can't identify and for which you do not have a recipe.

If food from the flower garden does not appeal, you can try to capture the fragrance. Where there is a plentiful supply of rose petals or other sweet-smelling flowers, the choice is between pot-pourri (page 238), flower perfumes (page 234) and herb pillows (page 228). If you do not have enough fragrant flowers but would still like a natural fragrance indoors, try your hand at a pomander using an orange, cloves and cinnamon (page 297).

You can be practical by making flower food, wine, perfumes or even cosmetics (page 232), or you may prefer to be artistic and create a pressed flower picture (page 241) or fern print (page 246). A large rag-bag of things to do indoors – enough to convince you that a love affair with flowers can be a year-round activity. There are so many things to do when the snow is on the ground … or when the sun is shining and you are feeling lazy.

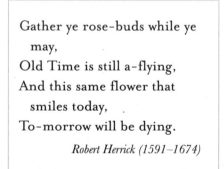

Gather ye rose-buds while ye
  may,
Old Time is still a-flying,
And this same flower that
  smiles today,
To-morrow will be dying.

*Robert Herrick (1591–1674)*

# HOW TO COOK WEEDS

## NETTLE SOUP, DANDELION COFFEE

USING WEEDS in the kitchen provides a double source of satisfaction – there is the chance to enjoy a new flavour and they are obtained free of charge. We do not have to buy them in the store nor do we have to cultivate them in the vegetable plot, but before getting too enthusiastic it is necessary to sound a note of caution.

> **Weeds can be gathered from your garden but picking wild plants in the countryside is now illegal**

Despite the enthusiasm of some self-sufficiency writers the flavours tend to be commonplace, and you must only cook weeds which you can identify and for which you have read a recommend-ation. On these pages only common garden weeds are considered although scores of wild plants can be used for cooking.

Weeds can be gathered from your garden but picking wild plants in the countryside is now illegal. Do not use plants which have been sprayed, and wash all the leaves and stems thoroughly before use. With these points in mind, you can now safely try the taste of the weeds which bedevil the beds and borders.

Stinging nettles have been used as a foodstuff since time immemorial, and there is evidence that they were once cultivated for the kitchen. Pick young shoots (using gloves, of course) before the

end of May – mature nettles have a bitter taste and laxative effect. Cook the young nettle shoots like spinach. **Nettle Soup** has a long history and has served as part of the staple diet in times of harvest failure. The Irish version contains oatmeal but the English version is simpler. Boil nettle shoots for about 15 minutes and then reduce to a purée in a food mixer. Stir 30 g of flour with a little melted butter and blend with 600 ml of milk or stock. Bring this liquid to the boil and add a cupful of the nettle purée. Cook slowly for about 5 minutes. **Nettle Porridge** is made by adding finely chopped and boiled nettles to an oatmeal gruel – Pepys recorded eating it and the Irish peasant survived on it during the Great Potato Famine.

> A weed is no more than a flower in disguise.
>
> *J. R. Lowell*

Dandelions, like nettles, are common weeds which have a place in the kitchen. You can grow cultivated varieties but it is much easier to pick young leaves from the heart of the weeds in your garden and serve them raw and chopped in salads and sandwiches or cooked like spinach. Dandelions have a high mineral and vitamin content but whether they clean your blood, improve the gall bladder and prevent kidney stones is a matter of debate. **Dandelion Coffee** is sometimes recommended as a caffeine-free substitute

– wash the roots and let them dry in the sun. Roast in the oven until they are brown and crisp, then grind and use in the ordinary way.

It is hard to believe that anyone should wish to grow Ground elder but it was cultivated as a vegetable in medieval times. It is cooked like spinach and has a strong and unusual flavour. Cooked plantain leaves also have a strong taste but boiled chickweed is delicately-flavoured.

Sorrel is widely cultivated in France for soups and salads. This dock-like plant grows in acid soil and if it infests your garden try making **Sorrel Soup** from the young leaves. Fry a cupful of sorrel leaves together with a chopped onion in butter until they are soft but not brown. Stir in the contents of a can of cream of chicken soup and cook according to the instructions. You can start from scratch and use chicken broth and cream, but there is a danger of curdling.

# HOW TO
# CRYSTALLISE FLOWERS

## GROW YOUR OWN CAKE DECORATIONS

CRYSTALLISED flower petals are widely used for decorating the tops of cakes, trifles and other desserts. Our source for these sweetmeats is the supermarket and not the garden, but it was different in earlier times.

Roses are now grown for their beauty outdoors and in flower arrangements, but they used to have to work for a living. Nicholas Culpeper wrote in his *Herball* that 'of red roses are usually made many compositions, all serving to sundry good uses'.

Pick a number of roses in full bloom – they need not be red ones. Make sure that the petals are clean, fresh and disease-free – they should not have been sprayed with a pesticide.

Beat the whites of two eggs in a bowl until they begin to stiffen. In another bowl place a cupful of caster sugar. Remove each rose petal gently from the dry blooms with a pair of tweezers, and dip it first into the frothy egg whites and then into the sugar. You should ensure that each petal is fully coated but avoid an excess of either egg white or sugar.

Lay the petals on a lined baking tray, ensuring that they do not touch each other. Put the tray in an airing cupboard for about 24 hours, by which time the petals should be crisp and brittle. Store them between sheets of grease-proof paper in an airtight tin. Properly stored they will keep indefinitely.

Rose petals are not the only plant material you can use. Crystallised violets are equally attractive and crystallised mint leaves make an excellent accompaniment for melon or grapefruit.

Even more popular than crystallised flowers for cake decoration are the candied green stems of angelica. If you grow Garden angelica (*A. archangelica*) you can make your own. Cut the stems into pieces about 5 cm long and scrape off the outer fibrous surface. Boil them in sugar syrup until tender and then drain. Coat the segments with sugar and then simmer again until the syrup is clear. Place the angelica segments on a tray, boil the syrup to thicken it and then pour the liquid over them. Leave them to crystallise and then they are ready for use.

# HOW TO
# SKELETONISE LEAVES

## REVEALING THE NATURAL TRACERY

SKELETONISED 'magnolia' leaves are available from some florists, and they provide an attractive background feature in floral arrangements. Unfortunately they are not easy to find and the range of shapes and sizes is usually limited.

With some patience and a little luck it is possible to skeletonise leaves at home. You may be lucky enough to find naturally-skeletonised leaves half-buried in the debris beneath bushes of camellia, laurel, holly or rhododendron. It is usually necessary, however, to start from scratch.

Choose large leaves – oak, camellia, holly, laurel, maple, pear, lime or rhododendron will make suitable subjects. The leaves should be free from blemishes and they must be mature – you need old, healthy leaves.

Stir a large handful of washing soda in rainwater in an enamel saucepan and boil the leaves for about an hour. Wearing rubber gloves remove one leaf and see if you can rub off the soft green surface

under a running tap. If the soft tissue is still firmly attached, continue the boiling process for another hour.

Remove the leaves one at a time. Lay each one in turn on a piece of newspaper and scrape off all the soft tissue with the back of a knife. Rinse under a running tap and repeat the process until a clean leaf skeleton is obtained. Do not remove the next leaf from the soda solution until you have properly skeletonised the first one.

Soak each skeletonised leaf in dilute bleach and then spread them on newspaper to dry. Attractive shapes can be produced by wrapping them round a pencil or candle. After a day or two they will be ready.

The leaf stem will be weak and you will have to wind florist wire around it for support. Now you have your own home-made skeletonised leaves – a talking-point as well as a thing of beauty for your next flower arrangement.

# HOW TO DRY FLOWERS

## KEEPING THE BRIGHT FLOWERS OF SUMMER

ALL GARDENERS have seen a beautiful flower at some time or other and wished that it could be preserved for months or even years.

Of course, you can grow one of the Everlasting Flowers such as *Helichrysum*. These are cut before the blooms are fully open and hung to dry in small bunches in a cool, dark and airy place – the garage is ideal. These dried blooms are useful for the flower arranger but their button-like heads and dry, chaffy petals have neither the beauty nor the delicacy of a rose or carnation.

It is possible to dry roses, carnations and many other garden beauties but it does take patience. Choose blemish-free single or semi-double blooms and cut off the stems. When quite dry lay the flowers face upwards on a 2 cm layer of oven-dry fine sand in a biscuit tin. Leave at least 2 cm between the blooms. Slowly add more dry sand until all parts of each flower are covered. This is the skilful part of the operation and you must do it carefully. Trickle the sand gently between the petals so that every bit of the flower is covered. Finally, cover the blooms with 5 cm of sand and replace the lid. Seal it with adhesive tape.

Store the tin in a warm and dry place for three weeks. Remove the blooms gently – they should now be dry and crisp. Turn each one upside down and

> It is possible to dry roses, carnations and many other garden beauties but it does take patience

shake out the sand – remove any remaining grains with an artist's paint brush. Insert a piece of stout florist wire into the base of each bloom and cover it with green florist tape.

# HOW TO DYE
# CUT FLOWERS

## ROSES ARE RED... AND SO ARE THE DAFFODILS

A RED-VEINED daffodil or a blue-veined rose is bound to create a dramatic effect in any flower arrangement, and it will certainly be a talking point. Only you can decide whether it is 'fair' or not – such flowers would probably not be allowed at your local flower show but for home decoration there would seem to be no reason why you can't add to Nature. We all accept such changes as the blueing of hydrangeas and the grafting of roses.

---

## White or pale roses, chrysanthemums, carnations and daffodils are particularly suitable subjects

---

Buy a small bottle of food dye from your local supermarket. There are many colours available, but do choose a really strong colour such as deep red or navy blue. White

or pale roses, chrysanthemums, carnations and daffodils are particularly suitable subjects – cut the stems just below a leaf joint and place them in plain water. The blooms must be open at the time of the colour treatment – it is not suitable for flower buds.

Make up the dye solution using 30 ml of food dye to 600 ml of warm water. Add 1 teaspoonful of sugar to the solution and pour an 8 cm layer into a suitable container. Stand the flowers in this dye solution and keep an eye on them – satisfactory coloration may take as little as one or as long as 24 hours.

When the desired intensity has been reached, remove the stems from the dye solution and wash the ends under running water. Cut off the bottom 0.5 cm and the flowers can then be used in the normal way to make a floral decoration. Bloom life might be somewhat shortened by the colour treatment, but you will have an eye-catching display while it lasts.

# HOW TO GROW
# A SALAD POT

## AN ALLOTMENT ON YOUR KITCHEN WINDOWSILL

IF YOU ARE keen on herbs in cooking and also have green fingers then you can follow the advice in the gardening magazines. Have a line of flower pots on the windowsill in the kitchen and fill them

## The kitchen windowsill is an excellent place for plants

with basil, rosemary, lemon balm, sage, thyme and so on in winter time. You will be able to pick your favourite seasonings without having to trudge through the snow. The kitchen windowsill is an excellent place for plants – the air is often steamy and you can't help noticing if they are in need of water – both you and the herbs are tied to the sink!

For most people the extensive herb garden is not a good idea. Your windowsill allotment should be restricted to just a few herbs and salad crops which you eat regularly, because if the plants are left uncut they

become leggy and unattractive. So don't be too ambitious at the start. Fill a few margarine tubs with seed compost – the pressed-down surface should be about 1 cm below the rim. The basic allotment consists of a mint pot (plant a rooted clump from the garden), parsley (sow seed), chives (again a clump from the garden or garden centre) and spring onions (sow seed). Water in the plants or seeds, and when they are growing water once or twice a week – or when they are beginning to flag.

Cut the mint, parsley or chives as required and pull the spring onions. Don't forget to mist the leaves two or three times a week. From these simple beginnings you can become more adventurous. Lettuce growing is the next step – raise the seedlings in yoghurt tubs and then transfer them to a wide and shallow plastic container. If you have space for a 15 cm pot you can grow a miniature tomato – Tiny Tim is the usual choice but Minibel is better.

# HOW TO KEEP GERANIUMS OVER WINTER

## THEY REALLY ARE TOO COSTLY TO THROW AWAY!

GERANIUMS remain a fundamental part of our summer bedding schemes. The bold umbels of red, pink and white flowers are seen in gardens, window boxes and balconies everywhere, but, as any botanist will tell you, the bedding 'geranium' is not a geranium at all; it is the Zonal pelargonium. Look closely at the leaves – you will see a distinct horseshoe marking or zone in nearly all varieties.

The Ivy-leaved pelargoniums are less popular but are no less useful, drooping

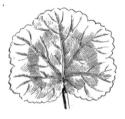

over window boxes and clothing hanging baskets. Unfortunately you cannot expect these geraniums to survive the average British winter – not for us the impressive perennial displays of shrubby geraniums which clothe balconies and even hillsides in more favoured climes.

Just because they are frost-sensitive does not mean that bedding geraniums should be thrown away at the end of the summer – they are far too expensive for that. Before the first frosts arrive dig out the plants and shake off the soil around the roots. Pot them up singly in seed and cutting compost, using pots which are no larger than necessary to house the roots.

Reduce the height of the stems by about a half and cut off yellowing leaves and dead flower-heads.

Put the pots in an unheated spare room or in a cold greenhouse. The plants will be exhausted after their summer-long activity

> As for our love of gardens,
> it is the last refuge of art in
> the minds and souls of
> many Englishmen: if we did
> not care for gardens, I
> hardly know in what way of
> beauty we should care for.
>
> *Sir Arthur Helps*

This standard procedure will allow you to overwinter your bedding pelargoniums and so save the expense of having to buy fresh ones in May or June. There are variations to this procedure, depending on the facilities you have available. If you own a greenhouse you can use the outdoor plants as a source of cuttings in September, which means that you can considerably increase the number of plants and so have a much larger display in the following summer.

## When spring comes the pots should be put in a well-lit spot and the amount of water should be increased

outdoors and you should not treat them as house plants to be coaxed into flowering. They need a rest and on no account should they be kept warm. Do not feed them and water only when it is essential in order to stop the leaves from flagging.

When spring comes the pots should be put in a well-lit spot and the amount of water should be increased, but do not force them into active growth by feeding and copious watering. As soon as the danger of frost has passed transplant the geraniums outside so that they can once again burst into growth and provide a summer-long display.

If on the other hand you have neither a greenhouse nor a spare room for pots of geraniums then you can try the old practice of hanging up the old plants in the garage over winter. There is some risk, of course, but you have nothing to lose. Dig up the plants before the first frosts arrive and shake all the soil off the roots. Tie a small bunch of the plants together and suspend them upside down from the roof of the garage. Dust lightly with fungicidal powder such as sulphur and leave them until the spring. Soak the roots before potting or planting outdoors.

# HOW TO MAKE
# A HOP PILLOW

## Curing Insomnia the Natural Way

THE PURPOSE of a herb pillow is to provide a soft headrest with the added advantage of a pleasant fragrance. The whole pillow can be filled with herbs, but it is more economical to place the aromatic leaves and flowers in a large muslin envelope which is then slipped between the pillow and cover. The warmth and pressure of your head increases the fragrance as time goes by, but you will probably have to renew the herbal mixture after a couple of months.

The best mixture is a matter of individual taste. Rosemary and lavender are popular ingredients, and so are thyme, marjoram and scented-leaved pelargonium. For a lemony smell you will need Lemon verbena and finely shredded lemon peel. Lady's bedstraw provides a hay-like smell and owes its name to the legend that it was the 'bedstraw' in the Manger.

There can be no doubt that the herb pillow provides a relaxing atmosphere at night, but the question of its medical value remains unresolved. A mint pillow is claimed to relieve headaches and the resin vapour arising from a pine needle pillow is supposed to clear a stuffy nose. The evidence here is not strong, but the belief that a hop pillow can relieve insomnia is much more firmly held.

The hop pillow may have changed the course of British history – the ailing George III found that he could at last enjoy a good night's sleep and so discussion

## Rosemary and lavender are popular ingredients

about the appointment of his son as Prince Regent was postponed. Of course the reason could have been his imagination, but hop cones do contain the natural tranquilliser *lupulin*. Sprinkle a little alcohol on the dried hop cones to prevent crackling in the pillow. If you suffer from insomnia it is worth a try, and the devotees claim extra benefits such as asthma relief and the removal of nervous tension.

# HOW TO MAKE
# A POT-ET-FLEUR

## LIVEN UP YOUR HOUSE PLANTS

FOR COUNTLESS people flower arranging is an absorbing hobby and their handiwork brightens up the home. For the uninitiated, and the lazy, there is much less attraction – a good deal of effort and skill is involved in producing a truly worthwhile display and it is inevitably short-lived. So they stick to growing pot plants – simple, straightforward and of course long-lived.

> You buy some flowers for
>    your table,
> You tend them tenderly as
>    you're able,
> You fetch them water from
>    hither and thither –
> What thanks do you get for it
>    all? They wither.
>
> *Samuel Hoffenstein*

## At the beginning of the year three or four daffodils against a living green backcloth look most attractive

More than 40 years ago Violet Stevenson came up with the idea of combining the two techniques. A group of foliage house plants is grown in a suitable container, and close to the front a cut-flower holder is embedded. Subsequently this tube is filled with water and used for a simple flower arrangement. This is the Pot-et-Fleur, combining the permanence and greenery of a house plant collection with the splash of temporary colour provided by a flower arrangement.

Surprisingly the idea has not become popular. The basic reason seems to be that the flower arranger finds the Pot-et-Fleur far too limiting for her skills whilst the pot plant grower finds a combined display unacceptable. It could help if we stopped regarding the Pot-et-Fleur as a hybrid. It is in fact a house plant display, and in order to brighten it up or to keep it seasonal a few flowers from the garden or the florist are popped in. At the beginning of the year three or four daffodils against a living green backcloth look most attractive. During summer a few flowers from the flower garden or shrub border are used … not a skilled arrangement, just a few strong points of colour to add interest to the pot plant group. Christmas calls for sprigs of berried holly or a small group of chrysanthemums.

---

## During summer a few flowers from the flower garden or shrub border are used

---

Choose your container carefully – it should be wide and deep. The house plants can be kept in their pots or planted directly into the compost – the essential feature is a deep layer of charcoal at the bottom of the container. At the back place the tall pinnacle plants – suitable examples are *Sansevieria*, staked ivy and *Ficus benjamina*. The list of suitable side plants is extremely long – *Begonia*, *Pilea*, *Peperomia*, *Neanthe* and so on, and the provision of trailing plants at the front of the container is essential; *Tradescantia*, *Zebrina*, trailing ivy and *Ficus pumila* are obvious choices. Between the pinnacle plants and the trailing plants insert the glass tube or metal florist tube for the cut flowers.

Try a Pot-et-Fleur – there really is no other way to display effectively two or three choice flowers from the garden unless you are a skilled flower arranger.

---

Take it from us, it is utterly forbidden to be half-hearted about gardening. You have got to *love* your garden whether you like it or not.

*Sellar & Yeatman*

# HOW TO MAKE
# A TERRARIUM

## Your own Mini-Jungle in a Fishtank

IT IS A great pity that somebody once decided to make a bottle garden out of a large carboy. The idea used to be popular – it appeared in every book on indoor gardening and it was a hardy annual in the gardening magazines, appearing at regular intervals. But planting through the narrow opening of the bottle is difficult, pruning is even more difficult and removal of dead plants is almost impossible.

The open-topped terrarium is a much better idea. You can use a large sweet jar, a giant brandy snifter or, perhaps best of all, a large fishtank. The essential features are that the glass should be clear, the container must be leak-proof and there must be a transparent cover – a lid for a jar, a sheet of glass for a fishtank.

Begin by placing a layer of gravel and charcoal at the bottom of the container and then add a 5 cm layer of seed compost. You can landscape the 'ground' into hills and valleys – use stones and pebbles if you wish but do not incorporate wood.

There is an almost limitless choice of suitable plants but do avoid cacti and succulents. It is a pity if you choose commonplace house plants for such an ideal home. Delicate ferns, crotons, *Fittonia*, *Maranta*, *Cryptanthus*, *Cordyline*, *Calathea* and *Rhoeo* will all flourish. Between the foliage plants add flowering varieties to provide splashes of colour – African violets and small orchids are ideal. Other suitable types are gloxinia and *Aphelandra* – always leave room between the plants so that they will be able to expand without becoming cramped.

When you have finished place a sheet of bevelled glass over the top. You have created a mini-jungle in which the air will always be still and moist. Plants will succeed here which might struggle in the conservatory of a skilled grower.

Stand the terrarium in a well-lit spot out of direct sunlight. If condensation on the lid is excessive, slide it open for a few hours, but keep it shut at other times. The compost should be kept slightly moist, and because of the enclosed system you will rarely have to water – once every few months at the most. Remove dead and diseased plants promptly and there is nothing else to do – this is the easiest way to grow exotic plants.

# HOW TO MAKE
# FLOWER COSMETICS

## THE FLORAL WAY TO IMPROVE YOUR SKIN

WINE MAKING at home has been a popular hobby for many years and the growing interest in herbal remedies can be seen by looking at the range of products now offered in health food shops. Home-made floral cosmetics, however, remain virtually unknown, which at first sight is rather strange.

You do not need any special equipment or skill to make simple lotions and creams, and the value of some plant extracts, such as Witch hazel, in such preparations is well established. But recipes rarely appear and there is a good reason for this lack of interest. Unlike their commercial counterparts, home-made cosmetics are often unstable as there are no added preservatives. This means that many of them can only be kept for a short time.

Do not let this deter you – if you have the flowers available, try one of the recipes for a natural skin treatment. The most important flowers for this purpose are those of the elder because of their mildly astringent properties. **Elderflower Lotion** is made by adding 220 g of fresh elderflowers to 600 ml of boiling water.

Simmer for about 60 minutes and then strain through muslin. Add a little eau-de-Cologne when cool and pour into bottles. This lotion is excellent for washing or for adding to the bath, and can be kept for about 3 weeks. You can make **Lime** or **Verbena Lotion** by substituting the appropriate flowers in the recipe for Elderflower Lotion, but these alternative lotions will only last for a few days. For an instant lotion you can use the dried chamomile flowers sold as Chamomile Tea at your local health food shop. To make **Chamomile Lotion** simply pour boiling water over a dessertspoonful of chamomile flowers in a cup. Allow it to stand for a quarter of an hour and then strain off the liquid. Use it as a skin lotion or hair rinse.

Instead of making a lotion you may prefer to produce a cream. For **Buttercup** or **Elderflower Cold Cream** add about 200 g of flowers to 200 g of unsalted lard and simmer for an hour. Strain through muslin and when cool whisk briskly to turn the mixture into a smooth cream. For fragrance pour in a little toilet water, beat again, and fill into screw-top jars. This cold cream can be used for chapped or rough hands, as it has been for generations in rural districts.

Cosmetic vinegars (skin tonics) are used to relieve dryness and itching by restoring to the skin the slightly acid coating which is removed by washing. For **Flower Skin Tonic** add a cupful of fragrant flower petals such as roses, carnations, violets or lavender to 600 ml of boiling water. Simmer for a couple of minutes and then add a cup of wine vinegar. Pour the mixture into a sealed container and allow it to stand in a warm place for about 2 weeks before straining through muslin. This tonic can be used as a lotion after bathing, a final rinse after shampooing or as a relief from sunburn.

---

For an instant lotion you can use the dried chamomile flowers sold as Chamomile Tea at your local health food shop

---

All the above recipes produce plain and simple lotions and creams which clean and soften the skin or remove the remnants of soapy film after shampooing. None of them has magical properties, but there are remarkable claims for some herbal waters made by boiling the flowers or leaves in water for about an hour. Parsley Water is supposed to remove moles and freckles, Rosemary Water strengthens the hair and Horsetail Water heals wounds and prevents brittle nails.

# HOW TO MAKE
# FLOWER PERFUME

## CAPTURING THE FRAGRANCE OF THE FLOWER GARDEN

JARS OF perfume more than 4000 years old have been found in Ancient Egyptian tombs, and since those far-off times the art of extracting perfume from flowers has been practised in countries all over the globe. It might seem that if early civilisations with no scientific knowledge could make flower scents then it should be an easy matter for people like us living in a technological age to make flower perfume at home. Sadly, this is not so.

The first problem is that large quantities of flowers are needed – many more than the average garden could provide. To make attar of roses, which is the essential essence of rose fragrance, it takes 1 hectare of roses to produce a single kilo of liquid. Secondly, we do not have the equipment at home – an efficient still is necessary. And our choice of flowers is rather limited – we have roses and lavender but the Eastern civilisations also had orange blossom, jasmine and frangipani.

Even so, you can try your hand at the ancient art of flower perfume making. The original method which was practised in Ancient Egypt and Greece was oil

extraction – they used sesame oil but you can use olive oil. The age-old recipe for **Rose Oil** is to take about 200 g of fragrant rose petals and crush them in a mortar and pestle – these days you could chop them up with a little olive oil in an electric food mixer. Add the crushed petals to 600 ml of olive oil in a covered pot, stir, and keep the mixture warm – the airing cupboard in winter or out in the sun in summer would be ideal. Stir occasionally and after a month heat the mixture to the temperature of a warm bath. Strain the liquid through a fine sieve and place it in a container with an airtight lid. Use this oil as a perfume or for making pot-pourri.

After the discovery of oil extraction came the method of boiling the flowers and condensing the steam. To make

**Lavender Water** by this distillation technique, half fill a large old kettle with water and add 500 g of lavender flowers and leaves. Fix a 1 m length of rubber tubing to the spout of the kettle and place the other end in a large jar on the floor. Submerge the middle part of the tubing in a bowl of ice-cold water on a chair – this will condense the steam passing through the tubing.

Keep the kettle on a low heat and allow it to simmer until it is nearly dry. Switch off and carefully drain the contents of the tubing into the jar. The clear liquid you have collected is Lavender Water – if you substitute fragrant rose petals for lavender flowers the resulting liquid will be **Rose Water**, which the knights returning from the Crusades brought back to Europe.

From ancient times Rose Water has been made in Persia and exported to China, India, Egypt and elsewhere. It was in Persia that **Attar of Roses** was discovered – the essential oil present in minute quantities in the petals and which gives the rose its perfume. According to legend, the Mogul Emperor of Persia in the 17th century had a canal filled with Rose Water for his new bride. As he walked in his garden he noticed an oily scum on top of the water – the heat of the sun had extracted the essence of the rose. The Empress called this exquisitely-scented oil

---

To make attar of roses it takes a hectare of roses to produce a single kilo of liquid

---

*Atar jehanghiri* (Perfume of Jehan Ghir) in honour of her husband, but it was soon called Attar of Roses and a new industry was born. Unfortunately it is quite impossible to make Attar of Roses at home, and so Rose Oil, Lavender Water and Rose Water will have to suffice. Don't expect too much – the modern perfume manufacturer uses a great deal of complex equipment and all sorts of solvents, so your efforts will certainly not match the perfumes you give or receive every Christmas.

# HOW TO MAKE FLOWER WINE

## BOTTLING THE TASTE OF THE FLOWER GARDEN

OUR ANCESTORS did not regard the making of flower wine as a symbol of self-sufficiency or as an enterprise filled with nostalgia – for them it was just one more chore required to provide the provisions in an age before the corner shop existed. They used simple materials to provide an unsophisticated brew – if you

---

### Wine making can be fun but it does take time and some skill

---

want to make homemade wine these days your best plan is to buy a book on modern wine making. You will learn about Campden tablets, airlocks, filters, fermentation jars and the rest. These aids take the risk out of wine making and ensure a better product, but of course our ancestors had none of these things.

If you would like to make a flower wine as they did in the old days, there are plenty of recipes. Perhaps the easiest is **Dandelion Wine**, once a favourite on both sides of the Atlantic. In America they called it 'bottled summer sunshine' and

drank it when the snow began to fall in the winter.

Pick 1 litre of fully open dandelion flowers and wash thoroughly. Put them in a large open container and cover with 2 litres of boiling water. Place muslin over the top and let it stand for 3 days, stirring each day. On the fourth day squeeze the flowers into the liquid and then throw them away. Add 1.5 kg of sugar and the chopped-up rinds of 3 lemons and 3 oranges. Put the mixture in a pan and boil for 30 minutes and then strain through muslin. When cool, add the juice of the oranges and lemons together with 30 g of wine yeast. Cover with muslin and let the brew stand for about 3 weeks. Filter when the bubbling has stopped and pour into wine bottles. These should be lightly corked at first – when fermentation has ceased the corks should be pushed in firmly.

You can use coltsfoot flowers instead of dandelions, but you may prefer to use the flowers from your own garden rather than hunting for weeds. To make **Rose Wine** you will need 1 litre of petals, the juice of 2 lemons and 1.5 kg of sugar stirred with 2 litres of boiling water. When lukewarm add the wine yeast and nutrient tablet you can buy from the chemist. Let the mixture stand for about a week, stirring daily. Strain through muslin and leave the brew in the earthenware crock or other container until bubbling ceases. Alternatively you can do the job properly and put it into a fermentation jar with an airlock. When fermentation stops bottle off the wine and leave for about 6 months.

Non-alcoholic **Elderflower Champagne** was once popular. The grated rind (not the pith) of a lemon and its juice are mixed with 1.5 kg of sugar and 2 tablespoonfuls of wine vinegar. Add

2 litres of cold water and 3 large heads of elderflowers – stir and let the liquid stand for 2 days. Strain through muslin and store in screw-top bottles, leaving at least a 5 cm air space at the top of the 'champagne'. Drink after 2 weeks – do not leave longer unless the bottles are sealed with wired-down corks.

Wine making can be fun but it does take time and some skill. A simple alternative is to make flower-flavoured wine – here you begin with wine or brandy and add flowers to give a distinctive taste. The best known is **Hawthorn Brandy** – fill a jar with open hawthorn flowers from which all the stalks have been removed. Cover them with brandy and let the liquid stand for about a month in a warm place. Strain through a fine sieve and bottle firmly. **Instant Rose Wine** is another example – mix 200 g of fragrant, red petals with 600 ml of hot water and squeeze through a fine sieve. Add more petals until the liquor is a rich red colour and then stir in 500 g of sugar and 300 ml of brandy. Bottle and serve as soon as you like.

# HOW TO MAKE
# POT-POURRI

## KEEPING THE SWEET SMELLS OF SUMMER

Pot-pourri is basically a mixture of dried flowers which remains fragrant for a long time. Usually it contains spices, oils, fixatives and sometimes dried leaves, and it is always welcome during the winter and spring months as a reminder of summer's fragrance.

Nowadays ready-made pot-pourri is frequently seen for sale, but this is not quite the same as preserving one's own flowers. Sadly it is now made in very few homes, as the skills and ingredients are no longer found.

> Every good housewife gathered herbs and scented flowers to make pot-pourri

It was once very different. Hundreds of years ago everyone was aware of the 'smells of summer'. Open drains, rotting vegetation and unwashed bodies forcefully reminded the citizen that his sense of smell was too acute for comfort. Every good housewife gathered herbs and scented flowers to make pot-pourri. Jars were placed about the house in an attempt to mask the evil smells of primitive sanitation. In stately homes the Pot-pourri Maker was an important member of the household in Elizabethan times.

The preparation of pot-pourri was lengthy and complicated, and the word 'pourri' from the French verb *pourrir* (to rot) gives a clue to the old process. Flower petals and salt were placed in alternate layers in a large glazed pot and the contents pressed down. After a few weeks the resulting brown slab was removed, broken into pieces and mixed with fixatives, oils and spices. The finished pot-pourri was unattractive in appearance but sweet-smelling.

This 'moist method' was joined in more recent times by the much simpler 'dry method'. Petals were allowed to dry until quite crisp and were then mixed with spices, fixatives and sweet essences. This way the petals retained much of their colour and the mixture was just as sweet-smelling.

Old recipes abound – some from as far back as the 16th century. As sanitation and

## The Pot-pourri Maker was an important member of the household in Elizabethan times

hygiene improved the need for such things as pot-pourri grew less, but even in Victorian times great heaps of fragrant flower mixtures were made in country houses. Interest continued to wane in the 20th century as flower hybridists searched for showier blooms and neglected the perfume of many plants.

Recently there has been renewed interest in natural scents. Rose growers offer fragrant collections and flowers which were once overlooked are being grown for their scent. The jar of pot-pourri now seems like a good idea – no longer to mask bad odours, but to fill a void in an increasingly artificial world.

Pot-pourri making is not really difficult by the dry method. Many recipes quote the need for sweet-smelling flowers such as jasmine, heliotrope, mock orange and so on, but in fact only fragrant roses, lavender and carnations retain their perfume after drying. Pick other petals for their bright colours when dry, rather than for their

scent. Useful ones are delphinium, cornflower and marigold.

Place a thin layer of petals and aromatic leaves on a mesh-bottomed rack in an airing cupboard. Stir occasionally, and they should be cornflake-crisp in a week or two. Now you need to add a mixture of sweet flower oils (to strengthen the perfume), spices (to enrich the fragrance) and a fixative (to stop the fragrance from disappearing in a short time). There are many recipes – a good basic one is:

30 g dried orris root

½ teaspoon allspice

½ teaspoon cinnamon

A few drops of flower oil (rose or violet)

Add the mixture to a litre of dried flower petals and shake the ingredients thoroughly in a plastic bag. Leave tightly closed for about three weeks. The pot-pourri is now ready and should be placed in attractive containers. Keep it in a pomander (a china or metal pot with a perforated lid) or place it in open bowls and large brandy balloons away from direct sunlight. Alternatively keep it in a decorative glass jar, removing the lid occasionally to scent the room.

However you use it, pot-pourri will bring back the smells of the summer garden to your home.

# HOW TO
# PRESERVE FOLIAGE

## KEEPING LEAVES FOR EVER

BEAUTIFUL INDOOR arrangements can be made by using foliage from the garden, but like all fresh material it soon fades and falls.

Many leaves can be dried to provide more permanent material for indoor decoration. Only trial and error will tell you which are suitable, but brooms, heathers and fine-leaved conifers can all be relied upon to produce everlasting display material. Tie the ends of the stems together with string and then hang the bunch upside down in a cool, dry place for a couple of months. They should then be ready for use.

The trouble with air-dried foliage is that it looks crisp and lifeless. The glycerine method is much better – it produces leaves which bear a satiny lustre.

Cut the branches when the leaves are firm – do not wait until the end of the season when the foliage is limp and has started to change colour. Wash the leaves if necessary. Beech is the favourite material but there are many, many others – oak, camellia, lime, laurel, poplar and evergreen magnolia are just a few. And it need not be restricted to shrubs and trees – you can use many herbaceous perennials, such as gladioli and irises.

Strip the leaves from the bottom 8 cm of the stems. Crush the ends and insert in about 6 cm of a 1 part glycerine/ 2 parts warm water solution. Make sure that air can circulate around the leaves, so do not put too many stems into one jug of solution.

When the colour of the leaves starts to change you will know that the preservative has arrived. The colour change may be slight or it may change markedly from deep green to brown. When the whole leaf surface has changed colour the leaves are ready for removal and use. This will take between one and six weeks, depending on the variety and conditions. Your glycerine-preserved foliage should last indefinitely, but do handle and store with care.

# HOW TO PRESS FLOWERS

## A Picture from your own Garden

Making a pressed flower picture is not an easy task. You have to select suitable specimens and then dry them properly. When ready the pressed blooms and foliage have to be mounted, which is a job requiring a delicate touch and some artistic skill. But it can be a rewarding hobby in terms of satisfaction, and even in terms of money if you are really talented.

Pick the material on a dry day – you will need flowers which will press flat and so you should avoid complicated and multi-petalled blooms such as camellias, roses, double marigolds and so on. Blue is a difficult colour – delphinium is the only successful material. The flowers should be fully open with no signs of decay. Pick more than you will require for your picture – some flowers change colour when pressed and become distinctly unattractive, others will crease and fold during the drying process and this means that losses are bound to occur. Don't forget to pick grasses, stems and leaves – the soft foliage of herbaceous plants is usually better than the leathery leaves of shrubs and trees.

There are several drying methods. Perhaps the simplest is to place the specimens between two sheets of blotting paper and insert between the pages of an unwanted book made of non-shiny paper. The plant material must be free from traces of surface moisture and before closing the book insert a name tag listing the varieties. You can, of course, insert several blotting paper sets in a single book before putting it on the floor of a dry room with a heavy weight such as a brick on top.

Leave the book undisturbed for at least a month, after which you can make your picture. You will need a mounting board (thin cardboard, not paper), tweezers, matchstick, camel-hair brush and a rubber-based adhesive. Arrange your design on the board and remember that curved stems can help to give the arrangement a better balance. There are all sorts of 'rules' about good design – don't use too many flowers, avoid colour clashes and so on, but really it is up to you.

Use the matchstick to apply a tiny amount of adhesive to the tip of the back of each petal. Place the dried bloom back on to the mounting board and arrange the petals very gently with the brush before pressing down. Continue until all specimens have been fixed. Your picture is now ready for framing.

# HOW TO UNDERSTAND
# THE CATALOGUES

## WHAT THE HORTICULTURAL TERMS MEAN

CATALOGUES are always useful and sometimes colourful, but seedsmen like many gardening writers seem to delight in technical terms. For the perplexed, this simple key may help. An **Annual** is a plant which is normally started from seed and produces its crop of flowers and seeds and then dies within one growing season. Many of our popular garden flowers and most of our vegetables belong here. In contrast to annuals, the **Biennial** takes two years to complete its life cycle. Flowering biennials are sown outdoors in late spring and transplanted in autumn into the site where they will bloom in spring. Examples are wallflowers, forget-

me-nots and Canterbury bells. They can sometimes be kept for more than two seasons but the flower display deteriorates. A **Perennial** will live for many years – **Trees** (single main stem at ground level) and **Shrubs** (several main stems at ground level) retain a woody framework in winter, but the stems of the **Herbaceous Perennial** die down and are removed.

Some plants will tolerate the rigours of winter but others will not. A **Hardy** plant is not killed by the freezing temperatures we can expect in Britain, but a **Tender** variety does not like low temperatures – it needs the protection of a greenhouse or windowsill for much of the year. Between these two extremes lies the **Half-hardy** plant. It can spend most of its life outdoors but it cannot tolerate frost, so it must be sown and grown indoors until all risk of frost is past.

**Early, Mid-season** and **Late** are confusing terms which are applied to vegetables. They do not refer to the time of year but indicate the length of time between sowing and harvest. Early varieties are quick-maturing and the late

HENDERSON'S
NEW BUSH
LIMA BEAN

GROWS ONLY
18 INCHES
HIGH.

Seed was once sold as Nature had left it, but this is no longer always true. **Dressed seeds** have been given a dusting to deter birds or protect them against disease or pests. **Pelleted seeds** are small seeds which have been given a clay or clay-like coating to make them larger and easier to handle.

> I cannot omit nor spare to deliver my mind, concerning the great and abominable falsehood of those sorts of people which sell garden seeds.
>
> *R. Gardiner (1603)*

(or main crop) ones take longer to reach maturity.

Plant **Species** such as the tomato (*Lycopersicon esculentum*) come in many **Varieties**, such as Moneymaker and Ailsa Craig. A special selection (a **Strain**) of the variety is sometimes made, and when the pollen from one variety or species is transferred to a different one by the technique known as crossing, the offspring is a **Hybrid**. Hybrids offered for sale will have been selected to possess health, size or appearance which is superior to their parents – they are the Olympic athletes of the garden. The **$F_1$ Hybrids** are the equivalent of the medal winners at the Olympic Games. **AGM** signifies that the plant has been awarded the R.H.S. Award of Garden Merit – the highest accolade that the Society can award.

# HOW TO WIN
# AT THE ROSE SHOW

## WHAT THE ROSE JUDGES WILL BE LOOKING FOR

OF COURSE nobody would enter the local flower show just for the prize money – it is most unlikely that it would cover all your expenses. The joy is to win an award, and in order to do that your exhibit must appeal to the judges.

So what are the rose judges looking for? If you are a beginner you must understand that a rose show is not like a 'giant vegetable' competition – the biggest blooms are not necessarily the winners. The second point is that the judges will not be looking for a single feature – they will award points for several aspects of your display and it is up to you to be aware of the features which will affect the scoring.

---

It is up to you to be aware of the features which will affect the scoring

---

The first golden rule is to read and follow the show schedule *carefully*. Sounds simple, but so many entries are disqualified

or seriously downgraded for a minor breach of the rules – leaves oiled, blooms wired, extra foliage added or petals removed when such actions are prohibited by the schedule.

Next, select the class you propose to enter and again take care. In a **Decorative Class** the roses are judged on the basis of the overall effect of the blooms together with the leaves and stems in a bowl or vase. Artistry and peak condition are much more important here than flowers which are above average size. In a boxed **Specimen Bloom Class** the roses are primarily judged as individual blooms and here the judges will be looking for flowers which are as near perfect as possible in shape and colour and which are also significantly larger than the average for the varieties shown. It is expected that all varieties staged should be named.

The third rule for catching the judge's eye is to pick your varieties carefully. There are a number of Hybrid Teas which regularly win prizes at local and national rose shows. They provide the large blooms with high centres that appeal to judges – a good rose book will include a list of Exhibition varieties and most rose catalogues include recommendations for the show bench.

## The judges will look for clean and undamaged leaves and they must be adequate in size and number

And now for the day of judgement. You will gain points for graceful balance and an artistic arrangement in which the flowers are neither crushed nor widely spaced and the stems are straight and in proportion to bloom size. The judges will look for clean and undamaged leaves and they must be adequate in size and number. The petals must be firm and clean if you are going to win an award, and there must be no 'blueing' of red varieties. The stage of flower development will also be important – Floribundas should be fully open but Hybrid Teas should be only half or three-quarters open. If you have removed, added or overdressed petals by bending them backwards in an obvious way then you will lose points.

In a Decorative Class the judges will award a maximum of 10 points for the form and size of the individual blooms, 10

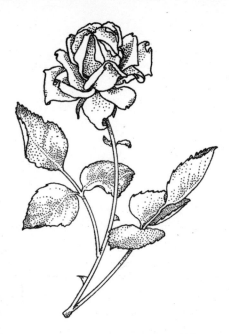

The rose looks fair, but fairer we it deem,

For that sweet odour which doth in it live.

*Sonnets (William Shakespeare)*

points for their freshness, brilliance and colour purity, and 10 points for the presentation, including leaf and stem quality. If it is a Specimen Bloom Class in boxes then at least 90 per cent of the points will be awarded for the form, substance, size, freshness, brilliance and colour purity of the individual blooms. And remember that winning isn't everything, but it is *much* better than losing.

# HOW TO MAKE
# A FERN PRINT

## A Picture that only Nature could Paint

EVERY PLANT lover has felt the need at some time or other to capture the beauty of flowers and leaves in a picture. Portraying plants in paint or pastel is beyond the artistic ability of most of us, but photography is the great leveller. Even so, though we can all focus and press a shutter release, a great deal of skill and expertise is required to create a truly worthwhile flower photograph.

Because photography is apparently so simple, many people look for a flower picture craft which is easier than painting but not as straightforward as a camera. The most obvious, of course, is the pressed flower picture and the technique involved is described on page 241. The quality of the result depends on the choice and arrangement of the leaves, and the same criteria apply in a much less popular art form, the fern print.

Fern prints are extremely simple to make and are therefore frequently regarded as a pastime for children, but in skilled hands the effect can be quite stunning. The first step is to pick a number of leaves from ferns or other plants with interesting foliage. Place the leaves between folded sheets of blotting paper and put several heavy books on top. After a week arrange the flattened leaves in an attractive pattern on a piece of thin white card. Sounds simple, but so does flower arranging …

Take a stiff nailbrush or toothbrush and dip it into a tray of watercolour. Hold it with bristles upwards and pull a thin stick towards you across the bristles. As they are released, tiny drops of paint are scattered on to the card. Repeat until there is an adequate cover of spots. Carefully remove the leaves when the paint is quite dry and the picture is finished.

The effect can be framable – or burnable. The artistic merit will depend on leaf arrangement, paint colours, droplet size and the number of droplets. It isn't really child's play.

# HOW TO COOK FLOWERS

## SOPS-IN-WINE, ROSE ICE CREAM...

*Y*OU MIGHT think it strange to pick the blooms in the flower garden and use them in the kitchen. There is nothing really odd about this – we happily eat the fruits of all sorts of flowers and the division between flowers and vegetables is a wholly artificial one. But we all have our prejudices – there are people who relish oysters yet would not consider eating snails.

THE BEST known flower food is the **Pickled Nasturtium**. Wash the seeds and soak them in a solution of 60 g of salt dissolved in 600 ml of water for 24 hours. Drain and place in jars which should then be filled with vinegar. These pickled seeds can be used in place of capers for garnishing. The rest of the nasturtium plant is equally useful – **Nasturtium Leaves** and **Flowers** add a peppery taste to salads.

---

## For most of us roses are the only flowers which are plentiful enough for kitchen use

---

Marigold flowers were popular in the medieval kitchen – petals were sprinkled into stews and soups or mixed with cheese. Violets were widely used in meat dishes and desserts and the carnation was the base of the once-familiar **Sops-in-Wine**. To make this syrup, gather 250 g of petals from a fragrant carnation variety and remove the white base from each petal. Pour 600 ml of boiling water over the petals and allow to stand for a day. Strain the liquid through muslin and heat gently in a pan with 250 g of icing sugar until a syrup is formed. Dilute this Sops-in-Wine with water or lemonade as a soft drink or add it to white wine as they did in the old days.

## Nasturtium leaves and flowers add a peppery taste to salads

For most of us roses are the only flowers which are plentiful enough for kitchen use, and there are lots of rose recipes – the following two are examples. To make **Rose Ice Cream**, remove the white bases from 2 cupfuls of red rose petals and stir the petals into 600 ml of boiling milk. Let the mixture stand and after a couple of hours strain through muslin. Add 2 beaten egg yolks and sweeten with sugar to taste. Heat (do not boil) whilst stirring. Leave the ice cream to cool and then place in the freezer. A more traditional rose food is **Rose Petal Jam**. Make a syrup by gently boiling 2 kg of sugar with a litre of water. Add about 500 g of rose petals and also the juice from 2 lemons to help the jam to set. Pour in a little rose water for flavouring and simmer gently until the jam thickens. Pour into jars and seal.

# THIS AND THAT

A PRACTICAL GARDENING book does not contain a This and That section. Such an omission is reasonable and unavoidable – there are so many instructions and so much advice to convey that there isn't room for general background and tit-bits of information which are of no practical use.

The purpose of this book is to look at gardens, plants and gardening from the pleasure rather than the practical standpoint, and so it is not surprising that the This and That chapter is longer than any of the other sections. It is not formally laid out like a classical French garden – it is instead a colourful and hopefully interesting jumble of bits and pieces which would have no place in a gardening textbook. This, then, is a cottage garden of information.

This chapter covers a wide range of plants and garden features. There is a group of articles which are indeed practical but are generally ignored in most gardening guides. There is the question of the effect of tree roots on house foundations (page 286s) and information on your legal position when neighbours, workmen or suppliers let you down (page 253). It may also be useful for you to know which plants can be harmful (page 270), which trees to choose for firewood (page 260) and which plants you can bring in

> I have read much and found nothing but uncertainty, lies and fanaticism. I know about as much today of the essential things as I knew as an infant. I prefer to plant, to sow, and to be free.
>
> *Voltaire*

from abroad without getting into trouble (page 251).

From the practical to the totally impractical – in the article beginning on page 288 you will find the story behind many common and not-so-common plants. It will not help you to know that kissing under the mistletoe once meant that you were proposing marriage and it is of no practical use to know that the beautiful garden lupins of today arose from the strain which a man bred on his little allotment. There are rose stories on page 302 and the story behind our national flowers on page 311.

> I have seen one clambering
> rose, one lingering
> hollyhock glorify a cottage
> home, arrest one's step,
> and prolong one's
> meditations, more than all
> the terraces of Chatsworth.
>
> *Alfred Austin*

The 'Looking Around' articles provide background information on many gardens and gardening facets, and some of this may certainly be useful. Page 275 tells you what to look for when visiting a garden open to the public and page 272 should help you to get the best out of your local garden centre. The articles on mazes (page 282), peat (page 284), the meaning of Latin names (page 318) and rose breeding (page 262) show that there is always something new to learn, and if you are interested in words there is the feature on gardening fallacies.

Reading about things you never knew before is all very well, but perhaps you would like to get up and do something. Specially for you, then, is the article on how to grow a selection of odd items in the garden – a loofah, Christmas decorations or a walking stick (page 268). A distinctly odd note to end on, and which is appropriate for the purpose of this chapter, is to show that gardening is *not* just a matter of digging, picking, buying, planting, feeding and weeding. It is also a wonderful world of legends, words and far-away places.

# ANYTHING TO DECLARE?

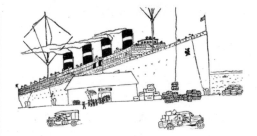

ONE OF the attractions of taking holidays abroad is the chance to buy things which you don't find at home. Strange wines, hand-crafted leather, dolls in national dress and so on, but for the flower-lover there is the added temptation to pick up plants, seeds and bulbs which are not found at the garden centre in Britain.

Unusual vegetable seeds from France, novel pot plants from Holland, a bunch of semi-tropical flowers from Malta ... a good idea, but many people are cautious because it might be breaking the law. They

> If you bring back a plant or even a rooted cutting from a prohibited area it will be confiscated at Customs

are quite right to be cautious. If you bring back a plant or even a rooted cutting from a prohibited area it will be confiscated at Customs. If you try to hide it – 'put it in that large string bag, nobody will notice' – you may be prosecuted.

These restrictions may seem like red tape – after all, countless tons of assorted fruits and vegetables are imported every day and nobody seems to care. What possible harm could a little tree in a pot do to anyone? The simple truth is that people *do* care about vegetable imports (there are strict rules and regular inspections) and your little pot could possibly introduce a new problem to Britain.

The rabbit was introduced into Australia by some well-meaning nature-lover. The Water hyacinth, which now plagues the waterways of southern U.S.A, was introduced from Japan by a gardener who wanted the pretty flowers in her pond. Dutch Elm Disease came over to Europe from America on an imported elm. The major concern of the authorities is that new pests and diseases could be introduced into Britain on imported plants.

So the rules have to be strict. If you want to import plants from abroad you must obtain a plant health certificate issued

by the government of the country in which the plants were grown. That's fine if your business is importing, but it's not worthwhile for the holiday-maker.

## The rules for bringing plants from your holiday are strict and are very complex

More recently there has been a second major concern – the need to conserve endangered species. In 1975 CITES (the Convention on International Trade in Endangered Species of Wild Flora and Fauna) was introduced – this forbids the import into Britain of many orchids and some cacti from non-E.U. countries unless you have obtained a permit.

The rules for bringing plants from your holiday are strict and are very complex. Fortunately this complexity concerns plants obtained outside the European Union – you can bring back any plant material, provided it was grown in the E.U. Coming back from a non-E.U. country you can bring back a bunch of flowers and 5 packets of seeds and perhaps some fruit and bulbs, but not plants which are growing.

The rules are complex but the advice is simple. Bring back seeds, bulbs or a plant which caught your fancy on your European holiday, but restrict your souvenirs to strange wines, hand-crafted leather and dolls in national dress if your holiday was in the U.S. or some exotic spot.

No man but feels more of a man in the world if he have but a bit of ground that he can call his own. However small it is on the surface, it is four thousand miles deep; and that is a very handsome property.

*C. D. Warner*

# BE YOUR OWN
# GARDEN LAWYER

Tᴴɪѕ ɪѕ the saddest feature in the book. Gardens are such pleasant places in which to work, potter or just laze . . . but occasionally disagreements do occur with neighbours or suppliers or others. The golden rule is to be as reasonable as you can and to try to settle the dispute by discussion.

If the trouble persists then you can seek advice from your Citizens' Advice Bureau or a solicitor, but do remember that going to law is a lengthy, exhausting and costly business, and even if you win against a neighbour you can lose in the end – continued hostility may force you to move.

Throughout this feature it has been assumed that the wrongdoer is male – this is for the sake of simplicity and does not imply any sex discrimination!

## Tʜᴇ Lᴀᴡ ᴏɴ Bᴏʀʀᴏᴡɪɴɢ

When you borrow your neighbour's lawnmower you take on certain responsibilities. If you damage it then it must be repaired and if you lose it the lawnmower must be replaced. However, the owner must not come over and collect it without permission – that would be trespassing.

If your neighbour expressly states that the lawnmower must be returned, then he can sue you in court for its return – otherwise, he can sue you for compensation of the cost of the lawnmower rather than its return.

## Tʜᴇ Lᴀᴡ ᴏɴ Wᴇᴇᴅѕ

There is generally little you can do to make your neighbour get rid of weeds in his garden. Nettles, dandelions and cow parsley may be his idea of getting back to Nature. However, he isn't quite free of the law. By the Weeds Act 1959 it is an offence to allow the spread of certain injurious weeds such as thistles, docks and ragwort. The local authorities can ask him to remove them and can fine him if he refuses. It is also possible that a neighbour who leaves his garden to go to pot could be served with an Anti-Social Behaviour Order (ASBO).

---

By the Weeds Act 1959 it is an offence to allow the spread of certain injurious weeds such as thistles, docks and ragwort

---

## The Law on Buying and Repairing

When you order plants or a piece of equipment you have entered into a contract. You can't simply cancel the order if you change your mind, even if the order was a verbal one. The seller must also honour his part of the contract – the goods he supplies must be of merchantable quality for the purpose for which they have been sold. This means that if the equipment is defective or the plants are not as described in the catalogue then you can ask for a replacement or a refund. If the goods fit the description and are not defective, you cannot ask for a refund merely because you expected something better (the laws on mail order are different – see page 258).

The law on repairs makes it quite clear that the repairer's job is to use the skill and materials one would expect from a person in his position. Note that it does not demand that he cures the fault. Secondly, you should agree a 'proper' price before the work is begun – if you don't then he will decide the proper price when the job is completed and it will be hard for you to disagree. He can hold on to your equipment until you pay.

## The Law on Taking it with You

When you sell your house your solicitor will provide you with a standard fixtures and fittings form. If you list the plants in your garden, or if the buyers want them listed and you agree, then they will have to stay. Generally plants which have rooted into the soil and garden features which have been attached to walls or cemented into the ground are considered fixtures, so it is best to clarify everything with the standard form.

If you do want to take some of the plants then it may be best to agree this with the buyers to avoid disagreements later.

# The Law on Pets

Your neighbour is allowed to keep any pet he likes (subject to the Dangerous Animals Act) as long as it is not judged to be a nuisance. If the animal comes on to your property and causes damage then the Animals Act makes his liability clear. As the owner, it is his duty to take reasonable care to ensure that the animal causes neither injury nor damage. If the animal is a dog or cat, however, the law takes a lenient view – cats are excluded from the Act and dogs are only covered if they go on to kill or injure livestock. You would be most unlikely to get a judgement against the action of a cat or dog unless your neighbour had been negligent – for example, taking a pet for a walk and allowing it to enter your garden and cause damage.

# The Law on Nuisance

There are many ways in which your neighbour's activities in the garden may make you unhappy. Bonfires on washdays, constant use of noisy machinery, rat-infested piles of rubbish, destructive children ... the list is a long and depressing one. Essentially, the law is basically simple. As an occupier you can seek a court order to stop your neighbour being a nuisance, and if you have suffered some form of loss you can claim damages. Unfortunately, both interpretation and findings under the current law are complex and sometimes puzzling. The deciding question in the mind of the court is 'Was neighbour A being reasonable in disturbing neighbour B?' You may not like your Sunday nap being disturbed by the power mower next door, but no court will stop it. Similarly, an occasional bonfire will not be considered an unreasonable nuisance.

---

**You may not like your Sunday nap being disturbed by the power mower next door, but no court will stop it**

---

Persistent and prolonged annoyance can be judged to be a nuisance, but much depends on where you live – machinery noise may not be judged to be a nuisance in a noisy, industrial area. You may also be able to apply for an A.S.B.O. to be made on the neighbour – this is a civil order, the breaking of which is a criminal offence.

Your first step if you feel your neighbour is creating a nuisance should be an approach to the council and not to a solicitor. If a bye-law is being broken then it is their responsibility to stop it. If it is not a council affair then a writ may be the only answer, but once again it is so much more satisfactory if the difference can be settled by discussion.

## The Law on Occupier Liability

If someone is hurt in your garden, then you can be sued for damages under the Occupier Liability Act. Whether he wins or not depends on whether you have taken 'reasonable' care to protect the person, and the difficulty is that nobody has clearly defined the word 'reasonable'.

Reasonableness depends both on the nature of the hazard and the type of person injured. If you leave a ladder against a wall then you may be judged to have failed to show reasonable care for a youngster who might climb it and fall, but this certainly wouldn't be the ruling for an adult, who could be expected to appreciate the risks involved. The presence of dead branches, loose steps, unguarded holes etc. could be judged to be unreasonable hazards for people of all ages and your liability doesn't only extend to your visitors. A workman could sue you if the risk was unexpected. Trespassers and those using private rights of way are covered by a 1984 amendment to the Act – they have a lesser protection, as the owner would need to be aware of the danger, have reasonable grounds to believe that people may enter the property, and believe that the danger is one that should be protected against. Of course, nothing like this will ever happen to you, but it is a wise precaution to make sure that your house insurance covers third party liability ...

## The Law on Trees

If your neighbour has an unsightly tree which is spoiling your view or a leafy one which is casting dense shade on your beloved roses, there is nothing you can do apart from appealing to his better nature. However, you can take action if his tree trespasses on to your property. Overhanging branches can be cut off, but they must be returned to your neighbour, together with any fruit on them! He is also liable for any damage caused to your paths or house foundations by trespassing roots, or for drainage blocked by trespassing leaves.

---

### Overhanging branches can be cut off, but they must be returned to your neighbour

---

Don't wait until a dangerous-looking branch on a neighbour's tree is blown off in a gale before complaining. If you genuinely and reasonably feel that a branch is a danger to your greenhouse, shed or house then have it lopped if it hangs over your garden or write and ask him to do it if the branch does not cross the boundary. Such a letter would greatly strengthen your case if damage did unfortunately occur at some later stage.

Local authorities can also prohibit the felling or lopping of an individual tree or group of trees with a Tree Preservation Order. Written notice of the Order must be given to the land owner, and only the local authority can enforce it, although members of the public can report possible Order violations.

## THE LAW ON FENCES

Boundary disputes are a common cause of ill-will between neighbours and it is useful to know your rights. It is unwise to guess who owns the fence – check the title deeds and plans to find out. If the deeds do not establish ownership, the property which has the fence posts is generally regarded as the owner.

If the fence is yours then it is up to you to maintain it if you wish. Some towns and some deeds say that fences must be kept in good repair – if this does not apply then your neighbour cannot insist on proper maintenance.

When you repair your fence you cannot demand that your neighbour should share the cost nor can you enter his property without permission. Of course, the type of fence and the time of fixing is up to you but height can be a problem – you need council permission for a pavement boundary fence over 1 m high and any other fence over 2 m. It is worth remembering the old adage – good fences make good neighbours.

## THE LAW ON HEDGES

Since 2005 you can take complaints about a neighbour's hedge (such as overgrown *C. leylandii*) to your local authority for adjudication under the Anti-Social Behaviour Act. This can only be done once all other attempts to resolve the dispute have failed. The local authority will decide whether the hedge is adversely affecting the reasonable enjoyment of your property, and may make a formal notice to your neighbour as to what they need to do to remedy the situation. Failure to carry this out can lead to a £1000 fine.

## THE LAW ON TRESPASS

You may need to trim the other side of the hedge or mend a broken window which can only be reached if you put a ladder in your neighbour's garden. No matter how pressing the need may be, the law on trespass is quite adamant – you cannot enter your neighbour's property without his permission. The only exceptions are if a right of way has been established by passing through your neighbour's garden freely and as of right for at least 20 years or if right of access appears in your title deeds. Both forms of easement are unusual – the best course of action is to remind your neighbour that his stubbornness could result in a similar response from you when your help is needed. The threat to withdraw your watchful eye when the neighbour's house is empty at holiday time may work wonders.

From the other point of view, if you want to take your neighbour to court for trespass, beware – the law of trespass is much more complicated than it might appear to non-lawyers!

## THE LAW ON CHILDREN

Children have no right to enter your property. The boy who climbs your wall to rescue his ball is trespassing and the children who take apples from the tree or conkers from the Horse chestnut tree are stealing in the eyes of the law. You can prosecute them or use 'reasonable force' to expel them from the garden.

Do be careful before using force or the courts. If you have let your neighbour's

---

By far the best action is to forcefully tell trespassing children to leave and then have a word with their parents

---

children collect their ball on previous occasions but today you've 'had enough', then the ruling may be that they have informal permission to enter your garden. The same goes for apple 'scrumpers' if you did not object in the past.

Force too has hidden dangers. A child can claim unreasonable assault and it is difficult to prove your innocence. By far the best action is to tell trespassing children forcefully to leave and then have a word with their parents, if necessary. Of course it's possible today to get an A.S.B.O. for scrumping!

## THE LAW ON MAIL ORDER

Buying plants, equipment and sundries through the post or internet is a satisfactory way of obtaining supplies, but things can occasionally go wrong. The first step to avoid problems is to keep a copy of the advert, catalogue or web page together with proof of payment (cheque stub, credit card details etc.). When your goods arrive inspect them carefully to see if you are satisfied.

You have grounds for complaint under the Sale of Goods Act if the goods do not correspond to the advert or are not of merchantable quality for the purpose for which they have been sold. If this happens to you, write or send an email to the supplier with precise details of your complaint and ask for a replacement or full refund – he is bound by law to replace defective goods or return the money. Keep a copy of this letter/email for future reference.

It may be that you are disappointed with your purchase even though it is suitable for the job and the advert was not misleading. It used to be the case that you had no claim, but under the Consumer

Protection (Distance Selling) Regulations, you are entitled to cancel the transaction as long as you inform the seller in writing (fax, email or letter) within seven working days of receiving the goods. Unfortunately, the regulations do not apply to perishable goods such as flowers. It should also be noted that you may have to pay the postage for returning the item.

---

## Never send cash in the post

---

Your problem may be a lack of delivery rather than defective goods. The Consumer Protection (Distance Selling) Regulations stipulate that if the goods have not been delivered within 30 days you must be refunded within another 30 days.

Mail order companies also follow the Advertising Standards Authority rules. If you don't get your money back, the ASA is your first port of call. The ASA offers a complaints service if you return an item and it is refused by the seller.

One other thing to remember is to never send cash in the post – it's too risky. Credit cards are the safest form of payment.

## The Law on Hosepipes

During times of water shortage, water companies can apply for banning orders which forbid the use of hosepipes and sprinklers connected to a mains tap. At present there are loopholes which allow hosepipes to be used for filling swimming pools, but there are new rules designed to prohibit the use. Customers who continue to use hosepipes during the ban can be liable to be fined by the water company concerned.

Welcome, sweet April! thou gentle Midwife of May's Pride and the Earth's green Livery. Sow your Garden Seeds and Plant Herbs, finish your grafting on the Stock. Open your Hives and give your Bees free Liberty to look into the Garden. You may bathe freely provided you be not under fourteen years or above fifty-six Old, or be exceeding fat or very lean; in such cases by all means abstain.

*M. Stevenson (1661)*

# BURNING LOGS

THERE ARE various charts which compare the cost and efficiency of the fuels which we use to heat our homes during winter. Some are cheaper than others, but only one is free for the taking – wood.

Firewood has other advantages, and these do not appear on the comparison charts. Well-seasoned logs produce a strong and pleasant aroma, and there are leaping flames and glowing sparks which neither coal nor natural gas can match. The best wood for grate and stove is both dead and dry. Never cut down trees or large branches just for firewood, of course, but when you have to fell a tree or lop off large branches then store the logs in a dry place if you have an open fire or wood-burning stove. When gathering wood from other people's land you must ask their permission. To take even dead timber off their property means that you are trespassing.

For a fast-burning fire with the maximum amount of flames you should stack the logs as upright as possible in the grate – laying the logs horizontally will produce a longer-lasting fire. A few words of warning – sparks can be a problem, so protect nearby carpets from costly damage.

Firewood offered for sale is often pine, and you must remember that some conifers have a high resin content. This will not be a problem in the case of an occasional wood fire in an open grate, but the heavy deposit of tar in the chimney of a wood-burning stove will require removal.

Dried logs produce a pleasing fire with dancing flames and sweet-smelling smoke … but not always. The quality of the blaze will depend on the type of wood you are using and there are many country rhymes which sing the praises of some woods and warn against others.

*'Applewood will scent your room,
with an incense-like perfume.'*

Apple is one of the best of the 'scented' woods but there are others – pear, cherry and juniper. If you have some logs of one or other of these trees, use them in a fuel cocktail. Make the fire from ordinary timber and place a single log of the 'scented' variety on top to provide the fragrance to fill the room.

*'Beechwood fires are bright and
clear, if the logs are kept a year.'*

Beech has a good reputation as firewood, but it should be stored for many months before use. Oak and chestnut have the same reputation.

*'Birch and fir logs burn too fast,
blaze up bright and do not last.'*

Birch is an excellent wood to use for kindling because it burns so easily. Several trees, such as birch, fir and holly, will produce a satisfactory fire with wood which has not been left to dry.

Some woods can be disappointing, producing little flame or acrid smoke. Elm logs were plentiful shortly after the ravages of Dutch Elm Disease, but it is unfortunately a poor wood for burning – *'Elm logs like smouldering flax, no flame is seen.'*

---

## Apple is one of the best of the 'scented' woods but there are others — pear, cherry and juniper

---

Alder and willow are also poor-burning woods, and poplar *'gives a bitter smoke, fills your eyes and makes you choke.'* There is a warning too about larch, which is *'of pinewood smell, but the sparks will fly'*.

In all these old country rhymes and sayings one wood stands supreme. It is a firewood which *'a king shall warm his slippers by'* – the ash.

*'But ash logs, all smooth and grey,
Burn them green or old.
Buy up all that come your way
They're worth their weight in gold.'*

# THE CRAFT OF
# THE ROSE BREEDER

ONE OF THE parents of *Josephine Bruce* was *Crimson Glory* – once the most popular red rose in Britain. Apart from its illustrious parent it can trace its ancestors back through generation after generation to the immortal Hybrid Tea Roses of Victorian and Edwardian times – *La France*, *Soleil d'Or* and *Mme. Caroline Testout*. This reads like an extract from the stud book of a racehorse or a pedigree dog, and roses are indeed bred with the same care and skill.

The scientific breeding of roses is surprisingly recent. The idea of crossing two known types so that the offspring would have a pedigree did not really become established until the last quarter of the 19th century – and the founder of the concept of selling roses with a family tree was not even a gardener.

## France was the centre of rose breeding throughout the 19th century

Henry Bennett was a cattle breeder in Wiltshire, and so was well aware of the need to prevent accidental coupling and also the value of keeping records of the crosses he arranged. In 1878 Bennett introduced a range of 'pedigree' Hybrid Tea Roses which had named parents. The modern age of commercial rose breeding had begun.

At this point in time there was no shortage of rose varieties even though marriages were not arranged. These varieties had been introduced by observant horticulturalists who had carefully selected promising seedlings which had arisen from natural crosses. In Persia and ancient China this type of selection had produced many beautiful named varieties before travellers from the Western World arrived, and in more recent times an accidental cross between *Old Blush China* and *Autumn Damask* in 1818 gave rise to the race of Bourbon Roses.

France was the centre of rose breeding throughout the 19th century and a vast number of seedlings were grown in the search for better varieties, and there was a feeling that this work should not be such a hit-or-miss affair. The facts of life for roses had been spelt out by Bradley in 1717 but nobody felt that it was necessary to give Nature a hand. The breakthrough came in 1848 when William Paul of Hertfordshire described the techniques of hybridisation in *The Rose Garden*. In this book he described how blooms should be prepared, how pollen should be transferred from the donor to the seed parent, how the rose hips should be treated and how the seedlings should be raised. He noted that he had learnt the technique from French gardeners and had begun to practise the craft in England in 1840. To him must go the title of the Father of Rose Breeding, although it was farmer Bennett who created the 'stud book' concept for such crosses.

The techniques employed by the great rose breeders of today have of course been refined since Paul's early work, but the principles remain the same. The breeder decides which rose will serve as pollen parent and which one will be the seed parent. The petals and then the stamens are removed from the seed parent before its pollen is shed – in this way self-fertilisation is prevented. Accidental cross-pollination would be equally disastrous, so seed parents are either grown in greenhouses away from pollen-producing males or their emasculated blooms are covered with bags or cones if grown in the open.

## Hips are harvested in autumn and the seeds sown in late winter or early spring

Fertilisation is now completely in the hands of the breeder. Pollen from the pollen parent is transferred to the stigmas of the seed parent by physical contact of the two blooms or by means of a fine brush. Hips are harvested in autumn and the seeds sown in late winter or early spring. Each seedling will be unique, but the chance of one being a winner is like the odds on winning a national lottery. The rose breeder does not leave it to chance – he uses a high degree of skill to find that needle in the haystack – the new rose of real merit amongst thousands of worthless seedlings ... and that is still a craft and not a science.

# GARDENING
# DOWN UNDER

FOR MUCH of Australia's past, garden-making has been an attempt to reproduce English styles and ideas with European garden flowers in an environment which was often quite unsuitable. It is impossible, of course, to generalise about so vast a continent with its reasonably temperate coastal strips, its semi-tropical areas and its baking deserts of the interior, but for so long Australian gardening was tied far too strongly to the English rule book.

This was not South Wales – it was New South Wales. It was not Victoria, London – it was Victoria, Australia. The immigrants from England had to face a factor which they had not known before – water shortage for part or even the whole of the year – and obviously features and techniques from Oriental gardens would have been useful. But the homesick early settlers wanted to be surrounded by a little bit of Kent or Yorkshire and not a Persian *paradiso*, and it was the same with the plants – they wanted the flowers they remembered and not the Australian 'weeds' which grew wild.

Even in the most difficult times and in the most inhospitable areas a sprinkling of fine gardens were created. The native flora was cleared and the roses, oaks, achilleas and so on planted – a touch of home in a strange land.

The real change came after World War II when the strong and widespread interest in creating *Australian* gardens began. A number of factors had come together – the economic boom meant that there was money to spend and there were now many native-born Australians who didn't feel the same twinges of nostalgia. Finally the English immigrant Edna Walling had started to publish her excellent textbooks.

The country garden of today is no longer a little bit of Yorkshire or Kent. You will find one or more of the 500 species of Eucalypts, which range from the tallest broadleaved plants on earth to rockery shrubs. Another vast plant family, the Wattles, so-called because they were used by early settlers to make wattle-and-daub buildings, will also be represented. No longer are the native shrubs and flowers regarded as weeds which should be removed – now they are accepted as plants which can equal or excel the exotics from Europe. The beautiful Boronias, the Flannel flower with its woolly-white blooms, the Waratahs with their great red heads and the Darling Pea with its small, pea-like flowers. Once the Australian envied the plants which grew so easily in England but struggled in the bright light, drought and sands of the Southern continent. Now the tables are turned – the European gardener must envy the Wax flowers, the Kangaroo paws, the Tea trees, the Silky oaks, the Palms and the Tree ferns which flourish there but do not like our cool and misty climate.

The country garden of today will probably contain mossy boulders and stone outcrops studded with flowers. This is one of the few home-grown gardening features and is a departure from the neat rockeries of the English garden. Natural grasses are no longer despised, and there is no longer the 19th century feeling that turf must look like a closely-shorn bowling green.

Another home-grown feature is the bush house, which is quite unknown in the Northern hemisphere. A frame of upright posts and laths is covered with wire-netting and the room is filled with ferns, climbers and some flowering plants. This, then, is the Australian country garden; a collection of plants from the old world – the indispensable roses, thymes, wisterias and so on blended with native plants such as the *Correa*, *Hakea* and *Helichrysum*. There is no standard 'Australian' style, but at least it is no longer a copy of a picture in an English textbook.

Within the town the courtyard garden has been developed. The garden is small, as was the tiny plot left behind by many of the immigrants who came from Kent or Yorkshire. But now there is much less desire to produce a Lilliputian grand garden – instead there is the idea of a courtyard, as you would find in the United States, Southern Europe or the Middle East. Pots and stones are important, and so are sitting-out areas and brightly painted walls.

A great continent, 800 x 1000 hectares. A vigorous, outdoor-loving people but no Australian style of gardening has developed. There has been no major contribution to the world of horticulture apart from some outstanding plants which have been accepted only lately in their native land. For most of its life the Australian garden has hung on the apron-strings of its English mother garden, and to understand why you have to look at Australian history – a history which Mark Twain described as the 'chiefest novelty the

country has to offer … it does not read like history, but like the most beautiful lies.'

The garden story began on 29 April 1770 when Captain Cook and his party landed at Botany Bay. The scientist Joseph Banks was not over-impressed with the place and it was originally called Botanist Bay in his honour, not Botany Bay in recognition of the plants there. Banks declared that 'It could not be supposed to yield much to the support of man.'

If the Botany Bay area could not be a place for people then it would have to be a place for convicts from England. The first shipload arrived with Governor Phillip in 1788. This was not a time for gardening – it was a time for survival. The colonists and prisoners cleared scrub, set out the plants they had brought from England and kept them watered in order to produce the vegetables and fruit needed to maintain the tiny group of settlers.

There were gardens – the Governor's estate at Rose Hill and the prisoners' tiny plots, but these were areas of vines, figs, fruit trees and vegetables which were generally maintained by the womenfolk. The early 19th century was a time of great activity in the colony by botanists such as Caley, Brown, Cunningham and Suttor but this merely served to strengthen the English connection with Australian horticulture.

The creation of pleasure gardens as distinct from food plots had to wait until a wealth-owning class was created. In 1807 free passage, land and convicts were offered to 'settlers of substance' and in the 1840s the transportation of prisoners stopped. Fine gardens were now built – Elizabeth Farm, Elizabeth Bay House, Camden Park and so on, but they were all English in character and contained as many Old World plants as possible. The reason is that colonists were often homesick and their gardens were created out of a sense of nostalgia and not just a desire to have a beautiful area around the house.

In the 1830s Australia had its first landscape designer, Thomas Shepherd, and he extolled the virtues of retaining native trees in the garden. This was a time of graceful garden building by wealthy landowners, pieces of restrained landscaping using sub-tropical fruits, English flowers and some Australian trees. There was little interest, however, in gardening at the cottage level.

The late 19th century brought the excesses found in Victorian England – around the mansions of the wealthy were the terraces, fountains, complex flower beds, lawns, topiary, conservatories and rose pergolas you would have found in the Neo-Italianate gardens being built in Yorkshire and Kent – a true Australian approach had not yet arrived.

As stated earlier, the birth of the Great Australian garden movement began after World War II. In the 1970s Australian horticulturalists stood back to look at their gardening heritage. They could be proud of their great Botanical Gardens – there were the Melbourne Botanic Gardens with 12,000 different species, the Adelaide Botanic Gardens with its representative collection of Australia's unique flora and the Darwin Botanic Garden commissioned in 1872. There was the newly-opened Canberra Botanic Gardens, but some of the old 19th century gardens were in great danger of being lost for ever. The Australian Heritage Commission and the Australian Garden History Society now seek to preserve some of the examples of old gardens.

## Another home-grown feature is the bush house, which is quite unknown in the Northern hemisphere

Pride in its heritage – pride in its old buildings, old gardens, native flowers, etc. – may be a new movement in Australia but it is a strong one. The Handbook on the Canberra Botanic Gardens sums it up neatly: 'The ruthless demands of economic progress in earlier times had small regard for the preservation of Australia's flora and fauna. Now, every day sees an increase in awareness of the urgent need to conserve these natural treasures.'

# GROW YOUR OWN...

## WALKING STICK

For more than 150 years the Giant Jersey cabbage has been cultivated in the Channel Islands for the manufacture of walking sticks. In its natural habitat the straight stalks grow 4 m or more and in the old days every part of the plant was used. The leaves were chopped up with other vegetables and added to beef stock to make Jersey cabbage soup, the roots were carved into thimbles and the stems were sold as canes for dashing Victorian gentlemen.

The trade has declined since the end of the war, but seeds are still available and you can grow your own walking stick. Seeds can be obtained from Thompson & Morgan, and they should be sown in August. Treat them in the same way as Spring cabbage at first – transplant them from the seed bed in September or October to their permanent quarters.

Now the fun starts. When they are about 50 cm high, pick off the lower leaves and they should reach 1 m by the end of the first season. In the second season they will flower and they are ready to harvest at the end of the third season. You will not match the Jersey heights but a 2 m cabbage is taller than you have ever grown before.

Cut the stalks into walking-stick lengths and allow to dry for 6 months. Lacquer each one and fit a handle to the top and a rubber tip to the bottom. It will be a little knobbly and may not be perfectly straight – but it will at least be home-grown.

## CHRISTMAS DECORATIONS

All you will need is a packet of seeds of Ornamental gourds. You will see them in the shops and catalogues, and the decorative fruits really are as bizarre as the illustration. Furthermore they are child's play to grow – just sow the seeds outdoors in late May against a south-facing wall or trellis. The seeds are large and easy to handle – just push them about 1 cm down into soil which you have enriched with lots of old compost. Seed germination is slow – help things along by soaking in warm water for about 48 hours before sowing – but once the shoots are through the plants will start to grow quickly. The tendrils will cling to almost anything so keep clear of other plants – all you have to do is to provide some form of support, water when the weather is dry and

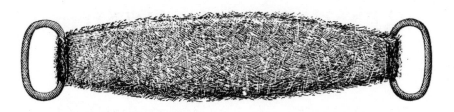

feed occasionally with a liquid fertilizer.

After the female flowers have faded the gourds will appear – some plants will bear round fruits – others pear-shaped, oval, bottle-shaped and so on. The colours are just as variable – red, yellow, half-green, orange and even white. Don't pick these colourful fruits too early – for best results the gourds should be allowed to ripen on the vines. When the stems have withered, pick the fruits and store in a cool, dark and airy place such as the garage. Three weeks later they are ready for polishing – rubbing with floor wax will give them a natural-looking shine but many people prefer to use a clear varnish to produce an attractive gloss. Your home-grown decorations are now ready for the festive season.

## LOOFAH

A loofah may look as if it has been made in a factory or harvested from the sea, but it is actually the fibrous skeleton of the fruit of *Luffa cylindrica*, a member of the cucumber family.

These rampant climbers are too tender to grow outdoors in Britain, but you will have no difficulty with them if you have grown greenhouse cucumbers – cultural instructions are identical.

The large, black seeds are obtainable from nurseries which offer unusual varieties and the time to sow them is April. Fill 8 cm pots with seed compost and plant a couple of seeds about 1 cm below the surface. Keep warm until they have germinated and then maintain a minimum temperature of 15°C. Discard the weaker seedling and when the remaining one has reached the 4th leaf stage plant it in a growing bag. A large bag will take 2 plants and growth should be restricted to a single stem trained up a vertical wire or cane. Like cucumbers they need plenty of water and moist air.

Young fruits will appear a couple of months after planting. Cook as courgettes; they are worth their weight in gold as a surprise at a dinner party – fried loofah! For their more normal use wait until the fruits are fully grown and have turned orange-brown. Harvest them and keep in a warm place until thoroughly dry – peel off the skin and squeeze under a tap to remove the seeds and internal tissues. Let the loofahs dry for a couple of weeks – they are now ready to take a bath.

# HANDLE WITH CARE!

IT IS A sad but true fact that a few garden plants and some wild flowers are poisonous. This does not mean that you will die if you touch them – they are not that lethal. But it does mean that eating their leaves, flowers, fruits or seeds can cause sickness, and even worse when a large amount of plant material and small children are involved.

> **The golden rule is to warn children not to eat leaves or seeds from any plant growing in the garden or in the house unless it is grown for food**

The golden rule is to warn children not to eat leaves nor seeds from *any* plant growing in the garden or in the house unless it is grown for food. Luckily most of us know the two main culprits in cases of accidental poisoning – laburnum and yew. All parts of laburnum are poisonous and particularly the seeds – grow the variety *L. watereri* 'Vossii' as very few seeds are formed. Yew can be more of a problem because the poisonous seed is surrounded by an attractive rosy case which makes it look like an appetising berry.

Laburnum pods and yew 'berries' are the major but not the only problem. There are several other plants which should not be eaten – avoid *Daphne mezereum*, *Nerium* (oleander), privet, ivy, Deadly nightshade, foxglove, Spindle tree, buttercup, monkshood, *Aquilegia*, *Datura stramonium* (Thorn apple) and Lily of the valley.

Avoiding trouble is so easy – just don't eat them. Plants which cause dermatitis are more of a problem because a sensitive person has merely to touch the leaves in order to break out in a rash of tiny blisters.

Some people are allergic to a few chrysanthemum varieties and there have been claims that celery, asparagus and globe artichokes have caused blistering on the arms of sensitive people. Fortunately there is only one flower which can really be considered a problem and that is the pot plant *Primula obconica*. Introduced about a hundred years ago from China, it has become popular for indoor decoration. The flower stalks bear clusters of large primrose-like flowers in white, pink, blue or red – attractive to look at but for some people most unattractive to touch. The hairs on the leaves will produce a painful rash if you are allergic to the irritant they contain.

---

## For those who suffer from hay fever the plants of the country-side are certainly a problem

---

*Primula obconica* is not the only house plant which has a bad reputation – *Dieffenbachia* (Dumb cane) is sometimes the feature of lurid articles describing the effect of swallowing the sap, but the risk may have been exaggerated. It is true that this sap was once used as a means of torture and swallowing it could result in a swollen tongue and a throat so inflamed that you would not be able to speak – hence the common name. But the chance of swallowing the evil-smelling sap of *Dieffenbachia* by accident is remote, and there is no need to avoid growing this plant unless you have children who habitually get into everything. As a simple precaution always wash your hands after taking cuttings from a *Dieffenbachia* plant.

There are no real worries of damaging your health by exposure to the few rogue plants in the home and garden – after all, you can see them and you don't *have* to eat them. Unfortunately, we *do* have to breathe the air around us and for those who suffer from hay fever the plants of the country-side are certainly a problem. The cause is pollen from wind-pollinated plants rather than from showy flowers, and the plants mainly responsible are grasses. The worst time is early summer, and the two grasses which cause most of the trouble are Cocksfoot and Timothy. It is different abroad – in some countries the hay fever season stretches from spring right through to autumn as reactive pollen is produced by a whole host of trees, shrubs and flowers as well as by grasses.

# LOOKING AROUND THE GARDEN CENTRE

<hr/>

## GARDEN CENTRE ASSOCIATION

Over 160 garden centres in the U.K. and N. Ireland belong to the Garden Centre Association. Each one has to achieve a high level of good business practice before it can be accepted, and each garden centre is inspected annually to ensure that high standards are maintained.

The G.C.A. Code of Practice serves to ensure the quality of the service, plants and associated products which the members provide:

* There is a guarantee that any hardy plant that fails to grow, provided that it has received reasonable care, will be replaced if it is returned within one year from the date of purchase.
* Trained staff are present to give sound advice.
* A comprehensive range of plants is offered all year round.
* Plants are maintained by professional horticulturalists.
* A wide range of gardening products is available.

## BEDDING PLANTS

The leaves should be firm and free from holes and spots. Growth should be bushy – avoid plants which are thin and drawn as a result of being raised in too little light and too much heat. There should be no roots growing through the bottom of the seed tray or pot, and the young plants should not be in full flower.

Whenever possible buy a whole box or pot rather than a clump of loose plants which may dry out before you have time to transplant them. The soil in the box or pot should be moist. Do not buy half-hardy plants before mid May.

## BULBS

Do not buy undersized bulbs. Make sure that they are firm and free from mould, holes and growing shoots.

## CONTAINER-GROWN PLANTS

Make sure that the plant has been grown in the container and not transferred into it from open ground. If the tree or shrub lifts out easily then take it as a danger sign. A few roots peeping through are not a problem, but avoid containers with a mass of long roots growing out of the bottom of the pot. Such specimens will be difficult to transplant.

Choose the most vigorous and healthy specimen. Shy away from ones with the danger signs:

* Shrivelled or cankered shoots.
* Diseased or abnormally pale leaves.
* Dying stems.
* Spindly branches.

## Fruit Trees

The variety named on the label will have been grafted on to the rootstock of another tree. Examine the area of the graft carefully – it should be dry and free from suckers. Never buy a specimen with suckers growing up from the roots.

## Garden Chemicals

The golden rule is to buy a pack which is large enough to last the whole season. Buying several small boxes or bottles is much more expensive but buying enough to last for several years can also be wasteful – many products deteriorate with long storage.

Don't just look at the pretty pictures and slogans on the front – read the instructions and precautions on the sides and back. Do make sure that you never use a pesticide without reading the label first. The range of insect killers on offer is much smaller these days – the choice of disease preventatives is now very limited.

## National Garden Gift Tokens

It is sometimes difficult to choose a present for a keen gardener – he or she probably knows the right plant to buy and you don't! In a case like this Garden Gift Tokens are a good idea and you can buy them at the garden centre. They are sold in £1, £5, £10 and £25 units and a range of greetings cards is available. These tokens can be exchanged at any of the outlets which display the sunflower sign.

## Rose Bushes

A container-grown rose provides instant colour, but it should be chosen for its sturdiness and bushiness rather than for the display of its few flowers. It is still a good idea to buy roses as bare-root plants in autumn or spring – dormant bushes with their roots packed in damp peat. Look at the stems – they should be no thinner than a pencil and they should be green and unwrinkled. Bare-root plants may be offered wrapped in polythene – check that the stems are not shrivelled and there should be no leafy shoots beginning to grow on the stems.

## Tools

Remember that tools come in a range of sizes and weights as well as prices. Always lift, handle and if possible try equipment before making your choice. Is the spade too heavy? Are the secateurs the right size for your hand? Are the handles of the lawn shears too long?

> Few lend (but fools)
> Their working Tools.
>
> *Thomas Tusser*

## Trees and Shrubs

First of all you should check that the plant is suitable for the spot you have to fill. To buy a sun-lover for a shady site is a waste of money and so is buying a lime-hater for soil which will not grow rhododendrons. Next, make sure that the plant is the right size, and that does not mean the size you are looking at. It might seem just right for the place you have in mind, but the 'pretty little Weeping willow' in the garden centre will become a spreading monster after a few years in a small garden. The rule is to check the expected height and spread at maturity of any tree or shrub before you buy it.

Having made your choice, look carefully at the specimens available. If it is a flowering shrub, don't let the number of blooms influence you. Look instead at height and bushiness – the golden rule is to choose a sturdy medium-sized specimen. It is a temptation to buy the largest plant you can afford, but you must remember that mature bushes and trees are often difficult to establish. A small or medium-sized plant will usually root much more quickly, but some plants may need careful nursing during their first year if you buy them as very small specimens.

Look for bushiness and an abundance of side shoots – avoid leggy specimens with bare branches. Pay for the plant you have chosen but your problems are not quite over – you have to get it home. Never bend firm stems in order to squeeze a plant into the boot or onto the back seat – it is better to pay a small delivery charge and get it home safely.

> There's rosemary, that's for remembrance; pray, love, remember: And there is pansies, that's for thoughts.
>
> *Hamlet (William Shakespeare)*

# LOOKING AROUND
# THE GRAND GARDEN

N O SINGLE garden contains all of the features described on these pages. These features span the whole history of the grand garden in Britain and the delight of one era often became a despised example of bad taste in the next.

A brief history of the various styles appears on page 95 and the gardens you will visit will be basically informal (aiming to produce a natural look) or formal (containing a mixture of geometric shapes such as squares, circles, triangles etc.). Many 21st century gardens are a mixture of both the informal and formal approach, including features from the many styles which the gardening architects of previous centuries had so slavishly followed.

The heyday of the informal garden was 1730–1830. During that period the Landscape style flourished. No beds, hedges, ornate fountains nor straight lines – instead there were artificial lakes, man-made hills, temples, ha-has, arcades and ornamental bridges.

The formal gardens of Britain were created either before or after these great Landscape estates of the 18th century. There are not many authentic examples of the early formal garden but several

't Konings Huis van de Tuin-zyde, met de Fontein van Venus.

excellent reconstructions have been created. The basic feature to look for here is either the knot garden of the early English garden or the parterre of the grand French design. Other features of these early formal gardens include the long canal, the avenues of stately trees, the gazebo and the patte d'oie.

The late formal gardens were built during Victorian times and are characterised by intricate flower beds filled with bright annuals. Look also for the shrubbery, fernery, the topiary, statues, grottoes and conservatory.

# FEATURES

**ALCOVE** A recess in a wall or gatepost, used to house statuary or a seat. When the use was to house a bee-hive, the alcove is called a **bee-bole**

**ALLEY** A broad path cut through trees, the branches of which may be trimmed. Like the avenue it is a feature of the French style

**ARBOUR** The smallest and most ancient of garden houses, dating back to the Middle Ages. It is a shady retreat or **bower**, large enough for a seat, and often covered by climbing plants

**ARCADE** A series of connected arches

**ARMILLARY SUNDIAL** A sundial with a set of linked hoops

**AVENUE** A broad road lined on both sides with trees planted at regular intervals. The most popular trees for this purpose have been the elm, lime and horse chestnut

**AVIARY** Structure containing birds

**BALUSTRADE** An important feature in the formal garden, consisting of a row of balusters supporting a coping or parapet

**BASON** The receptacle which collects the water issuing from a fountain

**BATH HOUSE** A small sunken pool with steps leading down into it and seats around the side. It was for cold-water bathing, not swimming

**BELVEDERE** A look-out tower commanding views of the surrounding countryside

**BOLLARDS** Short posts set at regular intervals to prevent the entry of animals or vehicles into restricted areas

**BOSKET** A block of closely-planted trees providing a dark background to the bright colours of the parterre

**BRIDGE** A decorative and/or purely practical feature

**CANAL** The proper name for the long rectangular pool of the formal garden

**CATTLE GRID** A metal grating set in a driveway to prevent access by cattle

**CHINOISERIE** Chinese-style buildings and ornaments, popular in the 18th century. The Pagoda at Kew is the most famous piece of *chinoiserie*

**CISTERN** Made for purely utilitarian purposes – the collection of rainwater. Now used as an ornament or as a plant trough. Types displayed are usually made of lead and bear date of manufacture

**CLAIR-VOYÉE** A wrought-iron screen set into a wall so as to extend the view

**COLONNADE** A classical feature, consisting of a row of columns

**CONSERVATORY** Like the greenhouse, a glass-covered structure for tender plants. Unlike the greenhouse it is sometimes accessible from the house and may be highly ornate, but the dividing line between the two is vague. The **palm house** is the largest type

**DOVECOT** One of the oldest garden features. Brick and stone-built pigeon houses or columbaria can be found

**EXEDRA** A semi-circular expanse of turf usually bearing statuary and with a hedge forming the curved boundary

**FERNERY** No longer popular now that the Victorian fern craze has passed

**FINIAL** The ornament placed on top of a gatepost, roof, tower or column. The **ball** is popular and so is the **pineapple** which was introduced at the end of the 17th century

**FISH-POND** Until the introduction of goldfish in the 18th century, the fish-pond was not an ornamental feature; it was for the raising of carp for the table

**FOLLY** A general term for the many types of decorative but useless structures such as sham castles, sham bridges, pagodas, temples, pyramids, stone circles and so on

**FOUNTAIN** The standard water feature

**GARDEN HOUSE** A general term for structures designed for housing people rather than plants. The **arbour**, less than room size, is the simplest and the **pavilion** is the largest and most ornate. The **gazebo** is between these two extremes, as is the more recent **summer house**

**GATEHOUSE** A building which houses the gates and through which the driveway passes

**GAZEBO** An early type of garden house. There are two storeys – the upper one serving as a viewing point and the lower one as a store

**GREENHOUSE** A glass-covered structure for the raising and protection of tender plants (see Conservatory). Originally the tile-roofed 'greenshouse' which protected evergreens during the winter. Glass roofing and proper heating did not appear until the 19th century

**GREENHOUSE CORRIDOR** A glass-roofed walkway connecting several greenhouses. Prevents cold air from entering the houses when the doors are opened and also acts as a support for exotic climbing shrubs. A popular feature of botanic gardens

**GROTTO** A cave-like structure (sometimes natural but usually artificial) often lined with shells or pebbles

**GROUNDS** A vague term covering the large estate where the word 'garden' is inappropriate. Called **policies** in Scotland and **demesne** in Ireland

**HA-HA** A basic feature of the Landscape garden. It is a wide ditch separating the garden from the surrounding countryside. The view is not interrupted but animals are prevented from straying

**HEATED WALL** Wall with hot water pipes

**ICE HOUSE** Igloo-like building with an underground chamber for storing ice. Very few remain

**KNOT GARDEN** Small and often rectangular beds bearing geometric patterns outlined in clipped hedges of box or other low-growing shrubs. The spaces between are filled with flowers or coloured stones

**LAKE** Area of water larger than a pond

**LODGE** Gatekeeper's house situated at the entrance to the driveway

**MAZE** See page 283

**MOUNT** A small artificial hill with an arbour or seat on top. A basic garden feature until 1650

**OBELISK** Common feature in grand gardens, usually erected at the end of an avenue to commemorate an outstanding event

**ORANGERY** Orange and lemon trees were the first tender evergreens to adorn British gardens. In winter they were housed in the Orangery, which became the most ornate of the early plant houses

**PALISADE** A line of deciduous trees with branches trimmed and interlaced

**PARTERRE** A large, intricately patterned garden feature constructed close to the house. Derived from the knot garden, its hedge patterns are much larger in scale and there are other features such as topiary, statuary and fountains. The **parterre broderie** is the most complex form

**PATTE D'OIE** A 'goose foot' is the fan-wise spread of avenues or walks from a single point. A feature of the French style

**PAVILION** The largest and most ornate of the garden houses. Derived from the Tudor **banqueting house**. Always architecturally designed, yet never approaching the mini-palaces of France

**PERGOLA** An arched structure which supports climbing plants. A popular feature ever since the earliest days of gardening. Rambler roses are the usual covering

**PLEACHED ALLEY** A tree-lined walk where the branches are arched over and interlaced

**PROSPECT** An attractive view covering a large area, both wide and long (compare Vista)

**SARCOPHAGUS** A stone coffin

**SCALLOPED WALL** Wall topped with a series of semi-circles

**SEAT** Earliest seats were turf-covered; good example in Queen's Garden, Kew. Many materials have subsequently been used – wood, stone, iron, concrete and so on

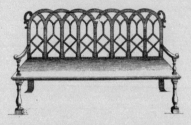

**SERPENTINE WALL** Snake-like (wavy) wall

**STATUARY** Animal- or human-shaped stone figures

**STILT HEDGE** A clipped hedge with bare trunks showing at the base

**SUNDIAL** Timepiece using shadow cast by the sun

**TAPIS VERT** A long rectangular strip of turf ('green carpet') between canals or driveways

**TEMPLE** Building of classical shape with roof supported by columns

**TERRACE** The level space between house and garden. Returned to the British garden early in the 19th century after its banishment by Capability Brown

**THÉÂTRE DE VERDURE** An open-air stage of turf and neatly-trimmed hedges

**TOPIARY** The clipping of trees and shrubs into geometrical or fanciful shapes

**TREILLAGE** Trellis used to produce an elaborate architectural feature such as an arbour or pergola

**TRELLIS** A framework of crossed slats or wires upon which plants can be trained

**TROMPE L'OEIL** A feature designed to enhance the appearance or size of the garden by optical illusion. The most popular trompe l'oeil is the narrowing of the far ends of beds and borders

**URN** A large ornate vessel which is narrow-mouthed and generally lidded. A common feature in the grand garden

**VASE** A decorative container, usually wide-mouthed, often used as a finial. The use of vases as plant containers was reintroduced at the beginning of the Victorian era

**VISTA** An attractive view stretching into the distance but with little width (compare Prospect)

**WELL-HEAD** An ornamental feature, although a few do stand over wells

# MAZES

TAKE AN adventurous youngster to a garden with a maze and there can be no doubt where the first port of call will have to be. The thrill of being lost in the hedge-lined puzzle and the frustration of moving from one blind alley to the next have been a feature of some of our grand gardens for centuries, but the history of the maze goes back much further and it has its surprises. As an example, the earliest mazes had a religious or deeply mystical purpose and were not designed for amusement, and the living puzzles at Hampton Court and Chatsworth are not really mazes at all!

---

## The earliest mazes had a religious or deeply mystical purpose and were not designed for amusement

---

A maze is basically two-dimensional. It is a winding and convoluted pathway which may be lined with low walls, logs or hedges of box, rosemary or lavender. Lined or not, you can always see right across it. When the walls or hedges lining the pathways are too high for you to see over them we have a three-dimensional maze or labyrinth. Thus a maze and labyrinth are not the same thing, but in popular usage the word 'maze' covers all types.

The story of the maze and labyrinth goes back to the beginning of civilisation – the twisting path represents the thread of life, paradise regained, death and rebirth, the search for the Holy Grail and so on. In Crete there was the Minotaur's labyrinth and its design appeared on Cretan coins from 1500 B.C. You will find mazes on Roman mosaic floors and on early carvings in N. America, India and Africa – there are mazes traced in the chalk on the Downs of southern England. We know they had a religious significance but we do not know exactly how the prehistoric mazes were used. Early churches on the Continent had mazes on their floors and penitents crept along the winding path on their knees as they said their prayers – an example can be seen at Chartres Cathedral in France.

Mazes were cut in the turf of English medieval gardens and there can be no doubt that these early single-line mazes were used in the same way as the church pavement versions – the turf maze at Wing in Leicestershire is built to the same design as the one inside Chartres Cathedral. Few of these turf mazes now remain, but an excellent one can still be seen at Hilton in Cambridgeshire.

The religious role of the maze disappeared in Elizabethan times and it became a place for people 'to sport there at times'. A variety of games were played on the paths, and in the 17th century the first labyrinths with tall hedge walls were created in England. Roses were the original screening plants but they were later replaced by yew and privet. The Wimbledon labyrinth made for Charles I was composed of 'young trees, wood and sprays of good growth and height, cut out into several meanders, circles, semicircles, windings and intricate turnings.'

The idea of 'windings and intricate turnings' declined and was replaced by interlinked paths and junctions with a series of blind alleys to tantalise the visitor. The famous Versailles Maze has gone but the Hampton Court Maze, laid out in about 1690, is still there and remains a favourite attraction. Some of the mazes in our stately home gardens are of more recent origin – Hatfield House Maze was planted in the 19th century and the Chatsworth Maze was made in the last century. For other labyrinths you can visit Somerleyton Hall in Suffolk, Hever Castle in Kent and Glendurgan in Cornwall.

# PEAT

ONE OF THE basic principles of good gardening is to ensure that there is adequate organic matter in the soil. All those glowing fertilizer advertisements may be very encouraging, but feeding does not replace the need for humus.

These days we rely on the garden compost we make from grass clippings, dead plants etc., and until recently peat which was bought in large bags or bales. But now peat is under a cloud and is completely shunned by many gardeners, and so there are a number of questions to be answered. What is peat, is the harvesting of peat an environmental sin, and is its use in the garden really necessary?

## The old question arises – which is better, farmyard manure or peat?

It is first necessary to understand the nature of peat, which consists of partly decomposed vegetable matter from bogs or heaths. This organic matter has not broken down like dead vegetation normally does because the process of decomposition has been blocked by very wet or very acid conditions, or a combination of the two. That is peat in general, but there are two distinct types of horticultural peat.

**Sedge Peat** is the type usually dug from English heaths and moors. The story begins in the bottom of a valley where the drainage is poor. Salts washed down from the hillsides create an environment which few plants like – nutrient-rich and very wet, so sedges and rushes start to take over. The dead plants do not decompose properly in the waterlogged conditions and this dark brown mass, made up of the remains of sedges, rushes, heather, a few tree roots and some mosses, has been harvested as sedge peat. The removal of this type of peat has scarred the countryside of areas in Somerset etc., and its use in gardening can never be justified.

**Moss Peat** (Sphagnum Peat) is quite different, and this is the type which is found in Ireland, Canada, Finland, Norway, Russia and Latvia. Here there is no downwash of salts from nearby hills and the bog rises above the level of the surrounding ground. This means that the bog is entirely dependent on rain falling on the surface to maintain its water content, so this type of deposit is associated with regions of high rainfall. The surface of the mounded area bears a mixed flora of plants but the body of the raised bog consists of dead sphagnum moss. Decay does not take place because of the very acid conditions, and it is this moss situated close to the surface which is cut, dried and then milled to produce moss peat for horticultural use. The lower levels of the peat in the bog are more compressed and have a higher wax content – no use for the garden but an excellent fuel.

---

## If you are going to buy peat for the garden, buy a large bale rather than little bags

---

This moss peat has quite different properties to sedge peat. It is lighter in both weight and colour and takes longer to break down in the soil. It is always acidic and has twice the water-holding capacity of sedge peat. It is fluffier and more pleasant to handle.

Now we can deal with the second question which was posed earlier – is the harvesting of peat for garden use an environmental sin? The situation with regard to moss peat is rather complex. Until recently moss peat from northern wastes in Russia and Canada was regarded like sedge peat as a non-renewable biomass. As such its harvesting and use was regarded by environment-alists as non-acceptable. However, the Intergovernmental Panel on Climate Change, a U.N. advisory body, has reclassified moss peat from a 'fossil fuel' to a 'renewable biomass' resource.

Which leaves us with the final question – is it now worth reconsidering its use in the garden? Nothing has changed – the reclassification does not remove the need for transporting the deposits long distances from out-of-the-way places, so the recommendations remain unaltered. Don't use peat for overall soil improvement – it is not efficient, and garden compost or manure will do a much better job. However, moss peat has a role to play in planting and seed composts where there are no substitutes of equal merit.

# PLANT ROOTS AND
# FOUNDATIONS

THERE IS something about trees and shrubs which turns a collection of flower beds and a lawn into a garden. These woody plants provide the permanent living skeleton of our plot, and many more trees and shrubs are being planted these days than ever before.

But not everything in the garden is rosy. Many homeowners have a vague fear that the tree or tall hedge growing close to the house must be 'doing something to the foundations'. We promise ourselves that one day, when it really gets too big, we will cut it down … and we leave it at that.

Should we be *more* worried than the homeowner just described, and get the tall conifer outside the window removed as

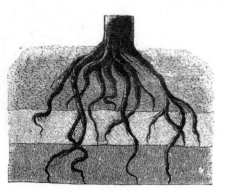

soon as possible, or should we be *less* worried, knowing that the idea of roots damaging foundations is just an old wives' tale? There is no simple answer – it all depends on a number of factors.

Of course it could not be true that any tree growing close to a house must damage the foundations. We have all seen hundreds of examples of large specimens growing close to fine old buildings with no problems arising, and in the U.S. there are many homes which have actually been built around a fine tree so that it becomes part of the structure. The point here is that foundations very rarely are affected by the pressure of the roots – tree roots just do not grow steadily underground until they touch and then dislodge the foundations.

The danger is much more subtle. The leaves of a large tree or hedge lose a considerable amount of water and this is drawn from the soil's reserves. With normal rainfall this is not a problem as the quantity lost is steadily replaced, but during a period of severe drought the soil may shrink and the reserves drawn up by the tree are not restored.

Note that the soil *may* shrink – whether it will or not depends on the soil type. If your house is on sand, chalk or non-shrinkable clay then the danger is remote. If, however, your soil is on a shrinkable clay, such as London Clay, then you can certainly have a problem with subsidence and the headache and heartache of disturbance and costly repairs.

---

## Subsidence is an ever-present danger with shrinkable clay in a period of drought whether or not trees are present

---

Subsidence is an ever-present danger with shrinkable clay in a period of drought whether or not trees are present – the presence of a nearby tree simply increases the water loss and so increases the danger of subsidence.

To lessen the danger there are various steps you can take. Don't plant trees closer to the house than the height you expect them to reach. Avoid the trees with a bad reputation (poplar, willow and oak) and keep other trees which may be close to the house pruned regularly so that the leaf area is kept under control.

It may seem that the obvious thing to do would be to fell a large tree growing close to a house built on clay. Unfortunately the sudden change in water balance can cause the trouble you are trying to avoid. Prune it by all means, but seek expert advice if you wish to remove a large tree growing near the house.

It is some consolation that trees need not be a problem, but this is little comfort to the houseowner on London Clay. Do check your Home Insurance Policy – damage by subsidence should be included.

Roots may not be a danger from nearby trees but branches certainly can be. High winds always bring a sorry tale of damaged roofs, walls and windows – it is a good idea to have dangerous branches removed *before* the wind does it for you.

# PLANTS WITH A STORY

## MYRTLE

When Adam and Eve left the Garden of Eden they were allowed to take three things. They chose a date to provide the best of all fruits, a grain of wheat to provide the best of all foods and a sprig of myrtle to provide the best of all fragrances. According to Moslem tradition, Adam took only the myrtle sprig.

The common myrtle (*Myrtus communis*) has been grown in Britain for over 400 years and thrives in a sunny and sheltered site. It is not very hardy, but your care will be rewarded in July and August with an abundant display of deliciously-scented, white flowers. The foliage is also fragrant, and the tradition of carrying myrtle in the bridal wreath began with the Jews during their captivity in Babylonia. It has spread to all countries and all climates, and received a Royal accolade from Queen Victoria. After her marriage to Prince Albert in 1840, she planted a myrtle sprig from her bouquet in the grounds of Osborne House on the Isle of Wight. The cutting rooted and the bush flourished – the progeny from this original sprig have produced myrtles for the wedding bouquets of Queen Elizabeth, Princess

Margaret, Princess Anne and the Princess of Wales. Planting myrtles from the bridal bouquet is an old country custom, but it is a job for the bridesmaid and not the bride.

## FLANDERS POPPY

Every November we wear paper or silk poppies, and wreaths of these flowers are placed at the bases of cenotaphs and war memorials all over the country. At the Festival of Remembrance in London's Albert Hall many thousands of petals flutter down on the silent gathering as it reflects on the dead from two World Wars. One of the young men who died was Dr. John McRae, a Canadian medical officer in World War I. One amongst millions, but it was McRae who was responsible for the adoption of the Corn poppy as the symbol of remembrance for the fallen.

In 1915 McRae was serving at a field hospital near Ypres, tending the injured and dying. Outside the windows he saw the red Corn poppies growing in profusion over the graves and between the trenches. He remembered the Greek legend that the poppy was created by the god of sleep and to McRae the weed symbolised the everlasting rest of the fallen. He turned this image into the poem *In Flanders Fields* which ended

> 'If ye break faith with us who die
> We shall not sleep, though poppies grow
> In Flanders fields.'

The need for remembrance of the dead and the symbolism of the poppy stayed with him, and when dying of pneumonia in 1918 he asked for these flowers to be strewn on his grave. Every year a wreath of poppies is placed by his tombstone in France and since 1921 the British Legion has sold artificial poppies in aid of ex-servicemen and their families.

## PARSLEY

Parsley is not a plant for the superstitious. There is a long tradition which labels it as the plant of the Devil, and the only safe time to sow seeds is Good Friday. The reason is that on this Holy day the Devil has no power over the living things on earth.

Cutting parsley and giving it to a friend will mean bad luck for you and an even worse fate for the recipient. A witch's curse was to cut parsley when speaking the victim's name and young lovers were warned not to pick the herb or their sweethearts would die. Of course, this nonsense will not affect you. Sow the seed in spring and wait for several weeks for it to germinate – it has to travel to the Devil seven times before it can emerge. And never boast if your parsley flourishes – it can mean only one thing …

## CHRYSANTHEMUM

The multi-petalled chrysanthemum did not appear in Europe until the middle of the 18th century, although its history in the Far East goes back for thousands of years. It was described in China in the 5th century B.C. and it became the emblem of the Mikado of Japan more than 1000 years ago. Chrysanthemum shows were being held in that country before William the Conqueror invaded Britain, and the 'Rising Sun' you see on Japanese postage stamps is actually a chrysanthemum flower.

The legend of the chrysanthemum originated in China. The girl Kiku-no-hana asked a spirit how long her forthcoming marriage to her betrothed would last. She was told that they would remain together for as many years as there were petals on the flower she would wear on her wedding dress. She searched everywhere, but could only find five-petalled flowers. At last she found one with 17 petals, and with her hairpin she divided each petal into two and then into four. This was the first chrysanthemum, and for 68 years she lived in bliss with Kiku-ri-bana. Since then the flower has been revered in the East as a symbol of purity and long life. From the legend it should also be the sign of female ingenuity!

The first chrysanthemum to come to Europe was probably the small, yellow-flowered *Chrysanthemum indicum* – hence its name, based on *chrysos* 'gold' and *anthos* 'flower'.

## SAGE

Today we only think of sage as a herb for mixing with onions to stuff the turkey, but once it was a valued medicinal herb – 'He that would live for aye, must eat sage in May.' Sage Tea has long been regarded as an excellent stimulant, with digestive properties, but in some countries of the world it was regarded as a brain stimulant – hence the common name. In the East they were quite convinced that this herb improved the intelligence – in the early days of the tea trade the Chinese were willing to exchange three chests of tea with the Dutch for just one chest of sage leaves.

To make Sage Tea, pour 600 ml of boiling water over 15 g of fresh sage leaves and 15 g of sugar. Simmer gently and add the juice of a lemon. Strain and serve – a great pick-me-up, according to its reputation.

## MISTLETOE

Kissing under the mistletoe began as a British custom – it has no counterpart on the Continent. Each year French farmers are delighted to get rid of the parasitic climbers which grow on their apples and hawthorns by sending them over to Britain. But the Christmastime sales of mistletoe have seriously declined in recent years – gone are the days when girls believed that they would remain old maids if not kissed beneath the waxy berries, and boys no longer feel the need for seeking permission from a sprig of mistletoe before stealing a kiss.

The origin of the kissing custom is unknown, but we do know that it was once a much more serious affair – to kiss a girl under the mistletoe in public meant a proposal of marriage. In later times a berry was removed every time a kiss was taken – a primitive form of kiss control.

Mistletoe has been used in herbal medicines since the Dark Ages. It was popular with the early herbalists – 'Good for the grief of sinew, itch, sores, toothache and biting of mad dogs or venomous snakes,' said Culpeper. Today it has

created interest in research circles by showing anti-cancer properties. A strange plant indeed – good for kissing and good for herbal medicines but once not allowed in Church. Its association with the heathen Druids was strong, and legend has it that the mistletoe was the tree on which Christ was crucified – it was cursed afterwards to become a weak parasite and an outcast.

## RUSSELL LUPIN

The lupins we grow in the herbaceous border belong to the Russell strain. Once the lupin was quite a plain flower but not any more. Russell lupins have large spikes of showy blooms in a vast assortment of hues, ranging from the most delicate pastel shades to garish bi-colours. The interesting story is that George Russell was not a trained botanist nor a professional nurseryman – he was a simple allotment holder who selected and re-selected seedlings on his little plot in York for over 25 years, and then produced a strain which put his name amongst those of the great plant breeders.

## ST. JOHN'S WORT

*Hypericum* is a popular garden shrub, growing in any garden soil and thriving in sun or shade. Its popular name is St. John's Wort, and the red spots on the leaves are supposed to have appeared when St. John the Baptist was beheaded. The Saint's Day is June 24, and this flower has special associations with Midsummer's Day. In earlier times it was believed that hanging flowers around the cottage on this day would protect the occupants from witches and thunderbolts, and the favourite flowers for this purpose were the bright yellow blooms of St. John's Wort.

## GLASTONBURY THORN

There is a hawthorn in Somerset which is world famous – it is the Holy Thorn of Glastonbury. It occasionally blooms on old Christmas Day (5 January) and in earlier times this was regarded as a miracle by simple people who were used to seeing hawthorn trees burst into bloom in May. When blooms do appear at Christmas the Vicar of Glastonbury sends a flowering branch to the Queen.

Its fame began in 1535 when the chief adviser to Henry VIII sent a doctor to investigate the rumour. The existence of the tree which 'blossoms at Christmas, mindful of our Lord' was confirmed, and the legend of Joseph of Arimathea sprang up. Joseph had buried Christ, and on one of his trips to the tin mines of Somerset he rested on a hill and laid down his staff. This staff had been cut from the tree which had provided the Crown of Thorns, and on this far-off Somerset hillside it took root and grew into the Holy Thorn of Glastonbury.

A lovely story, but the truth is that it is *Crataegus monogyna* 'Praecox', which grows in Southern Europe and the Near East. It is thought to have been brought to Glastonbury Abbey by a pilgrim many centuries ago, who would not have known that the early-flowering properties of his introduction would cause such a stir.

## OLD ENGLISH LAVENDER

Old English Lavender isn't English at all – it was brought to Britain by the Romans who used it to perfume their bath water. Hence the name lavender, from the latin *lavo*, 'I wash'. Its popularity has remained over the centuries – when dried it retains its fragrance longer than any other herb and it has been used in herbal medicines for all sorts of purposes, from curing fainting fits to the cure of 'all diseases of the head that come of a cold cause – flowers of lavender comfort the braines very well'.

Lavender has been a commercial crop for centuries. The flowers were distilled to produce Lavender Oil, and this still goes on today. The flowers were sold by street sellers, a trade which has now disappeared.

Lavender fields around London were once a common sight, and they are remembered in some of the district names which remain – Lavender Hill, Lavender Lane and Lavender Gate.

## CAMELLIA

Many people have fallen in love with the camellia (correctly pronounced Kam-*ell*-ia, not Kam-*eel*-ia). This is a distinction it

shares with the rose, the orchid and so on, but the camellia is unique because its first British grower died for it. The Jesuit monk Georg Josef Kamel, or Camellus, toured the Philippines and collected plants there – one of his discoveries was the handsome evergreen which now bears his name. The first two camellia plants in England were raised by Lord Petre in Essex, but his gardener treated them like stove plants to be grown under tropical conditions and they quite quickly succumbed. Poor Lord Petre died of a broken heart, but his gardener did not. James Gordon tried again with another plant in 1740 and this time he succeeded. The next step was to open a nursery, and this original camellia was the parent of all the early plants grown in Britain.

Lord Petre was not the only camellia lover to meet a tragic end. Alphonsine Plessis left her village in France and moved to Paris in 1840. The beautiful 15 year old was courted by Liszt, Dumas and other great names of the day – and was known for her passion for white camellias. Rich and famous, she died at only 22 and was immortalised as Violetta in Dumas' *La Dame aux Camélias* and Verdi's *La Traviata*.

## WHITE POPLAR

The White poplar (*Populus alba*) is an easy tree to recognise – the woolly underside of the leaves is immediately apparent when the foliage flutters in the breeze. Such an unusual effect was bound to attract a legend – the story is that Hercules was sent

to Hades to capture the guard dog Cerberus as his 12th labour. As he struggled through the underworld he paused by the nymph Leuce who had been turned into a tree by Hades' jealous wife. From the branches he picked some leaves and made a wreath for his forehead, and as Hercules continued to complete his labour the sweat from his brow bleached the undersides of the leaves.

## HIMALAYAN BLUE POPPY

Older readers may remember the excitement when the seeds of the Himalayan blue poppy first became available some years before the outbreak of World War II. The story of the pure blue poppies which grew high in the Himalayan mountain range began in 1886 when a French missionary found it growing in China and sent back a dried specimen to Europe. Many plant hunters sought it eagerly but it remained undetected until it was rediscovered in 1913 by Lt.-Col. Bailey. He was honoured in its original Latin name (*Meconopsis baileyi*) but once again only a pressed flower was collected.

We are indebted to one of the most successful of all plant hunters for the Himalayan blue poppies in our gardens. Frank Kingdon-Ward found a clump growing in the Himalayas in 1924 and later collected seeds which he brought to London. It became a popular garden novelty, and when he saw it blooming in

Hyde Park he later commented 'I found it growing on the roof of the world and now I saw it growing in the hub of the world.' This poppy is called *Meconopsis betonicifolia* these days and is grown as a short-lived perennial. It needs light shade and moist soil to succeed and produce its azure flowers in June and July.

## HOLLY

With prickles representing the Crown of Thorns and red berries symbolising drops of blood, it is not surprising that holly is a basic feature of our Christmas decorations. But there are rules to follow – it is unlucky to bring holly indoors before Christmas Eve and it must be put out on Twelfth Night – to break this rule is to court disaster. You also have to be careful to bring in the holly before the ivy on Christmas Eve if you are a male chauvinist – in that way you can ensure that the man will rule the household. To bring in ivy first would result in a woman-dominated house. Always allow both holly and ivy to grow freely in the garden – this will ensure protection from witches, fires and infertility.

The use of holly in religious festivals is much older than Christianity. Evergreens were widely used by the ancient Chinese, Egyptians, Israelites and so on, and holly was a feature in the December Saturnalia of the Romans before their conversion to Christianity.

## TRUFFLE

The truffle has been highly prized as a delicacy since Roman times, and truffle collecting is a thriving industry in France. They cannot be cultivated – hence their rarity. The best of all in the view of gourmets is the Périgord truffle (*Tuber melanospermum*), a dark brown underground fungus which can be as large as 12 cm across.

Truffles are rare in Britain, but they do occur. The species is the Summer truffle (*Tuber aestivum*) and it favours chalky soil around the roots of beech trees. They grow about 10 cm below the surface and the hunting season is between October and March. Look for cracks in the ground and an earthy aroma. Unfortunately your nose will almost certainly not be sensitive enough – trained dogs and pigs are used for sniffing out truffles. Without a truffle-hunting poodle you will have to search for truffles in the summertime when the small, yellow-coloured truffle flies hover above the ground before sunset. The professional truffle collectors who searched the beech woods of Hampshire, Wiltshire, Sussex, Kent and other southern counties before World War II have now disappeared, but the truffles are there for the keen (and lucky) amateur.

## FOXGLOVE

The 16th-century herbal written by Leonhard Fuchs contained the first reference to the medicinal properties of foxglove leaves, but his recommendation was for the use of this wild flower as a purgative. He called the plant *Digitalis* and never dreamt that one day the drug extracted from its leaves would play a major part in the treatment of heart disease.

The credit for this use must go to the 18th century physician Dr. William Withering. He noticed the part played by the foxglove in folk medicine and in 1776 wrote that 'a dram of it taken inwardly excites the heart muscle'. Dr. Withering treated 158 patients with an extract and found that there was a reduction in the pulse rate. This increased the efficiency of each heartbeat, and the health of over one hundred of the patients improved. A new specific medicine was created, and the work of the Foxglove Doctor is the favourite example quoted by herbalists of the benefits we have derived from plant drugs.

## MANDRAKE

This evil-smelling, poisonous plant is related to the potato. Although its home is the Mediterranean area, the magic and fear surrounding the mandrake was well-known to the British poets of the Elizabethan age. 'Shrieks like mandrakes, torn out of the earth' (*Romeo and Juliet*) refers to the belief that pulling a mandrake caused it to scream, and the sound made the listener mad. Digging up a mandrake was fatal – they were removed by black dogs roped to the roots.

These legends arose from the forked fleshy root borne by the mandrake. Its vaguely human shape plus its toxic properties meant that it was a plant of the Devil, but once out of the ground it could be handled without dire consequences. Safety to the handler, perhaps, but one of the practices was to boil up the roots to produce a popular poison of the Middle Ages. In small doses the mandrake extract was used as an anaesthetic – 'Give me to drink mandragora, That I may sleep out this gap of time my Antony is away' (*Antony and Cleopatra*). In smaller doses it was used as an aphrodisiac, an antidote to sterility and a cure for many diseases. A terrible plant with terrible legends, the worst being the medieval belief that the mandrake grew from the sperm of murderers who had been hung.

# GORSE

Throughout Britain you will find the prickly, evergreen shrub known as gorse, furze or whin. On inhospitable sites such as sandy, barren soils or steep slopes you will see its golden, fragrant flowers at any time of the year – 'When gorse is out of bloom, kissing is out of season'. This simple plant gave its name to a Royal family which ruled Britain for nearly 250 years, but its association with this line of kings began overseas with Geoffrey, Count of Anjou, who died in 1151.

Why Geoffrey adopted the gorse plant as his symbol is not certain. One story relates how he lost his helmet feather in battle whereupon he bent down, picked up a sprig of gorse and inserted it in his helmet with the cry '*Planta genista, planta genista!*' Alternatively it is claimed that he adopted the *planta genista* as a symbol of humility during his pilgrimage to the Holy Land. His son, Henry II of England, was the first of the House of *Planta Genista* or Plantagenet, and the Plantagenets reigned from 1154 to the removal of Richard II in 1399.

## THE CHRISTMAS TREE

The Christmas tree in Britain is a surprisingly modern custom. In 1840 the German Prince Albert cut a small fir tree on the Windsor Castle estate and brought it inside to amuse his young wife, Queen Victoria. This was decorated with candles,

sweets, small presents and paper chains. An angel stood on the uppermost branch – the Christmas tree had arrived.

It was not invented by Prince Albert – in his native Germany it was a common custom to have a tree indoors on December 24, the religious feast day of Adam and Eve, and fir trees decorated with apples had been used in this way for several hundred years. It is strange that this appealing custom should have taken so long to cross the Channel – German settlers in America were decorating their fir trees with presents and candles as early as the 17th century.

Spruce is the most popular Christmas tree, followed by fir. Our most famous Christmas tree is erected each year in Trafalgar Square – a gift from Oslo in gratitude for Britain's help during World War II.

# Rosemary

Rosemary was one of the basic herbs of the Middle Ages, widely used for cooking, making medicines and warding off the plague. It is recorded that during one plague outbreak the price of a rosemary sprig went up by 600 per cent, showing that the current laws of economics applied even then. Rosemary was popular for decorating churches at Christmas before holly became such a universal favourite, and it has long been associated with remembrance. Until Edwardian times it was common practice to carry rosemary at a funeral.

According to legend the flowers were originally white, but during her flight from Herod, the Virgin Mary covered a bush with her blue gown and since then the flowers have been blue. The name, however, is not derived from Mary – it comes from *ros* 'dew' and *Marinus* 'seaside'. It is an appropriate name because in the wild, rosemary grows on the sea cliffs of Southern Europe. It came to Britain in the 14th century and has been a feature of our herb gardens ever since.

## Lawson's Cypress

*Chamaecyparis lawsoniana* varieties are one of the most popular conifers in our gardens, and you will see them everywhere. They come in all sizes and colours – the compact 'Ellwoodii' and the blue 'Allumii', the pillar-like 'Columnaris' and the yellow 'Stewartii'. You will find a selection in every garden centre, and yet the native home of Lawson's cypress are two isolated small patches of land between Oregon and California in the United States.

The Scottish botanist John Jeffrey began collecting trees and shrubs in Oregon in 1850 – his discoveries bear the species name *jeffreyi*. In 1854 he disappeared, and a number of expeditions went to search for him. A fellow Scot, William Murray, joined in – but Jeffrey was lost in the wilderness. While trekking in the Sacramento Valley in search of the plant hunter, Murray came across a new cypress – he sent the seeds to the Scottish nurseryman Lawson and the plants which

were raised were called *Chamaecyparis lawsoniana*. One man died searching for plants, another was risking his life when he found them, but it was the seed house which got the name ...

## SNOWDROP

The little snowdrop is a welcome sight each year in early spring, its nodding white flowers serving as a promise that the floral year is about to begin. It has long been a symbol of hope – the legend is that Eve was weeping in her barren garden after the Fall of Man when an angel comforted her by blowing on to a snowflake and turning it into a snowdrop. A flower bloomed, and Hope was born.

Early monks travelling back and forth to Rome brought the flower to England and it has become naturalised in the vicinity of old monasteries. It became a church flower and on Candlemas (February 2) the image of the Virgin Mary was taken down and snowdrops spread in its place. In this way snowdrops earned the common names Maids of February, Candlemas Bells and Mary's Tapers, but their presence in churchyards gave them an 'unlucky' reputation for later generations. Even today many country people will not take snowdrops indoors and the sight of a single snowdrop blooming in the garden is taken to foretell an impending disaster.

## SAFFRON

The little Saffron crocus blooms in early autumn and within the pale purple petals are long golden stigmas. Time has passed the Saffron crocus by – it no longer figures prominently in books on herbs and the plants no longer bloom freely, but in the Middle Ages it was one of the most important of all flowers. In the 16th century it was the apothecary's standby, being used for jaundice, measles and depression, and it was also a major spice used for dyeing cloth (and hair) yellow and for baking saffron cakes. Spice sellers were known as 'saffron grocers' in those days and its production centre was Saffron Walden in Essex. It takes 100,000 blooms to produce a kilo of saffron, so large areas of land around the town were devoted to this lowly crocus. The fields have gone now that synthetic yellow dyes and better treatments for depression have been produced, but even today you will find the Saffron crocus growing wild around the town and people still make saffron cakes in the West Country.

This plant is not native to Britain – an early pilgrim is supposed to have smuggled some corms back from the Middle East in a hollowed-out staff and then planted them in his home town of Walden. The saffron industry flourished there and Walden extended its name.

# POMANDERS AND POSIES

At some stage the pomander and the posy changed their sex. In the Middle Ages they were worn or carried by men of rank rather than women – sweet-smelling accessories which were often decorative but always used with a practical purpose in mind. By the middle of the 19th century they were exclusively worn or carried by women and their practical role had given way to one of pure adornment.

The **Pomander** has changed its form over the years as well as its use, and it defies a simple definition. It began as a small nugget of ambergris (the *pomme d'embre* or 'apple of amber') in a small perforated case made from gold, silver, crystal, ivory or pottery. This pomander was worn round the neck, hung from a belt or attached to a ring, and its mention in the 14th century poem *Romance of the Rose* underlines its long history.

The purpose of the pomander was to protect the wearer from the 'foul, stinking air' of the day. By Elizabethan times it was part of the basic garb of the courtiers and all men of quality, as it was regarded as protection against the plague and other infections. The pomander had become highly decorative and the contents were now a waxy blend (**Pomade**) of fats, herbs and spices. Rotten apples were a popular ingredient – so were cinnamon and cloves.

---

## The purpose of the pomander was to protect the wearer from the 'foul, stinking air' of the day

---

Pomanders were far too expensive for the humble peasants, but they feared the plague as much as their masters. Cardinal Wolsey is credited with the invention of the poor man's pomander or **Comfort Apple**, and he carried these living pomanders on state occasions. An orange was covered with cloves and rolled in cinnamon – it is the version of this pomander we know today and serves as a sweet-scented novelty. To Wolsey it was a practical protection against the ills of the day.

In the 18th century the popularity of the pomander began to decline and was replaced by the **Vinaigrette** which had its heyday in Victorian times. The vinaigrette was a small enamelled container with a pierced lid which contained a piece of sponge soaked in a mixture of vinegar and lavender. It was the female equivalent of the male snuff box, and the pomander of the Elizabethan courtier had become the vinaigrette of the Victorian girl and matron … the pomander had changed its sex.

Many descriptions have been used for bunches of flowers which are carried or worn, and these terms are often interchanged or used indiscriminately. There are no clear-cut definitions for the various forms of these arrangements, but the purist makes the following distinctions.

A group of flowers which is tastefully arranged and then held or attached to clothing is basically a **Bouquet**. Such bouquets are generally small and compact with the exception of the **Wedding Bouquet**. Since pre-Christian times it has been the custom for a bride to carry flowers at her wedding and many flowers, including myrtle, orange blossom, rosemary and roses, have been associated with such bouquets over the years. A small bouquet of fragrant flowers and/or herbs which is carried in the hand is a **Nosegay**. When colourful flowers which may or may not be fragrant are surrounded with a paper frill, greenery or silver foil, the bouquet is usually called a **Posy** or posey, although the original meaning of 'posy' was a poem which accompanied a nosegay. A **Tussy Mussy** or tussie mussie is a small nosegay consisting entirely of fragrant flowers and some leaves in which a central bloom, usually a rose bud, is surrounded by the other flowers which in turn are encircled by the leaves.

When an exotic flower or small bouquet is worn by a woman rather than carried it is called a **Corsage**. According to legend the young Prince Albert slit the lapel of his jacket with a pocket knife in order to insert the rose given to him by his young bride. So the **Buttonhole** is supposed to have originated, but the custom almost certainly is older than the legend.

So far we have been discussing bunches of flowers or single blooms. Flowers and leaves may be woven into a band to form a **Garland**. When a garland is firm and circular it is a **Wreath** and when worn on the head it is a **Chaplet**. Finally, a soft and looping garland is a **Festoon** or swag.

The posy, nosegay and tussy mussy are no longer part of our everyday life, but in Victorian times a well-dressed lady would always carry one to a social occasion. It was part of her *ensemble* and for the young it was also part of their language – the choice of flowers could be used to transmit secret messages by the Floral Code (see page 144).

## When an exotic flower or small bouquet is worn by a woman rather than carried it is called a Corsage

Pure decoration and fun, but once the nosegay had a much more practical purpose. From medieval times it was carried by men of importance to protect them from the evil air. This practice, so common in Elizabethan times, died out amongst men long ago but the tradition is still maintained by the judge who carries his nosegay at the opening of the Sessions, and the Lord Mayor of London who carries a small posy at the Lord Mayor's Show.

The posy and nosegay became universally-popular female accessories in the 1800s but their popularity declined quite rapidly at the start of the 20th century. The corsage began much later than either the posy or pomander, but its popularity has continued into the present century.

Today we use flowers to adorn the house rather than ourselves. Now we give long-stemmed blooms to friends and relatives, either as simple bunches or in stylishly-arranged bouquets to mark some special occasion. We know that these flowers will not ward off the plague and we do not expect them to mask unpleasant smells. They have no hidden meaning as in Victorian times but the sentiment is just the same – flowers remain a sign of affection.

# ROSES WITH A STORY

## LA FRANCE

The textbooks will tell you that *La France* was the first Hybrid Tea Rose and the date was 1867. This may well be true – *La France*'s claim to the title is certainly as good as or better than any other claimant, but there was no dramatic introduction of a new type of bloom as occurred with the Hand-painted Rose in 1971.

In Victorian times the favourite rose was the Hybrid Perpetual. The blooms were large and fragrant but the group had its problems. The flowering period and colour range were limited, the growth was rampant and the flowers were inelegant in shape. Breeders began to introduce the tender but shapely Tea Rose into their crosses, and by 1880 it was clear that the Tea Rose blood was now so strong in some varieties that a new class was needed – the *Hybrides de Thé* (Hybrid Teas).

It was then necessary to look back and see which variety could claim to be the first. Britain's *Cheshunt Hybrid* was rejected – the decision went to *La France* raised 13 years previously, even though its parentage was unknown and its raiser, Guillot Fils, regarded it as a Hybrid Perpetual!

## MINIATURE ROSE

The story of the discovery of miniature roses is as fascinating as anything that the plant world has to offer. It started in 1810, when Mauritius was captured by the British from the French. Botanists with the Army discovered there a China rose, perfect in every detail and in full flower, yet

growing no more than a few centimetres high. This miniature rose was brought back to England, where Miss Mary Lawrance was at the height of her fame. Her flower paintings were in great demand, her book on roses the accepted authority on the subject and her lectures more popular than the theatre. Not surprisingly, this new introduction was called *Rosa lawranceana*.

Specimens were grown in many parts of Europe and the United States – *Pompon de Paris* was a well-known variety. Then they went out of fashion and disappeared at the end of the 19th century, apparently lost forever.

In 1918 Major Roulet saw a tiny rose with pink flowers growing happily in a pot on a windowsill in a Swiss village ... he was told that it had been there for over 100 years. This museum piece became *Rosa rouletti* and all our modern miniature roses are descendants of this plant. Many lovely hybrids have been produced – the first was *Tom Thumb* raised by Jan de Vink in Holland. Many others followed, bred by Pedro Dot in Spain and Ralph Moore in California.

## OMAR KHAYYÁM

There is perhaps nothing special about the plant itself. It is a Damask rose with very full, pale pink flowers which appear in midsummer. The fragrance is strong and the growth dense and bushy, but it is its origin which makes this rose so interesting.

In 1947 an old and decrepit rose was found growing on the grave of Edward Fitzgerald near Woodbridge in Suffolk. It was Fitzgerald who had translated the *Rubáiyát of Omar Khayyám* and a plaque near the rose stated 'This rose tree, raised in Kew Gardens from seed brought by William Simpson, artist and traveller, from the grave of Omar Khayyám at Nashipur,

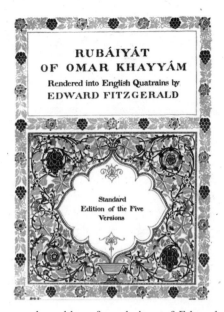

was planted by a few admirers of Edward Fitzgerald in the name of the Omar Khayyám Club, 7th October 1893.' Buds were taken from the branches of this old rose and new plants were propagated. *Omar Khayyám* is available from nurseries which specialise in unusual varieties.

## ROSA MUNDI

*Rosa Mundi* is one of the most popular of our old Shrub Roses, bearing striped flowers on twiggy, upright bushes for about a month in June or July. It is a sport of the Red Rose of Lancaster, and bears the Latin name *Rosa gallica versicolor*. There is an old story that Rosa Mundi was named after Fair Rosamund, the mistress of Henry II during the time his wife Queen

India Company's office at Canton. The roses had travelled by way of India and had survived the long journey. Amongst them was a new and exciting variety.

The roses were planted at the nursery in King's Road, Chelsea and bloomed the following year – the flowers were a delicate pastel shade and the fragrance was reminiscent of the inside of old tea chests – so the variety was appropriately named *Hume's Blush Tea-Scented China Rose*. Quite a mouthful, but it was the first Tea Rose of the Western World, and it would be hard to exaggerate its importance in the development of the modern rose. The flowers had weak necks and the bushes were not hardy, but *Hume's Blush* and the Tea Roses which arrived later provided the shapely buds, high centres and delicate fragrances we associate with their illustrious offsprings – the Hybrid Teas.

It had been thought for many years that *Hume's Blush* was extinct, but it seems that the variety is still preserved in the Rosarium at Sangerhausen in eastern Germany.

Eleanor was in prison. Rosamund, daughter of Walter de Clifford, died in 1176 in a nunnery and her grave was alleged to have borne the inscription *Rosa Mundi* (Rose of the World). Thus legends start, but there is no factual link between the Royal mistress-turned-nun and the rose. Experts prefer to believe the book written by Sir Thomas Hanmer in 1659 which recorded that the rose was 'first found in Norfolk a few years since upon a branch of the common Red Rose'.

## HUME'S BLUSH

In 1809 a consignment of roses arrived at Wormleybury in Hertfordshire, the home of Sir Anthony Hume. The plants had been sent from China the year before by his cousin, who was in charge of the East

## PERSIAN YELLOW

In 1836 the *Persian Yellow (Rosa foetida persiana)* was introduced to the Horticultural Society's Gardens from Iran. At that time there were very few yellow roses and there were no double yellow roses at all which could be relied upon to bloom freely in an average British summer.

Today's yellow and orange roses can be traced back to the *Persian Yellow*, and that has had a good and a bad effect. On the credit side it has helped to produce free-flowering roses in an infinite range of shades from palest cream to deepest orange, but on the debit side it brought black spot to our gardens. This disease did exist before the introduction of *Persian Yellow* but it was rare – the roses of the day were highly resistant. *Persian Yellow* was susceptible, and it has passed its weakness on to its progeny.

## PEACE

No other variety has ever captured the hearts of gardeners throughout the world in quite the same way. Both experts and novices were enchanted by the large, pinky yellow blooms of *Peace* when it was introduced as the fighting stopped at the end of World War II.

Its story epitomises the well-travelled nature of the modern rose. In 1935 François Meilland raised Seedling No. 3-35-40 at Lyons and a few plants were sent out on the last plane to America as France fell. This dramatic story may be a little theatrical, but we do know that plants were despatched to the Conard-Pyle Co. in America before the Occupation as well as to Germany and Italy afterwards. In France it was *Mme. A. Meilland*, in Germany *Gloria* and in Italy *Gioia*. In America it did not have a name – that had to wait until delegates gathered from all over the world in San Francisco to set up the United Nations. The American distributor placed a rose in every room – the rose was *Peace*. Britain entered the story at a late stage, but by 1951 over one million bushes had been sold in this country.

This rule in gardening never forget:
To sow dry and to set wet.

*John Ray*

# SAYINGS FROM THE PLANT AND GARDEN WORLD

***

## Here we go gathering nuts in May

Children have sung this nursery rhyme for generations, and the brighter ones have wondered about the month chosen for the little song – just which nuts can you expect to find in May? The original version of the nursery rhyme did not mention nuts at all – children used to sing 'Here we go gathering *knots* in May' as they gathered knots or bunches of flowers in readiness for the May Day festivities.

## By hook or by crook

To achieve your goal by one means or another. This phrase dates back to the time when farm workers had the right by ancient custom to gather firewood from the trees growing on the land owned by the lord of the manor. They could take branches from hedges and bushes by means of a hook or sickle and they could pull down dead branches from trees by using their shepherd's crook. So the tenant obtained his firewood by hook or by crook.

## Oak before ash, in for a splash, Ash before oak, in for a soak

An old rural weather forecast which predicts that if oak trees come into leaf before ash then the spring will be showery and the farming year will be a successful one. If on the other hand the ash trees are the first to come into leaf then a wet summer will result and the harvest will be a poor one. Unfortunately, the statistics of the Meteorological Office do not support the prophecy.

## The early bird catches the worm

Part of the feeding pattern of worms is to drag surface debris underground. They come above ground on mild, damp nights and are very sensitive to light – as soon as the sun begins to rise they start to move back to the safety of their underground tunnels. At dawn some birds leave the nest to hunt for food earlier than others, and it

## Buttercups make butter yellow

It was believed in medieval times that the rich golden colour of butter was derived from the buttercups which the cows ate when grazing in the fields – hence our common name for *Ranunculus*. This Latin name has an equally obscure origin – it means 'little frog', which is thought to be a reference to the damp, frog-ridden home of most buttercups.

## Under the rose

For thousands of years the expression *sub rosa* (under the rose) has meant 'in strict confidence'. Nobody is quite sure how it began – according to legend, Cupid gave the god of silence a rose to persuade him not to reveal the love affairs of Venus. During the Greek and Persian Wars the decisive battle against Xerxes was planned in secret in a rose bower. In Ancient Rome a rose hung over a table meant that nothing must be repeated outside the doors of the room.

By the 15th century the meaning of 'under the rose' was established in Europe. It appeared in books ('If this makes us speak bold words, anon, 'tis all under the rose forgotten') and roses were carved on confessionals as a symbol of secrecy. Roses were painted on the ceilings of banqueting halls and council chambers, and even today the attachment point of the centre light to the ceiling is known as a 'rose'.

will be the early bird which is able to catch the worm before it has been sufficiently well-illuminated to make it return to its burrow.

*Here we go round the*
*mulberry bush,*
*The mulberry bush,*
*the mulberry bush,*
*Here we go round the mulberry bush*
*At five o'clock in the morning*

A popular song of the playground, but once it belonged in the prison yard. James I encouraged the cultivation of the Black mulberry in the 17th century in order to stimulate a British silk industry. The experiment failed, but many mulberry trees were planted in prison yards and the inmates were exercised by having to walk around the tree in the early morning.

*A woman, a dog and a walnut tree,*
*The more you beat them*
*The better they be*

It is outside the scope of this book to discuss the wisdom of woman- or dog-beating, but there is some factual basis for the old practice of beating a nut tree to increase its fruitfulness. This thrashing was carried out with elder twigs, as elder was supposed to be a witch-repellent.

Leaving aside the magical aspect of ill-treating non-productive trees, it has been clearly demonstrated that one of the causes of poor fruit-bud production is over-vigorous growth. The way to overcome this trouble is to reduce the flow of food from the leaves to the roots and the grower does this by cutting out strips of bark around the trunk. Grazing animals can have the same effect, and so could a severe beating which removed some of the bark.

## Spinach makes you strong

Popeye helped to popularise the view that spinach gave you strength and many books noted that this vegetable was especially rich in iron. All of this arose out of a simple mistake by a scientist who put the decimal point in the wrong place when he determined the iron content of spinach over 100 years ago. We now know that spinach contains no more iron than many other green vegetables.

## Apple-pie order

Neat and tidy, but nothing to do with apples or pies. The saying arises from the French phrase *nappes pliées*, which means neatly laid out like folded linen.

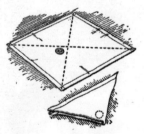

## Grass widow

In the days of the Raj the wives of British officers moved to the cool grasslands in the hills during the heat of summer. With the return of cooler weather these grass widows went back to their homes and husbands on the plains.

## They shall beat their swords into ploughshares

You will find the statement in Isaiah 2:4 but the people of the time could not have done such a thing. The Middle Eastern plough did not need such an attachment for their light soils – the ploughshare was developed in the 7th century to enable the ploughing of heavy grassland in Europe.

## To gild the lily

To 'gild the lily' is a well-known phrase meaning to add decoration or embellishment to something which is already sufficiently beautiful. We can never remember whether it was first used in the Bible or by Shakespeare ... the answer is neither. In *King John* by Shakespeare you will find 'To gild refined gold, to *paint* the lily ...'

## Cast ne'er a clout till May is out

The country saying that you should not remove your winter clothing until the end of May seems to suggest that our ancestors were a tender lot. However, the reference is to the flower of the may or hawthorn and not to the month. According to legend the hawthorn will not bloom until all danger of frost is past. Unfortunately facts do not bear out the legend.

## Not worth a fig

Worthless – but the reference is not to the fruit. It is to the Elizabethan expression *fico*, which was a gesture of contempt made with the thumb put between the first two fingers.

*Ring-a-ring-o' roses,*
*A pocketful of posies,*
*Atishoo, atishoo,*
*We all fall down*

Another nursery rhyme which may have a sinister meaning. Some people believe it is descriptive of the plague – the ring of red marks (ring of roses) was one of the symptoms and posies were carried to keep the 'evil airs' at bay. Sneezing (atishoo, atishoo) was another symptom and the last line refers to the effect on people throughout Europe during the great epidemics in the Middle Ages.

## As mysterious as the Willow Pattern

We have all seen the 'old' Chinese story portrayed by the blue Willow Pattern on porcelain. There is the mandarin, lovers, bridge, peach tree, cottage, river, fence and so on. In fact it was created by Thomas Turner in 1780 and it is neither Chinese in origin nor does it illustrate any Chinese legend.

# THE STORY OF OUR NATIONAL FLOWERS

*THERE IS no single or simple reason why a country should choose one particular plant as its national emblem. As a general rule the newer countries have adopted colourful flowers which grow abundantly within their borders whereas the older nations have chosen flowers which have close associations with either their kings or their saints. There are exceptions, and in the case of the British Isles half the national 'flowers' are not flowers at all.*

## THISTLE OF SCOTLAND

According to legend the Vikings were successful at the start of their war against the native inhabitants of Scotland. The customary raping and pillaging appear to have taken place and the country was in danger of being over-run. One night a large force of Vikings approached the sleeping Scottish army when one bare-footed Norseman stepped on a thistle (*Onopordon acanthium*).  His cry of pain woke the Scots and they routed the Vikings who never again returned to Scotland. A grateful nation adopted the thistle as its native flower.

## LEEK OF WALES

The legend of the leek depends on the story-teller. According to one version St. David had lived on bread and leeks when he had been a monk in Wales and he gave this unappetising fare to the Christian Celts before their battle against the heathen Saxons. The Welsh Celts won the day and adopted the leek as their emblem. Another version is pre-Christian – the Celtic god Aeddon had lightning as his sign, and the rather fanciful Celts believed that the smell of  leeks was similar to that of the ozone which develops in the air after a thunderstorm. Accordingly the leek became the plant emblem of Aeddon and later St. David.

During the 20th century the daffodil was adopted as a more attractive alternative to the leek as the national emblem of Wales.

## ROSE OF ENGLAND

The rose made its first royal symbolic appearance in England when Edward I adopted the flower as his badge, and we know that the Crusaders carved rose emblems on the buildings in the Holy Land, but it did not become our national flower until much later. In 1455 the series of civil wars now known as the Wars of the Roses broke out – so-called because the House of York adopted the White Rose (probably *Rosa alba semi-plena*) as its emblem and the House of Lancaster bore the Red Rose (*Rosa gallica*). The struggle finally ended in 1485 with Henry Tudor the victor at the Battle of Bosworth. Now was the time for reconciliation and a symbol of the re-unified nation was needed – Henry VII combined his Lancastrian Red Rose with the White Rose of his bride, Elizabeth of York, and the resulting combination was the Tudor Rose. From that day the Tudor Rose has remained the royal badge of England.

The description of this civil war as The War of the Roses first appeared in the 19th century.

## SHAMROCK OF IRELAND

As a young boy St. Patrick had been taken from his home in Scotland as a slave to Ireland, and as a fervent believer in the new faith he travelled to Tara one spring day in the hope of converting King Loaghaire to Christianity. He lit a fire to celebrate the Resurrection and the furious Druids dragged him before the king. The Christian missionary was given permission to speak before being sentenced for daring to light a forbidden fire, and Patrick told the king the story of the Trinity. But the ruler needed a sign, and Patrick bent down and picked up a shamrock with the words 'Look, three leaves in one leaf.' The king adopted the new faith and the shamrock became the basis of the Celtic Cross and the national emblem of Ireland. According to another version St. Patrick used the shamrock to drive the snakes out of Ireland, which even for a legend sounds improbable. Unfortunately for both stories, the word 'shamrock' is derived from the Arabic *shamrakh* which is the symbol of the Persian Trinity. Debate continues on the botanical identity of the shamrock – it is probably the Common trefoil (*Trifolium repens*) although the larger Wood sorrel (*Oxalis acetosella*) is often used … especially on St. Patrick's Day.

# LARGEST...
# TALLEST... OLDEST

## LARGEST

The largest tree in the world is the *Wellingtonia* 'General Sherman' in Sequoia National Park in California. It is 3000 years old, its girth is 24 m and height 84 m with a weight estimated at 2000 tonnes.

The largest flowering shrub in the world is a wisteria in California – it covers 0.5 hectares and produces hundreds of thousands of blooms during the flowering season.

The largest vine in Britain is the Great Vine at Hampton Court – its annual yield is about 500 kg of grapes.

The largest of all plant leaves belong to the Great Water lily (*Victoria regia*) with a diameter of over 2 m. The largest of all flowers is borne by the Monster Flower (*Rafflesia arnoldii*) of Malaysia. The evil-smelling flowers measure about 1 m in diameter and weigh over 9 kg.

The largest mushroom recorded in Britain had a cap with a circumference of 140 cm.

The largest flower picture ever created was the begonia carpet laid in the main square at Ghent (Belgium) in 1973. Nearly 2 million blooms were used to produce the multi-coloured, ornate carpet which measured more than 0.6 hectares.

## TALLEST

The world's tallest tree is a *Sequoia sempervirens* growing in California. At 110 m this species is a clear winner of the Tallest Tree title as no other type of tree exceeds 100 m. It is not the world's largest tree –

that title belongs to *Wellingtonia* 'General Sherman' – see the Largest section on page 313. It is thought that trees exceeding 120 m existed until recently.

The tallest tree in Britain is either a Douglas fir (*Pseudotsuga menziesii*) in Scotland or a Giant fir (*Abies grandis*) in the grounds of Leighton Hall in Wales. Both these giants are over 56 m high. No English conifer exceeds 50 m, but England holds the British deciduous tree record – there is a 47 m Common lime (*Tilia europaea*) in Yorkshire's Duncombe Park.

The tallest rose in the world is a climbing variety planted at the start of World War II in the garden at Kiftsgate Court in Gloucestershire. It is now nearly 20 m high.

# OLDEST

For many years the *Wellingtonia* 'General Sherman' in California was thought to be the world's oldest living tree. It is now known to be the Bristlecone pine (*Pinus longaeva*). A specimen in the White Mountains of California was shown to be 4600 years old and trees which are several hundred years older have been discovered in Nevada. The oldest tree outside America is thought to be a *Ficus religiosa* in Sri Lanka – it is thought to be about 2500 years old.

The oldest tree in Britain is a baby by comparison. The title is usually given to the yew growing in the churchyard at Fortingall in Scotland – it is well over 1000 years old. The oldest deciduous tree is probably the oak tree at Hatfield Broad Oak in Essex which is reputedly 800 years old.

The oldest rose in the world is the Hildesheim Rose growing in the grounds of Hildesheim Cathedral in Germany. According to legend it was planted by Charlemagne over 1000 years ago, but it is probably 400 years old.

The oldest viable seeds on record were palm seeds from Masada in Israel which were successfully germinated in 2008. They were found to be 2000 years old. Older claims have been made, including the germination of 'mummy' wheat from the Pyramids, but the Israeli palm seeds hold the record amongst scientifically-tested claims.

The oldest named bean variety is the White Aztec. It is believed to have been grown by the Central American natives before the landing of Columbus.

The first botanic garden was laid out at Padua in Italy in 1545. Britain's oldest is the Oxford University Botanic Garden (1621). The idea of town council-owned parks for the people is a relatively new idea

– the oldest Corporation park is the Derby Arboretum, presented by a benefactor in 1840. By 1870 every sizeable town in Britain had its park.

The oldest surviving colour magazine in the world is *Curtis's Botanical Magazine*, which started in 1787. The illustrations were still being hand-coloured in the 1930s and it is published quarterly by the Royal Botanic Gardens, Kew. The first journal in Britain to be devoted to gardening was the *Gardener's Magazine* (1826). It came out only four times a year – the first weekly magazine was the *Gardener's Chronicle* (1841).

The first illustrated seed catalogue published in Britain was the *Twelve Months of Flowers* issued by Robert Furber's Kensington nursery in 1730.

The first garden book written for flower lovers rather than herbalists was *De Naturis Rerum* by Alexander Neckham (1213). The first gardening book in English was *The Feat of Gardening* by Master Ian Gardiner (1400). This book of verses described the plants found in the medieval garden, but it was the book written by Thomas Hyll, Londoner, in 1563 that can claim to be the first English gardening textbook. Its title also gives it the record for being the English gardening textbook with the longest title - *A most brief and pleasant treatise, teaching how to dress, sow and set a Garden, and*

*what properties also these few herbs here spoken of, have to our commodity; with the remedies that may be used against such beasts, worms, flies and such like, that commonly annoy gardens, gathered out of the principallest Authors in this art.* The first gardening best-seller had a much shorter title – it was Thomas Tusser's *Five Hundred Points of Good Husbandry* (1573).

The first book in English on the flora of America was *Joyfull News out of the New Founde Worlde* (1577). An earlier work, written in Spanish by Dr. Francisco Hernandez in 1575, illustrated the dahlia for the first time. It is interesting that the first dahlia tubers sent to Europe were for eating and not for growing in the flower garden.

The oldest horticultural society in Britain is the Royal Horticultural Society, which began as the Horticultural Society of London in 1804. The oldest floral society is the Chrysanthemum Society (1846).

> I have often thought that if heaven had given me choice of my position and calling, it should have been on a rich spot of earth, well watered, and near a good market for the productions of the garden.
>
> *Thomas Jefferson*

# TOPIARY

THE SUBURBAN gardener neatly shaping his privet hedge on a Sunday morning probably has no idea that he is practising an ancient art. Topiary (the clipping of trees and shrubs into geometrical or fanciful shapes) dates back to early Rome. Of course, fruit trees are trimmed to increase their productivity and many flowering shrubs must be cut back each year to ensure a satisfactory display. This is the purely practical craft of pruning – topiary is a form of decorative folk art.

Simple topiary was popular throughout the monasteries of medieval Europe, and this led to the shaped trees and box-edged flower beds of the 15th century manor house. But it was not until the French landscape architect Le Nôtre took a ruler to nature that topiary became a key feature of the Grand Garden. The exiled Charles II and his court marvelled at Le Nôtre's skill and on their return the transformation of England's gardens began.

When William and Mary came to the throne topiary gained fresh impetus, for they brought the fanciful and fantastic designs from Holland with them. The King built a mock fort of yew and holly at Kensington Gardens, the firm of London and Wise sold vast quantities of clipped

trees, and topiary became a national craze by the end of the 17th century.

Such artificiality could not last and when fashion took a sudden swing to the natural landscaped look, many of the Grand Gardens were dug up and remade. This has deprived us of the opportunity to see more than a handful of examples of early topiary on the grand scale. Topiary lived on in Holland and also in the English cottage garden. In France there was much less of a swing to naturalism than in Britain. By the middle of the 19th century topiary was back in favour in the British garden. Back came the shears, the secateurs and the training wires, and most of the topiary to be seen around the stately homes of Britain is less than 100 years old.

Topiary is an art form and an important one in the story of European gardening. But is it ugly and unnatural or is it a useful element in garden design? The argument began a long time ago – 'Images cut in juniper, or garden stuff, they be for children,' wrote Francis Bacon in 1624. Five years later Parkinson described topiary as 'the chiefest beauty of gardens'.

Visitors to gardens with topiary are invariably intrigued by the designers' and the gardeners' craft. To see 18th century topiary, go to Levens Hall (Cumbria) for the best display in Britain – a fantasy of figures, birds, animals and geometric shapes. Early examples can also be seen at Packwood House (Warwickshire) and Chastleton House (Oxfordshire). For trees clipped to form a scene or picture go to Ascott (Buckinghamshire), Hasely Court (Oxfordshire) or Dunsborough Park (Surrey). Hedgetop tableaux are to be

seen at Mt. Stewart (N. Ireland), and Rockingham Castle (Northamptonshire). Modern topiary on a grand scale can be seen at Compton Wynyates (Warwickshire), Nymans (W. Sussex), Hever Castle (Kent) and Gt. Dixter (E. Sussex).

Figures and shapes are maintained, but the work involved in creating an extensive topiary garden from scratch must mean that there will never be a revival. The days when a stately home could employ a hundred gardeners have gone for ever.

> The best way to get real enjoyment out of the garden is to put on a wide straw hat, dress in thin loose-fitting clothes, hold a little trowel in one hand and a cool drink in the other, and tell the man where to dig.
>
> *Charles Barr*

# WHAT'S IN A NAME?

---

| NAME OF GENUS | NAME OF SPECIES |
|---|---|
| *Bellis* | *perennis* |
| from Latin *bellus* 'pretty' | from Latin *perennis* 'perennial' |

COMMON NAME
**Daisy**
from 'Day's Eye' – the white petals open during the day
and close over the yellow eyes at night

---

## WHAT THE GENUS NAMES MEAN

---

*Acacia* (Wattle)
Greek *akis* 'sharp point'
Many species are spiny

*Acer* (Maple)
Latin *acer* 'sharp'
Romans used maple for making spears

*Achillea* (Yarrow)
Named in honour of the Greek
warrior *Achilles*

*Aesculus* (Horse chestnut)
Greek *esca* 'nourishment'
Conkers were ground into flour

*Alyssum*
Greek *a* 'against', *lyssa* 'madness'
Early antidote for hydrophobia

*Anemone*
Greek *anemos* 'wind'
Grows in exposed places

*Antirrhinum* (Snapdragon)
Greek *anti* 'like', *rhis* 'snout'
Flower with face-like appearance

*Aquilegia* (Columbine)
Latin *aquila* 'eagle'
Flower with wing-like petals

*Aster* (Michaelmas daisy)
Greek *aster* 'star'
Flower with star-like petal
arrangement

*Aubretia*
Named in honour of the French flower
painter Claude *Aubriet*

*Azalea*
Greek *azaleos* 'dry'
First species so-named grew in arid
and frozen North

*Begonia*
Named in honour of
17th century Governor of
French Canada Michel *Bégon*

*Bellis* (Daisy)
Latin *bellus* 'pretty'
Surprising choice for the Latin
'pretty' title

*Buddleia* (Butterfly bush)
Named in honour of 17th century
English botanist Rev. Adam *Buddle*

*Buxus* (Box)
Greek *pyknos* 'dense'
Wood is closely-grained

*Calendula* (Marigold)
Latin *calendae* 'first day of month'
Like *calendae*, flowers appear all year
round

*Calla* (Bog arum)
Greek *kalos* 'beautiful'
Surprising choice for the Greek
'beautiful' title

*Calluna* (Heather)
Greek *kalluno* 'I cleanse'
Heather was once used for making
brooms

*Camellia*
Named in honour of 17th century
Moravian missionary Georg Josef
*Kamel*

*Campanula* (Bellflower)
Latin *campana* 'bell'
Flower with bell-like appearance

*Capsicum* (Red pepper)
Greek *kapto* 'I bite'
Apt name for the chilli, cayenne, etc.

*Cedrus* (Cedar)
Possibly Arabic *kedron* 'power'
Apt name for the most majestic of
conifers

*Cheiranthus* (Wallflower)
Greek *cheir* 'hand', *anthos* 'flower'
Wallflowers were widely used in posies

*Clematis*
Greek *klema* 'vine branch'
Apt name for this beautiful flowering
vine

*Cornus* (Dogwood)
Latin *cornu* 'horn'
Wood is extremely hard

*Crataegus* (Hawthorn)
Greek *kratos* 'strength'
Wood is extremely hard

*Dahlia*
Named in honour of
18th century Swedish
botanist Dr Anders *Dahl*

*Delphinium*
Greek *delphis* 'dolphin'
Flower with dolphin-shaped spur

*Dianthus* (Carnation)
Greek *dios* 'divine', *anthos* 'flower'
Apt name for this ancient beautiful
flower

*Erica* (Heath)
Greek *eriko* 'I break'
Old stems are brittle

*Euonymus* (Spindle)
Greek *eu* 'good', *onoma* 'name'
Surprising name for a poisonous plant

*Fagus* (Beech)
Greek *phago* 'I eat'
Masts were ground into flour (see
*Aesculus*)

*Forsythia*
Named in honour of 18th century
Scottish gardener and writer William
*Forsyth*

*Fritillaria*
Latin *fritillus* 'dicebox'
Flower with dice-like markings

*Fuchsia*
Named in honour of 16th century
German physician and herbalist
Leonhard *Fuchs*

*Galanthus* (Snowdrop)
Greek *gala* 'milk', *anthos*
'flower'
Apt name for this white
spring flower

*Gentiana* (Gentian)
Named in honour of King *Gentius* of
Illyria who discovered its medicinal use

*Gladiolus*
Latin *gladius* 'sword'
Apt name for this
sword-leaved herbaceous
border plant

*Helianthus* (Sunflower)
Latin *helios* 'sun', *anthos* 'flower'
Apt name for this sun-like flower

*Kerria* (Jew's mallow)
Named in honour of 18th century
English plant hunter William *Kerr*

*Lactuca* (Lettuce)
Latin *lactus* 'milk'
Milky sap, as every vegetable grower knows

*Lupinus* (Lupin)
Latin *lupus* 'wolf'
Old idea that lupins destroyed the soil's fertility

*Magnolia*
Named in honour of 17th century French botanist Professor Pierre *Magnol*

*Nicotiana* (Tobacco plant)
Named in honour of 16th century French Consul to Portugal Jean *Nicot*

*Orchis* (Orchid)
Greek *orchis* 'testicle'
Some species bear paired pseudobulbs at stem base

*Philodendron*
Greek *phileo* 'I love', *dendron* 'tree'
Apt name for this genus of tree-climbers

*Phlox*
Greek *phlox* 'flame'
Flower with bright-coloured petals

*Primula* (Primrose)
Latin *primus* 'first'
Apt name for this early spring flower

*Pyrethrum*
Greek *pyr* 'fire'
Early remedy for fevers

*Raphanus* (Radish)
Greek *ra* 'quick', *phainoma* 'appear'
Quick-growing, as vegetable growers know

*Rhododendron*
Greek *rhodos* 'red', *dendron* 'tree'
Red varieties were dominant in earlier times

*Saintpaulia* (African violet)
Named in honour of 19th century German discoverer Walter von *Saint Paul-Illaire*

*Sedum* (Stonecrop)
Latin *sedo* 'I sit'
Apt name for these low-growing plants

*Tulipa* (Tulip)
Persian *thoulyban* 'turban'
An apt name for this Oriental flower

*Zinnia*
Named in honour of 18th century German professor of botany Johann Gottfried *Zinn*

# What the Species Names Mean

## Colour

| | |
|---|---|
| *alba* | white |
| *argenteus* | silvery |
| *aureus* | gold |
| *caeruleus* | blue |
| *candicans* | hoary white |
| *candida* | shining white |
| *cardinalis* | red |
| *cinerea* | pale grey |
| *cochineus* | scarlet |
| *cruentus* | blood red |
| *cyaneus* | blue |
| *discolor* | two-coloured |
| *erubescens* | blush |
| *ferrugineus* | rusty |
| *flavidus* | yellow |
| *glaucus* | grey-coated |
| *griseus* | grey |
| *nigra* | black |
| *niveus* | snowy white |
| *picea* | pitch black |
| *purpurea* | purple |
| *rosea* | rosy red |
| *sulphureus* | sulphur yellow |
| *violacea* | violet |
| *viridis* | green |
| *xanthina* | yellow |

## Miscellaneous

| | |
|---|---|
| *acris* | sharp-flavoured |
| *affinis* | related |
| *amabilis* | lovely |
| *annuus* | annual |
| *assimilis* | similar |
| *baccata* | berry-bearing |
| *bellus* | pretty |
| *catharticus* | purgative |
| *conformis* | symmetrical |
| *decora* | beautiful |
| *edulis* | edible |
| *elegantissima* | beautiful |
| *flore-pleno* | double-flowered |
| *floridus* | flowery |
| *foetidus* | foul-smelling |
| *fragrans* | fragrant |
| *impatiens* | short-lasting |
| *inodora* | odourless |
| *insignis* | remarkable |
| *lactus* | milky |
| *major* | greater |
| *minor* | lesser |
| *odorata* | fragrant |
| *officinalis* | useful to man |
| *ornatus* | beautiful |
| *perennis* | perennial |
| *pictus* | ornamental |

| | | | | |
|---|---|---|---|---|
| *plenus* | full | | *davidii* | Abbe A. David |
| *praecox* | very early | | *douglasii* | D. Douglas |
| *pungens* | pungent | | *farreri* | R.J. Farrer |
| *radicans* | rooting | | *forrestii* | G. Forrest |
| *sativa* | cultivated | | *fortunei* | R. Fortune |
| *speciosa* | splendid | | *griffithii* | W. Griffith |
| *spectabile* | spectacular | | *hookeri* | Sir W.J. Hooker |
| *splendens* | bright | | *jackmanii* | G. Jackman |
| *trivialis* | ordinary | | *lemoinei* | V. Lemoine |
| *utilis* | useful | | *linnaei* | Prof. C. Linnaeus |
| *variegata* | variegated | | *meyeri* | C.A. Meyer |
| *versicolor* | changing colour | | *sellovianus* | F. Sellow |
| *vulgaris* | ordinary | | *sieboldii* | Dr. F. van Siebold |
| | | | *thomsonii* | Dr. T. Thomson |
| | | | *willmottiae* | Miss E.A. Willmott |
| | | | *wilsonii* | E.H. Wilson |

## Resemblance to Plants or Animals

| | |
|---|---|
| *acerifolia* | maple-leaved |
| *acetosa* | sorrel-leaved |
| *amygdalina* | almond-like |
| *apifer* | bee-like |
| *fagineus* | beech-like |
| *gramineus* | grass-like |
| *jasminoides* | jasmine-like |
| *linifolia* | flax-leaved |
| *malacoides* | mallow-like |
| *platanoides* | plane-leaved |
| *primulina* | primula-like |

## Size and Shape

| | |
|---|---|
| *acaulis* | stemless |
| *acculeatus* | prickly |
| *alatus* | winged |
| *alternus* | alternate |
| *angulatus* | angular |
| *apertus* | open |
| *apiculatus* | small-pointed |
| *arachnoides* | cobwebby |
| *arboreus* | tree-like |
| *ascendens* | upright |
| *auriculatus* | eared |
| *barbatus* | bearded |
| *bulbosus* | bulbous |
| *caespitosus* | tufted |

## People

| | |
|---|---|
| *baileyi* | Bailey (various) |
| *banksii* | Sir J. Banks |

| | | | | |
|---|---|---|---|---|
| *campanulata* | bell-shaped | | *hirsuta* | hairy |
| *canina* | common or spiny | | *horizontalis* | prostrate |
| *capillatus* | hairy | | *humilis* | small |
| *columnaris* | columnar | | *indivisa* | undivided |
| *comosus* | hairy | | *lanata* | woolly |
| *compacta* | compressed | | *lanceolata* | spear-shaped |
| *compressa* | closely packed | | *macrocarpa* | large-fruited |
| *conica* | cone-shaped | | *maculata* | spotted |
| *contorta* | twisted | | *mollis* | soft |
| *cordata* | heart-shaped | | *nana* | dwarf |
| *crenata* | scalloped | | *nervosa* | veined |
| *crispa* | curly | | *nitida* | shiny |
| *cristata* | plumed | | *nutans* | nodding |
| *cuneata* | wedge-shaped | | *plicata* | folded |
| *decumbens* | lying down | | *plumosa* | feathered |
| *dentata* | toothed | | *procumbens* | prostrate |
| *depressa* | flattened | | *pubescens* | downy |
| *diffusus* | loose | | *pumilis* | dwarf |
| *effusus* | loose | | *ramosa* | branching |
| *elata* | tall | | *repens* | creeping |
| *erecta* | upright | | *reticulata* | netted |
| *falcatus* | sickle-like | | *scandens* | climbing |
| *fimbriatus* | fringed | | *sempervirens* | evergreen |
| *fragilis* | brittle | | *stellata* | star-like |
| *fruticosa* | bushy | | *striata* | striped |
| *fulgens* | shiny | | *stricta* | rigid |
| *glabra* | smooth | | *terminalis* | tip-flowering |
| *gracilis* | slender | | *tomentosa* | woolly |
| *grandis* | large | | *vagus* | rambling |
| *heterophylla* | differing leaves | | *zonalis* | ringed |

## SEASON

| | |
|---|---|
| *aestivus* | summer |
| *aprilis* | of April |
| *autumnalis* | autum |
| *vernalis* | spring |

## HABITAT

| | |
|---|---|
| *agrestis* | field |
| *alpinus* | alpine |
| *aquaticus* | water |
| *arenarius* | sand |
| *argillaceus* | clay |
| *arvensis* | farmland |
| *calcareus* | chalk |
| *campestris* | field |
| *hortensis* | garden |
| *marinus* | sea |
| *maritima* | seaside |
| *montana* | mountain |
| *palustris* | marsh |
| *pratensis* | meadow |
| *rupestris* | rock |
| *saxatile* | rock |
| *sylvatica* | forest |
| *terrestris* | earth |

## COUNTRIES AND PLACES

| | |
|---|---|
| *antarctica* | Antarctica |
| *arabis* | Arabia |
| *arctica* | Arctic |
| *atlantica* | Atlas mountains |
| *australis* | Southern |
| *borealis* | Northern |
| *canariensis* | Canary Isles |
| *capensis* | S. Africa |
| *chinensis* | China |
| *gallica* | France |
| *hibernica* | Ireland |
| *hispanica* | Spain |
| *indica* | India |
| *japonica* | Japan |
| *libani* | Lebanon |
| *occidentalis* | America |
| *orientalis* | Orient |
| *pontica* | Black Sea |
| *sibirica* | Siberia |
| *sinensis* | China |

The secret of improved plant breeding,
apart from scientific knowledge, is love.

*Luther Burbank*

# YOU ARE WRONG
# ABOUT THAT!

## Hoeing is good for the soil

Not so – the sole benefit is the destruction of weeds. A necessary task in most gardens, but it is not always effective. Perennial weeds soon sprout again and it is essential that the stems of annual weeds are severed just below ground level. All too often the weeds are merely uprooted and left to re-establish in the moist soil.

Removing weed competition helps the nearby garden plants, but the 'dust mulch' created by hoeing is not beneficial – water conservation is an old wives' tale. Frequent hoeing can result in some loss of soil structure. The biggest danger is root damage if you push the blade too deeply into the soil.

## A deciduous tree always loses its leaves in winter

Not necessarily – some deciduous trees, such as beech hedges, may retain their leaves throughout the winter. These plants are not evergreens, of course, because this winter foliage is brown and lifeless – the correct definition of a deciduous tree is one which loses its *living* leaves during winter.

## You should buy the tallest plants you can afford if you want to establish a hedge as quickly as possible

Never – mature plants generally take a long time to become established after transplanting. For quick establishment, shun both newly-rooted cuttings and tall plants which may be several years old. Pick medium-sized specimens which appear healthy and vigorous.

## Adding worms will improve the soil

Very unlikely – worms are symptoms rather than stimulators of fertile soil. As every gardener knows, worms do have a beneficial action in the garden by dragging fallen leaves etc. below the surface and by mining tunnels which help to aerate the soil. But they are not really pioneers – if the soil is fertile they will arrive and breed rapidly without any help from you. Just dig the soil below the compost heap and you will see this in action.

If the soil is infertile and low in humus, worms will shun the area – adding worms to such soil leads either to their death or their rapid departure to richer pastures. If you want better soil then add lots of organic matter – the worms will find it!

## John Innes developed the first seed and potting composts

Not so – he died long before J.I. Composts were developed. John Innes was a wealthy property developer with a deep interest in horticulture. On his death in 1904 he bequeathed his home at Merton in Surrey to the Board of Agriculture with the request that it should be used as a gardening school.

Instead of a school a research establishment was founded – the John Innes Horticultural Institution. It was here between 1934 and 1939 that Lawrence and Newell developed the composts which were named after the Institution. A set of simple formulae were devised for sowing seeds, taking cuttings and for filling pots of various sizes. The basic ingredients are sterilised loam, peat and coarse sand, and to this mixture fertilizers and chalk are usually added.

## Cuttings should be planted as soon as possible after separation from the parent plant and you should always use a rooting hormone

Not necessarily – cuttings of cacti and succulents should be left to dry out for several days before insertion in cutting compost, and geranium cuttings should not be dipped in rooting hormone powder or liquid.

## Jordan almonds come from the Middle East

Not so – their name has nothing to do with either the country or the river. It is a corruption of the early English name *jardin* (or garden) *almande*.

## Ivy will harm the walls of the house

Not likely – the wall may actually be protected from the action of frost and rain on exposed sites by the presence of a covering of ivy. Trouble only occurs on old houses where the bricks are no longer sound and the mortar between them has started to crumble.

## Mammoth vegetables are just a matter of expert care and heavy feeding

Not so – there is much more to it than that. You will need fertile soil, and that means an abundance of organic matter and not just fertilizers. Then there is the choice of the right variety – the basic key to entry into the record books. If you choose a giant carrot variety such as Zino or Flak, then you will produce large roots in average soil and with average skill. Most of the record-breakers have evolved their own high-yielding strains over the years, and these they jealously guard.

Feeding is usually on a little-and-often basis with a liquid fertilizer. Weekly and even daily feeding is practised.

## A native British plant is one which has grown in this country for millions of years

Not necessarily – some of the plants which grew here in very early times (before the Glacial period) are not regarded as native British plants. Tropical trees flourished in those early days when conditions were much warmer than at present. A native British plant is one which arrived in this country without the help of man and has grown here in the wild in the period *after* the Ice Age. It may or may not have been present before that time.

## Nettles are bad for the garden

Not necessarily – a flourishing crop of stinging nettles is a sign of excellent soil beneath. The roots and fallen leaves of the nettle plants will have helped to create this fertility over the years and you can take advantage of it by planting vegetables or flowers in the nettle patch. To do this you will first have to dig out the weeds, roots and all. Do not use a long-lasting weedkiller or one of the hormone type if you plan to use the land in the near future – use a good fork and a lot of hard work instead.

## Vegetables taste better if you use organic manures rather than inorganic fertilizers

Not so – tasting trials have shown that the flavour of fruit and vegetables is affected by the amount of nutrient elements present in the soil but not by their source. This does not mean that organic manures are unimportant – feeding year after year with just chemical fertilizers can lead to trace element deficiencies and loss of soil structure. Regular application of compost or manure is vital – peat is not enough because it is quite lifeless and does not stimulate the bacteria.

Several factors affect flavour, such as the choice of variety, soil type and weather conditions. Loss of flavour is usually due to ignoring one or more of the three golden rules – pick at the right stage, which is often far below maximum size, eat the produce as soon after picking as possible and don't overcook.

## Sewage sludge is good for the garden

Not necessarily – it can be a good and cheap source of humus for the vegetable plot, but you must make sure that it has been sterilised and that it has been analysed and tested for use in the garden. Sewage sludge obtained from industrial areas may contain a high content of heavy metals which could poison the land and perhaps taint your vegetables.

## A power mower will give a better cut than a hand one

Not necessarily – it will do the job more quickly and more easily, but not more effectively than a good-quality hand-driven mower. The quality of the cut produced by a cylinder mower depends on the sharpness and setting of the blades and the number of blades on the cylinder. Five blades will give you an average sort of cut, but you need at least 8 blades to give a bowling-green effect. It's all a matter of blade number and not the source of power.

## Petrified wood is a tree which has turned to stone

Not so – there is no trace of organic matter in petrified wood. Water seeped into the wood ages ago and filled the plant cells. The minerals in the water formed 'stone' within the cells, and when the wood rotted away the stone image remained.

The Englishman loves to see everything on the tree. They hate to pick the flowers, they loathe to pick vegetables, they hate to dig potatoes. It is only the French who will cut the thing when it is young and tender.

*Rosa Lewis*

# ACKNOWLEDGEMENTS

At the end of *The Armchair Book of the Garden* I expressed my gratitude to all the people and organisations which had helped to make it possible.

This updated and revised version has once again involved many people – without them it would never have appeared. My special thanks go to the small team who devoted so much time and care to *The Bedside Book of the Garden*. At the top of the list there was the book-mother Susanna Wadeson (Transworld Publishers) and Gill Jackson (my girl Friday). In addition there was the team at Transworld Publishers – Deborah Adams, Rich Carr, Larry Finlay, Manpreet Grewal, Sam Jones, Sheila Lee, Phil Lord, Gareth Pottle, Kate Tolley, Eliza Walsh and Katrina Whone.

In addition I am grateful for the contributions made by the following people and organisations – Angelina Gibbs, Dr Steve Dowbiggin OBE (Capel Manor College), and Gillie Westwood (Garden Centre Association).

# ILLUSTRATIONS

6: Palm House, Kew; 9: John Bartram, from Howard Pyle's *Bartram and His Garden*; 11: William Robinson, drypoint by Francis Dodd; 12: *Kalmia latifolia*, calico bush; 13: *Magnolia grandiflora*; 16: Blenheim Palace from across the lake; illustration from *Rarorium Plantarium Historia*; 19: man wearing a hemp cloak from Robert Fortune's *A Residence among the Chinese ... from 1853 to 1856*, 1857; 20: Bleeding Heart; 21: 'a remarkable tree' from Robert Fortune, ibid.; 26: Château de Malmaison; 30: clock-face with flowering times of day of plants; 35 and 36: view of Versailles; 37: house and vista improved by Repton, from *The Landscape Gardening and Landscape Architecture of Humphry Repton ... by* J. C. Loudon, 1890; 38: clumps of trees planted by Repton, ibid.; 40: 'Solomon Seal and Herb Paris, in copse by streamlet' from William Robinson's *The Wild Garden ...*, 1895; 41: 'The White Japan Anemone in the Wild Garden', ibid.; 42: Rothschild family crest; 43: Nathaniel Rothschild; 44: Lionel Rothschild; 48, 49: tradescantia; 51: Handkerchief tree; 55: Spanish moss; 67 top: Sundew, 67 bottom: pitcher plant; 69: *Lilium longiflorum*; 70: tiger lily; 71: variegated holly; 72: variegated euonymus; 75: roof garden in Verona, c. 1708; 77 bottom: poplars; 81: *Chamaerops humilis*; 82: *Cordyline australis*; 86: santolina; 104: INTERFOTO Pressebildagentur/ Alamy; 105: water garden, Persian miniature; 106: Lion Court, Alhambra; 109: *Lavandula spica* 'Hidcote'; 111: cabbage palm; 113: William Hooker from *Illustrated London News*, 26 August 1865; 115: poinsettia; 117: *Rhododendron keysii*, a variety grown at Nymans; 119: Wellingtonia; 120: 'The spruce fir tree' from John Evelyn's *Silva*, 1776; 121: Richard Colt Hoare; 122: Woolverton Studios; 135: Iris Hardwick; 142: view of Wimbledon House, Surrey, from John Loudon's *The Suburban Gardener and Villa Companion*, 1838; 147: Crystal

Palace, view of transept; 148: Crystal Palace, view of the transept from *Illustrated London News*, 25 January 1851; 150: an apothecary's garden, c. 1500; 151: prickly herb aloe from John Gerard's *The herball or Generall historie of plantes*, 1597; 153: from *Punch*, 13 September 1879; 157: The Great Temple Show from *Gardener's Magazine*, 1 June 1907, RHS, Lindley Library; 158 and 159: Chelsea Flower Show, 1913 and 1933, both Getty Images; 165: peony from John Gerard's *The herball or Generall historie of plantes*, 1597; 190 top: bullfinch, bottom left: goldfinch, bottom right: chaffinch; 194 both: coal tits; 205 top: cabbage white; 206: peacock butterfly; 224: carnation; 225: parsley; 232: elderflower; 233 top: camomile, 233 bottom: buttercup; 238: lavender; 239: pink; 240: heather; 247: nasturtium; 248: marigold; 252: water hyacinth; 264: Banksia; 265: Melbourne Botanic Gardens; 266: wattle; 270: foxglove; 271 top: yew, 271 bottom: Timothy grass; 275: view of Het Loo and the Venus Fountain by Carel Allard, late 17th century; 285: sphagnum peat; 313: 'The Gigantic Water-Lily (*Victoria regia*), in Flower at Chatsworth' from *Illustrated London News*, 17 November 1849.